Writing Straight with Crooked Lines

Writing Straight with Crooked Lines

A Memoir

JIM FOREST

ORBIS BOOKS
Maryknoll, New York 10545

ORBIS BOOKS
Maryknoll, New York 10545

Fathers and Brothers
MARYKNOLL™

Founded in 1970, Orbis Books endeavors to publish works that enlighten the mind, nourish the spirit, and challenge the conscience. The publishing arm of the Maryknoll Fathers and Brothers, Orbis seeks to explore the global dimensions of the Christian faith and mission, to invite dialogue with diverse cultures and religious traditions, and to serve the cause of reconciliation and peace. The books published reflect the views of their authors and do not represent the official position of the Maryknoll Society. To learn more about Maryknoll and Orbis Books, please visit our website at www.orbisbooks.com.

Library of Congress Cataloging-in-Publication Data

Names: Forest, Jim (James H.), author.
Title: Writing straight with crooked lines : a memoir / Jim Forest.
Description: Maryknoll, NY : Orbis Books, 2020. | Includes bibliographical
    references and index. | Summary: "The autobiography of a noted
    peacemaker, including accounts of encounters with famous figures,
    including Dorothy Day, Thomas Merton, Daniel Berrigan, and Thich Nhat
    Hanh"—Provided by publisher.
Identifiers: LCCN 2019042855 (print) | LCCN 2019042856 (ebook) | ISBN
    9781626983571 (paperback) | ISBN 9781608338221 (ebook)
Subjects: LCSH: Forest, Jim (James H.) | Christian authors—United
    States—Biography. | Christian biography—United States. |
    Pacifists—United States—Biography. | Orthodox Eastern converts—United
    States—Biography.
Classification: LCC BX342.F67 A3 2020 (print) | LCC BX342.F67 (ebook) |
    DDC 281.9092 [B]—dc23
LC record available at https://lccn.loc.gov/2019042855
LC ebook record available at https://lccn.loc.gov/2019042856

For my children,
Ben, Dan, Wendy, Thom, Caitlan, and Anne

and grandchildren,
Zackary, Kara, Noah, Joshua, Lux, Dylan, Sara,
Sam, Julia, and Maya

Family gathering in Rotterdam, Christmas 2015

God writes straight with crooked lines.
　　—Portuguese proverb

Jim and granddaughter Julia

Contents

Prologue: Telling the Truth • 1

Red Diaper Baby • 3

A Kid with a State Name • 12

A Day-Late Saint • 21

An Apprenticeship in Saying "No" • 25

Deciphering the Alphabet • 29

Treasure Island • 32

The Circus • 35

Growing Up Radioactive • 37

Discovering God • 39

Sci-Fi • 44

Route 66 • 46

The Family of Man • 49

A Transcontinental Bus Ride • 51

Dream City • 57

Running Away • 61

In Uniform • 68

True North • 71

A Bus Ride up the Hudson • 75

Navy Weatherman • 77

The Works of Mercy • 79

Conscientious Objection • 84

Getting to Know Dorothy Day • 91

Books, Borscht, and Icons • 97

Working with Dorothy • 104

Hospitality of the Face • 109

Mail from Merton • 111

Hitchhiking to Gethsemani • 116

Dorothy Day University • 123

A Derailed Train • 129

Liberation • 133

The Night Side • 137

The Catholic Peace Fellowship • 140

The Spiritual Roots of Protest • 146

Loneliness, the Sixties, and War • 153

A Round of Irish Whiskey • 156

Draft Cards on Fire • 160

Dan in Exile • 165

Hard Times • 168

From Protest to Resistance • 172

Thich Nhat Hanh • 177

The Milwaukee Fourteen • 187

Trial • 192

Sabbatical • 203

On the Road to Emmaus • 212

A Sojourn in Paris • 220

Apprentice Father • 230

Al Hassler • 233

An Island Surrounded by Footlights • 237

No One Should Die • 241

To See, or Not to See . . . • 249

European Migrant • 243

Caring for Marigolds • 255

A Ceremony in Oslo,
a Meeting in Rome • 258

Beggar-in-Chief • 262

Lost and Found • 266

Let It Begin Here • 270

Tunneling under the Iron Curtain • 273

Border Crossing • 276

Pilgrims in the Holy Land • 279

Standing on Cracking Ice • 284

A Change of Address • 292

Miloserdia • 298

The Family Farm • 303

A Pilgrimage of Illness • 308

Peace Activist? • 315

Mentors • 317

Acknowledgments: A Few Words of Thanks • 321

Index of Names • 323

PROLOGUE

Telling the Truth

One of my childhood ambitions was to be an archaeologist when
I grew up. Photos in *National Geographic* magazine of archaeologists sifting earth for fragments of earlier civilizations and lost cultures
fascinated me: foundations of forgotten cities, buried temples, secret
graves, yellowed bones, faded wall paintings, bright mosaics, golden
coins. . . . The past was a vast, barely mapped continent. I wanted to
be one of the explorers.

Writing an account of one's life is a kind of archaeology, but instead
of digging trenches into multilayered tells, I'm digging into the rubble of my own memory which, like earth, hides more than it reveals.
One of my discoveries is how many fields of memory resist the shovel.
There are acres of my gray matter where signs have been posted that
warn, "Do not enter." It doesn't take long to realize that these are signs
I've created myself, protective barriers that surround areas of pain and
failure, lies and deceptions, selfish choices and unhealed wounds. Sins.
I've discovered that my memory is a scrapbook full of blurry and doctored photos and torn-out pages.

I sometimes think of Father Mikhail Zhakov, a fierce monk with
a wild red beard whom I met in the north of Russia in 1988. I was
writing *Religion in the New Russia*, a book about religious life in what
was still the Soviet Union, a state in which vast numbers of Orthodox
priests, monks, nuns, and lay people had been imprisoned, tortured,
enslaved, and murdered. Studying my face, he asked, "Will you tell
the truth in your book?" Even at the Last Judgment I doubt I will be
subject to a stricter scrutiny. Father Mikhail was a living outpost of
uncombed, God-haunted, ready-to-be-martyred old Russia. I had to
gather my thoughts before replying. "It isn't easy to know the truth," I
answered, "and even harder to tell it, but I will try to know the truth
and try to tell it." With the gaze of an icon, Father Mikhail charged
me, "Truth, truth, but only truth!"

Knowing the truth and telling it are both challenging tasks. Having seen a barn from one or two sides, I might say with confidence that the barn is red only to discover later on that the unseen sides are blue. In testifying that the barn was red, I haven't lied, but neither have I told the truth. Guesses became assumptions, and memories are unreliable. I was sincere and was attempting to be honest, but I was mistaken. Would that it were as simple to describe the architecture of myself. I am not only one color, and I have more than four sides. Even what we have witnessed with our own eyes and ears and have vivid memories of is not 100 percent reliable. Innocent people have been executed because of the faulty memories of sincere and honest witnesses. Writing this memoir I've repeatedly found my memory in error. Whenever I can, I have tried to check my memories against the memories of others and look for verifying evidence.

According to a Portuguese proverb, "God writes straight with crooked lines." It's a truth that my life bears witness to. God wastes nothing, not even our mistakes.

Chicago, 1942

Red Diaper Baby

I was a "red diaper baby"—both my parents were members of the Communist Party during my childhood, though Mother resigned somewhere in my teens. What exactly a Communist was I couldn't have explained to anyone, except that it meant occasionally walking with my mother for an hour or two on Saturday afternoons as she went door to door, trying, with no success that I can recall, to enlist subscribers to the *Daily Worker*, a paper published by the Communist Party from its headquarters in New York. My brother Richard and I were also sometimes brought along to the monthly meetings of her Communist cell group, made up of six or seven local people. Their living-room discussions, to my young ears, sounded very dull indeed. No uprisings were being planned. "Revolution" was a word I heard only in school, and there it was highly approved of: the American Revolution of 1776.

That Mother would turn out to be on the left edge of politics was certainly not what her parents had imagined or intended. She was born May 26, 1912, to a family that had money in the bank. Marguerite Hendrickson was the daughter of Charles Hendrickson, a lawyer of Dutch descent whose father had been a justice of the New Jersey Supreme Court.

Our first ancestor in the New World was Utrecht-born Hendrick Hendrickson, who earlier, if Mother's narrative is correct, had been navigator of *De Halve Maen* (*The Half Moon*) on Henry Hudson's first New World voyage in 1609. *De Halve Maen* was a Dutch ship with a Dutch crew; the only non-Dutch person on board was Hudson, an Englishman who had been hired by the Dutch East India Company to find a "northwest passage" that would greatly shorten the trade route to Asia. Instead Hudson won a place in history by sailing up the river that was later named after him.

The Castello map of Nieuw Amsterdam—today's New York City—provides a bird's-eye view of the most important Dutch settlement as it was in 1660 and also indicates property ownership. A house belonging to a Hendrick Hendrickson is shown on the southeast corner of Breedstraat, now Broadway, and Waalstraat, today's Wall Street. Far from being an artery of finance, the original Waalstraat was a quiet lane just inside the wall that served as the town's northern defense. Today the plot of land where the house stood is the location of a bank as well as a subway station entrance. Who lived in that long-gone house? Was it the same Hendrick Hendrickson who had been Hudson's navigator? Or a son? These are unanswered questions.

The only physical fragment of our Dutch roots that came down to us was a battered, centuries-old, dark red Dutch wooden shoe that served as a silent reminder of where some of our ancestors had originated. My mother kept it on a window ledge in the living room.

Even before entering high school, Mother aimed not for marriage but for higher education and a career, far from a common choice for women in those days. More than once she told my brother and me that her acceptance by Smith College in Massachusetts had been front-page news in the *Red Bank Register*. Searching the web, I recently found that front page; it was dated September 18, 1929. Four years later, Mother graduated *summa cum laude*, another front-page news item in the local paper. She went on to study social work at Columbia University in New York, but it was her undergraduate years at Smith that pleased and shaped her most. In one of my favorite photos of her, taken when she was in her eighties, she is proudly wearing a Smith College T-shirt.

It was also at Smith that Mother took a leftward turn, as did so many people during the Depression, from the down-and-out to the privileged. Soon after graduation, she signed up as a Communist. She met my father through the Communist Party and married him in New York in June 1934.

Communism is dense with ideology, yet Mother never struck me as an ideologue. I can't recall her ever trying to convince my brother or me of any Marxist dogma. For her, Communism boiled down to doing whatever she could to protect people from being treated like rubbish. She had meekly accepted the doctrine of atheism simply because it was part of the Marxist package. Yet in my experience neither of my parents were at war with God or Christianity.

Probably because she had grown up in a home without economic worries, Mother's adaptation to ascetic Communist ideals wasn't 100 percent successful. While we lived in a small house on the south edge of Red Bank, New Jersey, with only three cramped rooms plus kitchen and bathroom in a mainly black underclass neighborhood and had no car, not every economic choice suggested voluntary poverty. Although Mother spent money very carefully most of the time, it wasn't because there was no money to spend. In fact, in addition to having a good job as a psychiatric social worker, Mother had inherited an investment portfolio from her parents. Along with the *Daily Worker*, dividend checks and stock reports came steadily into the mailbox on our porch. Checking the financial pages of the *New York Herald Tribune*, Mother kept an eye on the value of shares in AT&T, Bell Telephone, and Standard Oil. One of her bywords, inherited from her father, was "never touch the principal, spend only the interest"—not a Marxist maxim. Thanks to the inheritance, our house had been purchased for cash—not a penny was owed the bank, nor did Mother buy anything on credit. She was dead set against debt.

Throughout her life she was devoted to her neighbors and would do anything for them, but dealing with behind-the-counter staff in stores betrayed her well-to-do upbringing. She expected *Service* with a capital "S," and complaints were delivered with hurricane force. I didn't envy the powerless sales people who were her usual target.

My brother Dick and I with our mother circa 1954

On the occasions when she went to the movies, she brought Dick and me with her. At times we were the only children in the audience, as was the case with *The Moon Is Blue*, a comedy about two playboys, each attempting to coax a young woman into bed but finding in their target an anthracite determination to remain a virgin until her wedding night. It was 1953; I was not yet twelve. Though the story left virtue triumphant, the film industry's Breen Office, responsible for enforcing the Motion Picture Production Code, judged the script as having "an unacceptably light attitude towards seduction, illicit sex, chastity, and virginity." Bucking the censors, director Otto Preminger refused to pasteurize the film. It was banned in three states, but that only enlarged audiences in the other forty-five. At the time I was unaware of the controversy, though I knew there were no matinee showings and that I was the only kid in my class who had seen it. What I remember best about the film is not its story but Mother's laughter. Afterward I asked her what the word "virgin" meant. "A woman who is determined to sleep alone," she said, then adding a joke. "Do you remember those huge stone lions that guard the main entrance to the New York City Public Library?" "Sure," I responded. We had walked by them many times on day trips to the city. "Those lions," she said, "roar whenever a virgin passes by."

Mother's laughter, at its most extreme, seemed to me life threatening and, when delivered in public, embarrassing.

But laughter was needed. Outside the theater, the Cold War and the McCarthy era meant that people like my parents were living in very unfunny times. Dad was one of a number of leading Communists who were arrested in September 1952. Uncle Charles, Mother's only brother, delivered the news the same day. He parked his black Buick in front of our house, knocked on the front door as if with a hammer, refused to come in when invited, and instead waved a page-one headline in Mother's face: FIVE TOP REDS ARRESTED IN ST. LOUIS. The principal "Red" was my father. My uncle shouted out his rage at the scandal of his being linked to such people (even though my parents were long divorced by then), stormed off the porch, and drove away. I don't recall Mother having managed to say a single word. I watched the scene from an adjacent window. I never saw my Uncle Charles again.

"Your father is in jail charged with 'conspiring to advocate the overthrow of the United States Government by force and violence,'" Mother explained to my brother and me that evening. "But you have to look at those words very carefully." She then pointed out that Dad was not charged with any violent act or even with advocating violence but "conspiring to advocate," which meant talking with other people about advocating violence sometime in the undated future. "But it isn't true," Mother added. "Your father hates violence and doesn't own a gun—he hates guns." At least I understood the last sentence. (After half a year in prison, Dad was freed on bail. Several years later, when the case was pending before the US Supreme Court, the Justice Department dropped all charges.)

In that period, we became aware that two FBI agents had been assigned to interview not only Mother's employers and co-workers but also our neighbors. One weekday, while Mother was still at work, the two blue-suited agents knocked on our front door and, displaying their badges, walked in. They then proceeded to fingerprint my brother and me. "Say hello to your mother," one of them said. They both laughed. Dick and I were left with the challenge of scrubbing the ink off our finger tips.

One of the nightmare experiences of my childhood was the electrocution of Julius and Ethel Rosenberg, the couple convicted of helping the Soviet Union obtain US atomic secrets. Mother was convinced that the Rosenbergs were scapegoats whose real crime was being Communists and Jewish as well. I doubt it ever crossed Mother's mind that either of them might in fact be guilty. Their conviction, she felt, was meant to further marginalize American Communists along with anyone even slightly to the left. The letters the Rosenbergs sent to their two sons from prison were published from time to time in the *Daily Worker,* and some of these Mother read to my brother and me. How we wept that morning in June 1953 as she read aloud newspaper accounts of their last minutes of life.

It's a safe guess that we were the only people in the neighborhood receiving the *Daily Worker.* A thin tabloid, it came rolled up in a plain wrapper without a return address. But as the chilly winds of the McCarthy period began to howl, the time came when, far from attempting to sell subscriptions, Mother began to worry about being on the mailing list at all. It was no longer thrown away with the trash like other newspapers but was saved until autumn, then burned with the fall leaves.

In the early fifties the FBI was systematically informing employers if someone on their payroll was a Communist or "a Communist sympathizer." In either case, the usual result was that the employee was fired. Thousands lost not only their jobs but, unable to meet mortgage payments, their homes as well. I know Mother worried about what would happen if she, a single parent with two children, were suddenly unemployed. Her inheritance wouldn't last long. Providing her employers with no excuse for firing her was the reason that she was never late for work and never took off a sick day. I doubt that the State of New Jersey ever got more from an employee than they got from her. "Why don't we have a car—everybody else has a car," I asked Mother when I was old enough to be puzzled that we depended so much on getting around by foot and bus or in my Aunt Douglas's car. "I don't want us getting used to having something," she explained, "we couldn't afford to keep if I lose my job."

I'm not sure when Mother resigned from the Communist Party and we stopped getting the *Daily Worker.* Her resignation wasn't something she told us about at the time. At the latest it would have been in 1956. I recall how shocked and disgusted she was by the Soviet Union's brutal suppression of the uprising in Hungary, an intervention slavishly supported by the Communist Party in the United States. But it may be that her resignation occurred earlier.

Demonstrating with my mother toward the end of her life

Even though an ex-Communist, Mother held unalterable, radical social values. "'From each according to his ability,' as she told me; 'to each according to his needs.' Only we're not ready for that yet. But I've never changed my mind that we should aspire to this."[1]

She battled local politicians for many years over a wide range of issues—racial integration of the local all-white volunteer fire department, roads, water mains, zoning issues, transportation for the old and handicapped, food

---

1. The quotation, though pure Marx, has a distinctly biblical ring. In the Acts of the Apostles, the community of first-generation Christians in Jerusalem is described as holding all things in common, with distribution made to every man according to need. "And the multitude of them that believed were of one heart and of one soul. Neither said any of them that ought of the things which he possessed was his own, but they had all things common. And with great power gave the apostles witness of the resurrection of the Lord Jesus. And great grace was upon them all. Neither was there any among them that lacked, for as many as were possessors of lands or houses sold them, and brought the prices of the things that were sold, and laid them down at the apostles' feet: and distribution was made unto every man according as he had need" (Acts 4:32-35).

banks, housing for the poor, etc., with many a walk in the neighbor-hood collecting signatures for petitions.

Christianity became central to Mother during her last four decades. A key event in her return to the Methodist Church in 1960 had been reading, at my suggestion, Thomas Merton's autobiography, *The Seven Storey Mountain*. When I told Merton about this, he laughed: "Your mother is my book's first convert to Protestantism!" No doubt there were other books, plus an inclination that had roots in her childhood, that were also important factors. She had been an occasional, back-door Methodist even while a Communist, but from about 1961 onward Mother never missed a service unless she was ill. She also took an active part in all sorts of adult activities, becoming one of the church's most engaged members.

When she was in her mid-seventies I took her out to lunch at a par-ticularly nice restaurant—One Potato, Two Potatoes—in Nyack, New York, the town where I was working at the time. A few nights before I had seen the film *Reds*, a remarkably accurate portrait of American radicals and writers in the early years of the twentieth century. I was trying to remember the lyrics of the socialist anthem, "The *Internatio-nale*," which she had used as a lullaby when Dick and I were children and which had been sung in Russian in the movie. I asked, "Do you remember the words?" Though the restaurant was crowded, and in any event wasn't a place where anyone but my mother would burst into song, without hesitation she sang the *Internationale* straight through: "Arise ye prisoners of starvation, arise ye wretched of the earth, for justice thunders condemnation, a better world's in birth. . . ." At the end—tears glistening on her cheeks and me still scribbling away on a napkin—she said, "With a hymn like that, how could you not be a Communist?" A hymn? For Mother it was.

After her retirement in 1977, Mother became a student at nearby Brookdale College and took classes there on wide-ranging subjects for about twenty years, until she was too weak to continue. Conversations with her during those two decades would invariably turn to what she was studying at the time, which might be history, sociology, anthropology, theology, or law. Even when she lost all but her peripheral vision and had become legally blind, she was undeterred, reading with the help of a scanning device that hugely magnified letters on a TV screen. A word of more than four of five letters would often overflow the screen area, but Mother doggedly read on word by word. For nearly ten years she used this machine in the college library for hours at a time, often five days per week. The librarian showed us a book in which users signed up for the device. With only a few exceptions, page after page was packed exclusively with the signature "Marguerite H. Forest." Finally the college, when upgrading library equipment, gave her the older machine to have at home. For a decade afterward, it was anchored to the dining room table.

During visits late in her life, I was repeatedly struck by Mother's "one day at a time" way of life. She had never been nostalgic. She had little interest in either past or future, but a tremendous engagement with the present. Her opinions hadn't mellowed or faded. Over lunch she expressed her pleasure about a letter to the editor my aunt had sent to a local paper, a protest against capital punishment. Aunt's point was that we should leave the taking of life to God.

In the summer of 1997, while doing a few errands in Red Bank, I stopped at a free food kitchen called the Lunch Break to drop off a box of unused light bulbs Mother had found in the cellar. One woman at the Lunch Break asked me, "Is Marguerite still going door to door?" This was a reference to my mother's frequent efforts to gather signatures for petitions. I assured her that she was still going strong. The volunteer laughed—"You sure got yourself some mother. Nothing can stop that lady!"

On my next visit I found her in surprisingly good shape and spirits. She couldn't get around easily, but you would hardly notice that the world she saw was increasingly a blur. Nothing was in focus. Her hearing was good. She was very alert, though when tired she couldn't quite remember if I was Jim or my son, Ben, who lived nearby. She was slower in doing things and used her four-footed cane inside the house. I found her dismayed that her text-magnifying device was broken; it had become unplugged, as I discovered. The book she was reading at the time was about life in Israel-Palestine at the time of Christ.

In old age, the ideals of her youth and young adulthood sprang back to life with renewed vigor. Despite being an ex-Communist, once again she often spoke of Communism in glowing terms. When I told her the ideals were fine but that in practice every country that had tried Communism quickly ended up being a hellish place to live, she was resistant to hearing it, though when I described visiting a forest near Minsk where, in the Stalin years, truckloads of people were shot and killed each and every day, year after year, their bodies filling many pits, she was horrified. But by the next day, what I had told her about Lenin's and Stalin's atrocities was forgotten.

Mother in her Smith College T-shirt

During her last few years I could see that Mother was much less able to get around, much quicker to tire. The television was on most of the time, mainly tuned to the Discovery Channel. Her world had shrunk to about the size of the house. Recent news wasn't in her thoughts, except during those moments when it was mentioned. She was amazed to be told how many great-grandchildren she had. "Goodness! Imagine that!" I once told Mother that her granddaughter Anne took great pride in having "so adventurous a grandmother." She responded, "Yes, I am adventurous." It struck me that even then, when she could hardly cross the kitchen without becoming exhausted, she put it in the present tense.

Mother's beloved sister, my Aunt Douglas, died in August 2001, age ninety-four. Though face-to-face visits had become infrequent because of the distance between their two homes, they would be in touch with each other by phone several times a day. Her sister's death was a signal that it was time to go.

Death came the night of December 8 of the same year. Earlier in the evening Mother repeatedly asked Norma Whisky, the live-in Jamaican woman who was caring for her day and night, to leave the front door unlocked "because my sister is coming to get me." My son Ben was with her when she exhaled her last breath. She was eighty-nine.

A Kid with a State Name

Dad never discovered what his family name would have been had his parents been married and had he not become an orphan. The name he was known by as an adult, James Frederick Forest, was two-thirds made up. Only James was there from the start.

He was born on August 8, 1910, in Boston, Massachusetts. His mother was an auburn-haired, brown-eyed, impoverished Irish immigrant who, as best Dad could discover, had worked as a seamstress, a maid, and an artist's model. It was only as an adult that he learned her name was Rose Murray and realized Murray had once been his own last name. The source of that desperately sought information was Catherine Smith, a social worker who had been a vital source of encouragement and practical support during his childhood.

When Dad spoke of his mother, there was grief in voice. He had no memory of ever living with her. "Sometime in my first few years she arranged for me to stay with a family—a good family, very kind—who were living on the upper floor in a Boston tenement," he recalled. "Why didn't you live with her?" I asked. "I don't know, but I saw her often and felt her sadness that we were living apart." What was unsaid was that perhaps her poverty had driven her to become a prostitute.

Dad's stay in the tenement ended abruptly when the building caught fire. "I was lifted by a fireman through a window on the top floor and carried down a long ladder to safety. I remember the fireman holding me over his shoulder. There was fire and smoke and it was nighttime. I was terrified. Afterward my mother arranged for me to board with another family."

Dad's last memory of his mother was her taking him to an amusement park near Boston. "I was four. I think she was saying goodbye. I never saw her again." Later in life he succeeded in finding her death certificate. Rose Murray died by drowning. Suicide? It's not certain but Dad thought so.

Following her death in 1915, Dad became a ward of the State of Massachusetts. It was at this point that he was given Frederick as a last name. "Perhaps that week they were giving out last names that started with an 'F.' I was a state kid with a state name."

His early life resembles a Charles Dickens narrative. "As soon as I became a state kid, I was put in the care of a man and woman, an older couple, who made their living providing care for orphans, up to six at a time. Supposedly they were seeing after our basic needs, but in fact they spent as little as possible on our needs and kept as much as possible for themselves. The two of them could have stepped out of the pages of *Oliver Twist*. The soup we were given was hardly more than water—water flavored by the shadow of a pigeon. The six of us had one room to sleep in, two to a mattress, and a single swing to share in the tiny back yard."

Fortunately, Catherine Smith, his social worker, came to visit and saw how undernourished he was. For a brief period she took him into her own home while making arrangements for him to be placed with an honest, attentive family. In 1916 she put him into foster care with the Drown family in East Pepperell, Massachusetts, a town forty-five miles northwest of Boston near the New Hampshire border.

"The head of the family," Dad recalled, "was Fred Allen Drown, a Yankee with deep roots in New England who had been born in Vermont in 1868. He worked at a local paper mill. His wife was Margaret Loretta Drown, an Irish immigrant with a strong Irish accent who also spoke Gaelic. The Gaelic songs that I know I learned from her. The family received three dollars a week for each state ward they took in; the state also paid for our clothing and medical expenses."

"My foster parents were shocked by my malnourished condition when I arrived. 'Look at him, just skin and bones!' I wasn't their only state kid. There were other foster children in the household for shorter or longer stays, but I was the only state kid who remained with the Drown household throughout my childhood. I gradually became part of the family, at least up to a point. I never felt loved but I did feel valued."

One of his first memories after coming to live with the Drown family was walking into the small barn on their property and discovering the cover of a popular magazine—possibly *Collier's*—tacked up on a wall. "There was a painting of a beautiful woman on the cover. I had not a moment's doubt it was my mother! I was overwhelmed with joy. I think the painting gave me the idea that perhaps she was still alive. I ran into the house and told my foster parents, but Mr. Drown was far from pleased. The cover was taken off the wall, and I never saw it again."

For years, fear was a constant in Dad's life. "I was terrified of being sent to an orphanage, which my foster parents reminded me could easily happen and which sounded like being sent to prison. My solution from early on was to become the 'can-do kid,' always looking for ways to be helpful, assisting with every aspect of household work as well as with the garden. The older I got, the more I took on. We had a cow and a horse and I took care of them as well. With my two paper routes and the chores I did for neighbors, mowing lawns in summer and shoveling snow in winter, I was able to contribute to family finances. When I got to high school, I also made a little money working as assistant janitor."

In 1925, after nine years with the Drown family, Dad—now fifteen—was legally adopted, a goal he had long sought. In fact he had worked so hard to make himself adoptable that, once the goal was achieved, he never felt sure whether the Drowns loved him as a son or as a hard worker who did more than his share.

Living in a Catholic household in a largely Catholic neighborhood, he developed strong ties to the Catholic Church. He was active in the local parish, serving as an altar boy. Mass was an event of consequence to him, as were the Gospel stories and parables. Inspired by an admirable pastor, Dad decided that once he had finished high school he would go to seminary and become a priest.

The Boy Scouts were an equally serious interest. He had started hanging around with the local troop when he was ten and officially joined the day he turned twelve. He loved camping and accumulated numerous merit badges, eventually becoming an Eagle Scout. Oddly enough, he never owned or desired a Boy Scout uniform, only borrowing one occasionally when it was essential, as when he was appointed to recite Lincoln's Gettysburg Address at the town's annual Memorial Day celebration.

It was his link to the Scouts that triggered his break with the Catholic Church. The parish priest Dad had so greatly admired was reassigned; his successor was a recently ordained man with rigid views on many topics. In those days of religious cold war, the new priest had an ice-hard objection to Catholics being involved in anything remotely Protestant. His strict eyes picking out my father at Mass on Sunday, he declared that the local Protestant-sponsored Boy Scout troop was off limits. Dad, then age fifteen, walked out of the church and didn't attend another Mass until half a century later when visiting me in New York. "It was a bitter moment in my life, changing my thoughts about the future and my ideas about religion," he told me. "If churches could be so narrow, if Christians could be so set against each other, I didn't want to be part of it." Yet I gradually became aware that underneath the bitterness he had acquired toward Catholicism was grief at having lost contact with a church that, in many ways, had shaped his social conscience. Far from objecting to my own religious awakenings, he cheered me along.

Dad was paying close attention to the world beyond East Pepperell. "I did a lot of reading, including books on utopian societies that, for a time in the nineteenth century, had flourished in America, and also about the recent revolution in Russia. I knew about various social protests going on and about the Communist Party. I was aware of the controversy that was raging over the convictions of Sacco and Vanzetti."

Though he graduated second in his senior class at high school, Dad wasn't able to enter college after his graduation. While his principal had succeeded in getting him a full-tuition scholarship to Harvard, no grant was provided for living expenses. This put Harvard out of reach. Instead, in the fall of 1928 he began a course at the Bartlett School of Tree Surgery in Connecticut. The school arranged for him to serve an apprenticeship as part of a team working on Long Island, an assignment that brought him to the Phipps estate in Westbury, one of the most palatial properties on Long Island's "gold coast" and known as "the richest square mile in the world." "Never in my life had I seen such wealth," Dad told me. "A mansion with cooks, maids, butlers, gardeners, mechanics, and chauffeurs! But I also learned about the advantages of not chasing money. One of my fellow tree surgeons introduced me to Thoreau and Emerson."

In the late summer of 1929, Dad moved to New York City to pick up credits at Columbia University with the intention of entering the New York Forestry School. "Once in Manhattan," he recalled, "I slept in thirty-five-cents-a-night flophouses on the Bowery and ate at Bowery restaurants that served soup at five cents a bowl, which I paid for with income from odd jobs. My first job was as an usher and bouncer at a movie house in the Bronx. I remember chasing a big guy out of the theater—lucky for me he didn't decide to turn around and fight!"

His plans to study at Columbia evaporated with the Wall Street Crash on "Black Thursday," October 24, 1929. The following day, Black Friday, he went down to Wall Street to witness what was happening and was only a block away when one of the men who had seen his fortune go up in smoke jumped to his death from a window ledge.

With the Great Depression under way, Dad decided it was time to make contact with "the revolutionary movement." The United States was, he felt, approaching a time of dramatic change. "Revolution was in the air," he recalled. "Many people spoke openly of the need for systemic change."

"In late November I saw a poster in Battery Park advertising a talk by a woman, Nina Davis, who had just returned from a trip to the Soviet Union. I attended, was impressed by what she had to

Dad about the time I was born

say, and afterward talked with her about joining the Communist Party. She signed me up at her office the following morning and gave me several dollars so I could buy a few basic Communist books at the shop downstairs. I sure needed those books! At the time I knew almost nothing about Marxism, but I was convinced that the solution to America's economic and social problems—the way to a more equitable society—was socialism, with the people owning the means of production. I saw in the Communist Party people taking up the challenge of the Depression and fighting for the immediate improvement of the needs of the people."

In those days one got a "party name" when joining the Communist Party. Dad chose "Forest" as a new last name. "I no longer felt a connection with the Drown family," he explained. "I was also aware that in earlier times names were often based on what you did. I was a tree surgeon and always felt at home in the forest. It seemed the perfect name for me."

Bright, highly motivated, and with a gift for public speaking, his talents were quickly noticed. He got involved with a party-supported Unemployed Council based at a center on the Lower East Side. His sleeping place was a couch in a vacant office. Then, when the couch was no longer available, his nighttime shelter was the back of a derelict truck. Hard up for nickels, he ate his meals at free soup kitchens. Even with the occasional banana or apple as a supplement, it was far from an adequate diet. Speaking at a rally on Union Square one day, he passed out from hunger, after which distressed friends took him to a nearby Russian restaurant for what might have been the best meal in his life so far.

In the spring of 1932, age twenty-one, Dad was asked to join the Communist-backed City Unemployed Council and was appointed editor of its publication, the *Hunger Fighter*. "I was well suited for the job," he told me. "God knows I had plenty of experience being hungry!"

One of his tasks was to help organize a demonstration at City Hall. Thousands turned out for what they hoped would be a peaceful event. Instead there was a police attack, complete with a horse charge. One of the horse's hooves landed on one of Dad's feet. "I limped for months afterward but counted myself lucky that no permanent damage was done. I narrowly escaped a blow with a police baton the size of a baseball bat. It would have crushed my skull."

Later that year, no doubt on party orders, Dad joined the Army. "I was excited—I had been dreaming since childhood of seeing more of the world," he told me, "and this was my chance. Thanks to a merit badge in telegraphy I had gotten as a Boy Scout, I spent two years in the Army Signal Corps, stationed at Fort Monmouth, New Jersey, not far from Red Bank. So much for travel to faraway places!" Had he been stationed anywhere else the author of this book would not be here to write it.

"Your mother had just graduated from Smith," Dad told me. "One of the first things she did once she returned to her parents' home in Red Bank was send a letter to the Communist Party headquarters in New York asking to become a member. As the party knew I was based nearby, I got a letter asking me to meet this Marguerite Hendrickson and see if she was well suited to party membership. Not only did I find her well suited, but I fell in love with her."

Despite the reservations of Mother's parents—Dad was far from the son-in-law they had envisioned—the two were married in November

1934, shortly before Dad's discharge from the Army. Their honeymoon was a long hike along the Appalachian Trail.

My parents settled in Manhattan, first in a room on West Fourteenth Street, then a larger apartment on Sullivan Street in Greenwich Village. Dad was now working full-time for "the party," which meant long hours and little money. Mother, the real bread winner, was hired by the city as a social worker based in Harlem. She loved the job. In the process, she helped organize a local branch of the Municipal Employees Union.

In 1937 Dad was appointed party organizer for the state of Utah, based in Salt Lake City. As his salary was not enough to live on, he worked part-time as a self-employed tree surgeon while Mother was hired as a social worker.

It is while they were living in Utah that I enter the story, a small item with a long name: James Hendrickson Forest, born November 2, 1941.

I have no memories of Utah. I was less than a year old when Dad's political work brought him to Chicago. In 1943, we moved again, this time to Denver. It was in Denver, on January 24, 1943, that my brother, Richard Douglas Forest, was born.

Early in 1944, Dad began an affair with Dorothy Baskin, a co-worker. He had been, he told me many years later, "swept off his feet." Dorothy gave birth to my half sister, Rosanne, on November 30, 1944, in St. Louis, Missouri, where Dad had moved after the divorce. Drafted into the Army in January 1945 and stationed in Hawaii, he remained in uniform until demobilization in December 1945, after which he returned to party work, first in Los Angeles, next in St. Louis, where his life took a different sort of turn. In September 1952, Dad was one of five Missouri Communists arrested under the Smith Act, charged with conspiring to advocate the overthrow of the US government by force and violence. He was in the city jail from the end of September 1952 until early February 1953.

The trial in Federal District Court, St. Louis, began in January 1954. Dad made the unusual decision to act as his own lawyer. In his opening statement he told the jurors that he wanted to speak for himself so that he could personally explain what he believed and what the Communist Party stood for. Describing his youth, he said, "The ideals of the American Revolution were my ideals and still are." On June 4, 1954, the "St. Louis Five" were convicted. Dad was sentenced to five years.

My father (second from right) with other members of the "St. Louis Five"

The judge ordered that the defendants, then out on bail, be sent back to prison while their conviction was appealed. Dad remained there from June to mid-August, a long, hot summer, until freed again on bail. (In April 1958, his conviction was reversed by the Federal Court of Appeals. In October 1958, the US Department of Justice, anticipating defeat at the Supreme Court, abandoned the prosecution of all such cases, including that of my father.)

After Missouri, California became Dad's permanent home. During the last years of his life, his home was a housing cooperative he had cofounded in Santa Rosa, California. Until stopped in his tracks by cancer early in 1990, Dad had been a builder, a handyman, a carpenter, a fixer, an inventor and improviser who couldn't get through a single day, as long as he had the strength to lift a hammer or turn a screwdriver, without improving or repairing something. "I was always fascinated," he said when he was hardly able to raise his head from his bed, "with how things worked and how to fix them when they didn't work."

When told he had cancer, Dad responded, "This ought to be interesting."

Visiting him in his final days, we talked several times about heaven. "Do you think there really is a heaven?" he asked me. I told him that God does not erase what he has made, least of all those who have loved creation and cared for it day by day. He reached out and gripped my hand with intensity. With tears in his eyes, he said a heartfelt "yes." I said that he would at last see his dear mother. "I will be so astonished," he said. I told him that he had always been a love-centered person. "I hope so," he responded.

While with him that last week, I wrote a biographical text about his life and read it to him. He was alert throughout, the longest stretch of being fully awake during the week that I was there. He was deeply moved. Time and again he said, "Did I really do that?" "Yes, you did." "Well, that wasn't so bad," he replied each time.

During those days he often didn't know where he was, though generally he recognized everyone who came to visit. I was impressed how caring he was about the people who came to see him—friends, the home hospice nurse, ambulance drivers. No matter how much pain he was struggling with, he wanted to know how each person was, how their children were doing and about past adventures in their lives.

The day I had arrived at his bedside, Dad had immediately noticed the crucifix I was wearing. He asked if he could borrow it. I told him I would give it to him as a gift. "No, just to borrow," he responded. "I won't need it very long." We talked about what the cross meant: the link between his suffering and the suffering of Christ, the suffering of countless people down through history, and the connection of the cross with the resurrection. From that moment on, the crucifix was next to him, hanging from the railing at the side of his hospital bed as his skin was too sensitive to wear it. He sometimes told visitors it was from me;he told others it had been given to him by a priest. The crucifix was in his hands when he died. It was mid-morning, May 7, 1990.

Dad and my stepmother Lucy take Wendy, Thom, and Dan to the circus in 1985

A Day-Late Saint

I was born just past midnight on November 2, 1941, at Latter Day Saints Hospital in Salt Lake City, Utah. Mainly Mormons are born in that dry, underpopulated state, but there isn't a single Mormon anywhere in my family tree. In Salt Lake City, which has exported thousands of young black-suited Mormon missionaries to every corner of the earth, my parents were missionaries of another kind with all of Utah their mission territory. They had come there four years before my birth because Dad had been appointed to serve as regional organizing secretary by the Communist Party.

Growing up in an Irish milieu and having once wanted to be a priest, my father would have remembered that November 2 is the Feast of All Souls, the day following All Saints' Day. Perhaps Dad joked about me being, if not a latter-day saint, then a day-late saint, a son who might have been delivered complete with halo had I only taken the trouble to arrive an hour earlier.

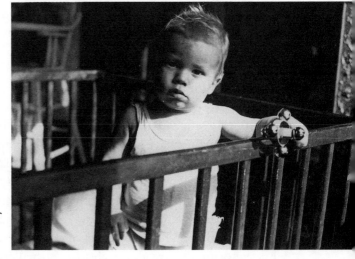

My arrival happened just five weeks before the Japanese attack on Pearl Harbor. During the first thirty-six days of my life, I was in a country on the brink of war but not yet in it, while in Europe a calamitous conflict had been raging for two years. But I have no memories of World War II. I was three when it ended.

Before my memory became retentive, we moved from Salt Lake City to Chicago. Somewhere in our house we have a photo of me that Dad took when I was about a year old, an earnest expression on my face, standing in a Chicago park next to my mother, a young woman wearing a dark beret, smoking a cigarette, and looking determined to change the world. In another photo, I am standing in a crib, a bell-studded rattle in my left hand and an interrogative countenance on my face suggesting that I am already pondering the meaning and purpose of life.

A year later came a move to Denver. It was in Denver, age two, that my memory began to kick in. We were living in a small, two-story house. What may be my earliest memory is inserting one of Dad's screwdrivers into an electric socket in the living room—an opening that seemed to cry out for a screwdriver's insertion—and then being astonished when sparks exploded from the opening and smoke emerged. I was an accidental arsonist at an early age. Luckily I had only touched the screwdriver's wooden grip, not the metal shaft. Damage to the house was slight. I have no memory of being punished or even yelled at. Mother was, in practice as well as principle, a pacifist parent. On this occasion I suppose the main thing on her mind was the happy fact that I hadn't killed myself or burned the house down.

Another early memory is using a chair in the kitchen as a platform from which to watch oatmeal cooking in a pot on the stove. Standing still as a flagpole, I gazed with intensity, hypnotized by the slow-motion bubbles rising, breaking the moon-like surface, at last bursting open, leaving short-lived craters in the oatmeal.

One of my great experiments in Denver had to do with raisin bread. My best guess is that I was three. I rose at dawn one morning to do something I realized had best be done while the rest of the family was asleep. There must have been a good deal of premeditation on my part. My target was a loaf of raisin bread. First, I placed a large bowl on a stool beneath the meat grinder, which was clamped to the counter. Turning the grinder's handle with my right hand, I fed in slices of bread with the left, while the bowl received the results. I then shifted the bowl to the kitchen table, picking out and eating all the raisin bits while ignoring the bread crumbs. I was thrilled at having successfully solved a daunting problem: how to get at the raisins without having to bother with the bread. I was discovered at the scene of the crime, but again there was no punishment. Mother laughed. After that she saw to it that we had a supply of little red-and-yellow packets of Sun-Maid raisins.

I recall a day when we went for a picnic in the Rocky Mountains. The tall grass and flowers were at my eye level and had an ultrabright, razor-edged intensity about them. I was fascinated by the snow-crested mountain tops we were ascending toward and the fiercely blue, cloudless sky over our heads. How high did we climb? What was the picnic like? Who else was there? I don't remember.

My brother Dick was fourteen months my junior. While I suppose I initially regarded him as uninvited competition delivered to the wrong address, he grew from bothersome infant into cheerful companion. I spent many hours playing with him and other kids in a wood-walled sandbox in the back yard. Probably Dad, a jack-of-all-trades, had built it. Sand flew over our hair, and into it, like snow.

Dad asked Mother for a divorce in June 1944. How much my mother knew about Dad's affair with Dorothy Baskin, and when, I have no idea. My earliest vivid memory of Dad is of his final departure from

With my brother Dick

our house in September. Of that bitter event, all that survives is a mental photo of Dad standing at the front door, suitcase in hand, looking back into the house apologetically and waving a sorrowful goodbye to me as I watched from halfway down the staircase. I still can feel the tears on my face and hear myself pleading, "Dad, please take me with you." I was not yet three. After his departure, it must have been a year or two before I saw him again. We remained in Denver until March 1946, when Mother received her master's degree in social work from the University of Denver.

Then comes a sweeter memory, a great railway journey east that is still so fresh that it remains forever in the present tense: My mother, my brother, and I are on the train going halfway across the country, from Denver via Chicago to New York. I seem to be awake all the way, my four-year-old nose pressed to the window pane making islands of fog-like condensation while watching the ever-changing view: farms, houses, horses, cows, trees, rivers, bridges, fields of corn and wheat, gullies, huge clouds, lightning storms, cloudless skies, train stations, islands of rust and rubbish, blurred villages, fast-passing towns, snapshot glimpses of window-framed lamp-lit people in their homes, all the while the train rushing relentlessly forward, the steel wheels beating a sweet jazzy music out of the tracks. Even long after sunset, it was a constant visual adventure, better than any movie. Is there a finer way to see the world than from a train?

My excitement about moving swept aside for a time the bewilderment and dismay I felt. I was oblivious to how acute was my mother's distress. She hid it well. It wasn't until many years later, after my own experiences of marital failure, that it dawned on me how desolate she must have felt.

Waiting for the three of us at the train station was my Aunt Douglas and her husband, Robert Inglis. We got into their dark purple Packard sedan and drove to my aunt and uncle's home in Red Bank, New Jersey, a river town not many miles from the Atlantic Ocean. Red Bank had been my mother and aunt's childhood home. Until Mother found and bought a house, we rented an apartment in the same building in which my aunt and uncle lived.

An Apprenticeship
in Saying "No"

A few years ago, the *Smithsonian* magazine published a list of "twenty best small towns in America." Red Bank was not only on the list but in third place. It's a town that has aged gracefully, with many of its streets lined with well-preserved nineteenth-century brick or clapboard buildings. Despite competition from the web and shopping malls, the stores and cafes on Broad Street remain open, though the businesses they house are different from those I remember. In broad strokes, Red Bank today is much as it was in my childhood.

One factor for the *Smithsonian* in weighing up the town's pluses is the Count Basie Theater, named after Red Bank's most famous native son. The theater now provides a venue for some of America's best performers. In my childhood it was called the Carlton, a gilded cathedral of cinema with a frescoed dome and spacious balcony. Occasionally the movie screen was raised and the deep stage behind it revealed. One of the memorable events of my childhood was seeing a production of Gilbert and Sullivan's *Mikado* performed by the London-based D'Oyly Carte Company. The theater's acoustics are remarkable. "This hall is to a singer what Steinway is to a pianist," Art Garfunkel has commented. Count Basie himself, with his orchestra, played there before I was born.

Just down the street, near the railroad station, now stands a bronze bust of Count Basie, the jazz genius himself. How times have changed. When I was a kid I recall no local politician suggesting a memorial celebrating Count Basie or any other member of Red Bank's substantial black community.

If Mother as an adult could have chosen her skin color, it wouldn't have been white. It was not by accident that the house she bought on

A drawing I made of Red Bank's train station

Newman Springs Road in Tinton Falls, on the south border of Red Bank, was in a mainly black neighborhood. On the Tinton Falls side of the road, where we lived, not all the roads were paved, and there were no sewers. We had a cesspool under our backyard. A few nearby homes still had outhouses.

Besides having chosen a neighborhood she was pleased to be part of, Mother had the convenience of being on a bus route that took her to her work every morning and back home at the end of the day. She had been hired as a psychiatric social worker at the state mental hospital at Marlboro, twelve miles to the west.

My brother and I quickly formed bonds with the neighborhood kids. Nearby fields and woods served as a playground. Inspired by westerns and war movies, we found an empty lot where we dug trenches, then covered them over with old boards and dirt—an underground fort with secret tunnels stretching out in several directions. In winter, snow forts arose on the same location, and wars were fought with snowballs. In summer, inspired by the legends of Robin Hood found in books and seen on screen, the local woods became Sherwood Forest in which we hid in trees and bushes, taking turns being Robin's Merry Men or the evil Sheriff of Nottingham and his thugs. In reality our only real enemies were poison ivy and poison sumac. At the cost of many an itch and rash, we learned at an early age to identify their toxic leaves. Green asparagus and wild strawberries grew in the fields—I brought home shoots of asparagus for cooking and ate strawberries where I found them.

On a dry summer day in a weedy field conveniently near the firehouse, I accidentally started a fire by applying a pinprick of sunlight produced by a magnifying glass to a small pile of grass and leaves. A flame burst from the heap and spread more quickly than my shoes could stamp it out. A fire truck was needed to put out the blaze. I watched at a distance, ashamed of what I had done and in dread of being caught. It was a terrifying lesson in what a spark can become.

I made a bumpy landing in school. There were early intimations that I was destined to commit occasional acts of civil disobedience later in life.

Getting to school meant taking daily rides in yellow buses that had the impressive power, thanks to their blinking red lights, of stopping traffic in both directions while kids got on and off. Less admirably, school buses were also ideal hunting grounds for bullies. Two older boys decided I needed to be moved from the part of the bus where they were to another section, but I was determined not to cooperate. There was a floor-to-roof vertical bar in reach. I grabbed it and hung on like a barnacle. My grip and stubbornness turned out to be enough. I proved unmovable and never again was troubled by those particular bullies. I felt like a victorious prizefighter.

Another collision of wills happened one day at lunchtime in the school cafeteria. Food was spooned into the compartmentalized tin trays that we held in our young hands. Normally I dutifully ate what I was given, but one day found the grayish green peas heaped in one corner of my tray tasted rotten and left them untouched. When I tried to return the tray with its island of peas, I was ordered to go back to the table and finish my meal. "But the peas have a bad taste," I explained. The kitchen manager responded, "You will not leave this cafeteria until the last pea is eaten." She was a substantial woman who seemed never to smile. My course of action was obvious to me. I sat alone at the table in silence the rest of the afternoon, ignoring a series of demands from several people, including the school principal. At 3 p.m., the school buses now being loaded, the kitchen manager gave up. Trailing clouds of glory, off I went to my bus, leaving the tray and its cold gray peas behind.

My first-grade teacher, Mrs. Stega, was a woman who later reminded me of the archetypal enemy of children, Miss Trunchbull, in Roald Dahl's novel *Matilda*. When she noticed that I was making my capital Js with squared corners at the base rather than a standard curved line, she decided, correctly, that my calligraphy was a declaration of war directed at her. The harder Mrs. Stega fought to get me to round off my Js—a letter of special importance to me as it was the first letter in James—the more determined I was not to comply. Though only six, I found myself in a position of power, intoxicated with the awareness that there was no way Mrs. Stega could force me to mend my letter-shaping ways. After some weeks, her outrage at my insubordination reached its climax with my being expelled from first grade and being sent back to kindergarten.

Dick and I

My obvious glee over my demotion must have disappointed her, but for me it was a gold-medal Olympic victory. Once I had a teacher I liked, I abandoned squared Js. A year later, skipping first grade and Mrs. Stega, I was returned to my own age group.

Such episodes in my early life were, I realize in retrospect, experiments in resistance—saying no to both adults and peers in a determined but nonviolent manner and refusing to budge. I was a Gandhian before I knew there was a Gandhi.

From early on I was also a budding patriot. Reciting the pledge of allegiance, my right hand over my heart and my eyes on the flag, was something I did without reserve. I can still sing a song we were taught in second or third grade: "I love the United States of America. / I love the way we all live without fear. / I love to vote for my choice, / speak my mind, raise my voice. / Yes, I like it here!"

Deciphering the Alphabet

I can't remember a time when books weren't important in my life. Our house was full of them, shelf after shelf of volumes of history, psychology, and literature—three floor-to-ceiling bookcases plus three more half as high. Part of the library dated back to Mother's student days at Smith College. A bound set of the complete works of Mark Twain had once been Grandfather Hendrickson's, and a similar set of all the Dickens's novels. A complete collection of Jack London's books had once been Dad's. There was also Carl Sandberg's four-volume biography of Abraham Lincoln and a *Webster's Dictionary* bigger than a bread box.

Before I began deciphering the alphabet, Mother read aloud from a wide range of books—the adventures of Winnie the Pooh as well as A. A. Milne's related poetry, Beatrice Potter's tales of Peter Rabbit and his neighbors, the escapades of Raggedy Ann and Andy, collections of stories by Hans Christian Andersen and the Brothers Grimm, such classics as *Aesop's Fables*, and many more.

I was so intrigued by the mystery of the alphabet—symbols linked with sounds—that I improvised an alphabet largely of my own design and used it to create a family newspaper, which unfortunately only I could read. It wasn't till I was four or five that I began to make sense of the alphabet, thanks to which I was able, beginning in first grade, to read the remarkably dull life of Dick and Jane, two white children living in a solidly white neighborhood—this in a school where half my classmates were black.

Once I had cracked the alphabet code, I was so thrilled with the achievement that I made a great nuisance of myself by reading aloud all the billboards we passed when Aunt, or sometimes Uncle Bob, was driving: "Pepsi-Cola! More bounce to the ounce!" "Coca-Cola! Every drink a fresh delight!" "Glad we're a Ford family!" "Be happy! Go Lucky!" "Lucky Strike means fine tobacco!" "Healthful, refreshing, delicious! Doublemint Gum!" "I'd walk a mile for a Camel!" "Wonder Bread builds strong bodies twelve ways!" "Keds—the shoes that winners choose!" "Schlitz! The beer that made Milwaukee famous!" "See the USA in your Chevrolet!" Exclamation marks were often in the ads but always in my readings. Before long Aunt would say, "That's enough, dear." But I never stayed silent for long.

By the time I was seven, the town librarian knew me well. While initially books had to be borrowed by my mother, at last came the happy day when I was old enough to be given my own library card. I would borrow several books at a time, often making choices suggested by the librarian. I'd love to see a list of all the titles that came home with me. In one period, aware that I was reading anything that had to do with pirates, the librarian diagnosed me as having "buccaneer fever."

One element in my early and urgent desire to read was my desperate need to become comic book literate. Once the cipher was broken, many a dime was spent on comics. One of my early favorites was Disney's "Uncle Scrooge" series.

As I became more literate, one of my devotions was *Pogo*, Walt Kelly's creation, a daily comic strip carried in hundreds of newspapers including the one Mother subscribed to, the *New York Herald Tribune*. Pogo lived in Georgia's Okefenokee Swamp along with a menagerie of animal friends, whom Kelly referred to as "nature's screechers." Heading the cast was the strip's namesake, Pogo, a level-headed, pure-hearted, and philosophically inclined possum who wore a striped shirt and was overflowing with good will. Pogo's most famous line was, "We have met the enemy and he is us." It would have been a Pogo-like child who pointed out to the emperor that he was clothed in nothing but his bare skin. Every four years Pogo cam-

paigned for the US presidency—many people, I among them, wore "I go Pogo" buttons.

Kelly's strip had a daring political edge at a time when the "funny papers" carefully avoided controversy. In the fifties, Wiley Cat, a menacing bobcat, morphed into Simple J. Malarkey, who had an unmistakable resemblance to Joseph McCarthy. If roses were red, Simple J. Malarkey saw Communist sedition in each rose petal. You had to be a brave cartoonist in those days to make fun of the junior senator from Wisconsin—being laughed at was not something that warmed McCarthy's cold-warrior heart.

Kelly took on an even more dangerous target, J. Edgar Hoover, head of the Federal Bureau of Investigation. Portrayed as a bulldog, in one series of *Pogo* strips he had a string of top-secret paper dolls locked in his briefcase. The real Hoover was not amused. Suspicious that Kelly was up to no good, Hoover reportedly had FBI cryptographers analyze the strip's lettering in search of encrypted subversive messages. I kid you not.

It was a time when newspapers and television programs were bursting with information about the Communist menace. Thousands of people in all walks of life were losing their jobs on suspicion of having once been either a Communist (a Red) or, just as bad, "a Communist sympathizer" (a Pinko). Not only people but books were suspect. Texts were being evaluated on the basis of possible contamination by leftist ideas. McCarthy's researchers found that the US-sponsored Overseas Library Program contained thirty thousand books written by "Communists, pro-Communists, former Communists, and anti-anti-Communists." After the list was made public, those books were banished from many libraries. If few were actually burned, there was the smell of smoke in the air.

Treasure Island

For years Dick and I saw Aunt Douglas not just for hours at a time but, during our summer vacation, for weeks on end, staying at her bungalow in Island Heights, an hour's drive south of Red Bank. Island Heights had in fact once been an actual island until the channel on its north side silted up. The town's year-round population was less than two thousand. Mother and Uncle Bob would join us on weekends.

Just a few houses away from our bungalow was an open space known as "the camp meeting." Beginning in 1878, Methodists had gathered here in summer for weeks at a time to listen to preachers, sing and pray, camping out in tents in the early days and later buying land and building first cabins and later houses on all sides of the meeting place. My maternal grandparents, fervent Methodists, had been among the town's founders. The Hendrickson bungalow was a second home that Aunt Douglas had inherited from her father.

By the time Dick and I became part of the town's summer population there were no more camp meetings, but the meeting field and open-air shelter remained hallowed ground, a grassy rectangle in the heart of the community. If I had pressed my ear against the ground, perhaps I would have heard Methodist hymns whispering in the grass. The Methodist church, a brown-shingled building of many gables, was a two-minute walk from Aunt Douglas's bungalow.

Aunt Douglas would wake us in the morning with the summons, "Rise and shine!" These three words were a compact summary of her philosophy of life. When we appeared at the breakfast table, she always announced, "Another country heard from."

For Dick and me, each day centered on playing, swimming, and catching crabs on the dock that stretched out into the Toms River. To go crabbing, all we needed were two poles with nets at the end plus a bucket for our catch. When the bucket was full enough, we carried it up to the bungalow, boiled the crabs in a large pot of water until the shells turned red, immersed the crabs in cold water and then—this was the hard part—broke open the shells to pick the meat out. Many an evening meal resulted: crab cakes, crab salad, crab chowder. Later in life, boiling a crab alive or killing any animal would present troubling ethical issues, but, during boyhood, my conscience was not yet raising such annoying questions.

For a year or two, pirates fascinated me. I had read *Treasure Island* and seen its translation into a live-action British film produced by the Disney studio. I could easily imagine a pirate ship skippered by peg-legged Long John Silver sailing down the Toms River. Island Heights was just a few miles inland from the Atlantic, which in my judgment made it ideal for pirate use. Even more convenient, there was a small islet in the river that Dick and I sometimes waded out to. I wondered if there might be a chest of buccaneer booty somewhere close at hand if one only knew where to dig. We even dug a few exploratory holes in places that looked promising but found no pieces of eight.

I sometimes went swimming with an eye out for sunken treasure and on one occasion thought I might have struck it rich. There, resting on the sandy bottom, was a blue box about a foot wide with brass-fitted corners. I managed to get it to shore, but opening it was a disappointment—there was nothing inside but water. Then came a moment of vision. What about making it into a treasure chest? I talked several of the neighborhood women into loaning me their costume jewelry—necklaces, brooches, bracelets, and earrings. It looked like treasure to me. All this went into the blue box, which I then buried on the islet.

Next came the making of the all-important pirate map. I found a sheet of watermarked cotton rag paper in my aunt's desk, then drew a map of Island Heights and the river as I imagined they might have been in the 1700s. To make it look convincing, the lines and legend were drawn using a metal-tipped pen and a small bottle of raven-black India ink purchased from an art shop. In the best tradition of pirate maps, X marked the spot. There it was on the west side of an islet just offshore from a larger island on a river just inland from the ocean. After folding the map came the aging of the paper using repeated immersions in tea, then putting the map in a hot oven to add another century or two. The final touch to my work of cartographic art was using a match to burn the edges. The end result looked every bit as good as the treasure map that guided Jim Hawkins and his collaborators in *Treasure Island*.

Then there was the question about how this long-lost map could be "discovered" by Dick and me. I decided to encase it in plaster, creating a kind of white stone. Once it hardened, I placed this on the shoreline of the islet, then got my brother engaged in playing a game of finding interesting rocks. Dick, as I had hoped, picked up the large oval white stone. "It looks soft," I pointed out. "I bet it's easy to break!" Using another rock, we cracked it open and, to his amazement and my feigned surprise, found the treasure map, complete with an X, a document that was obviously centuries old. "A large island and a small island, and a river," I said. "It could be the Toms River and Island Heights!"

We hurried to the bungalow, got a shovel out of the garage, raced back to the islet, and then dug a hole in a spot that seemed to match the map's X. Dick did the digging and heard the rewarding hollow clunk as the shovel struck metal. Out came the blue box. Inside it we found about a pound of pirate treasure. Great day in the morning, we had struck it rich!

Dick and I were as wealthy as King Midas for about an hour, until I could no longer delay the return of our treasure to the ladies from whom it had been borrowed.

The Circus

In the fifties Red Bank was one of the towns where the Ringling Bros. and Barnum & Bailey Circus paid an annual visit. Once a year my mother, brother, aunt, and I squeezed into Uncle Bob's Packard to drive to the fields on the west side of town where "The Greatest Show on Earth" set up its traveling universe of clowns, jugglers, acrobats, trapeze artists, lions and tigers, stately elephants, and riders who did handstands and somersaults on the backs of galloping horses. The oval-shaped principal tent was vast enough to contain three performance rings and to seat five thousand people.

When I was ten or eleven, I discovered an item in the *Red Bank Register* reporting at what early hour the Ringling Bros. circus train would be pulling into the Red Bank station the next day. Hardly able to sleep, I got up well before dawn to meet it, watching the colorful carriages pull in. Next came the unloading of the many wagons and trucks, then lining them up for the long procession to the edge of town. The stars were still shining. Almost no one else was watching, which struck me as a great waste, like sleeping through a total eclipse of the moon. Pedaling like mad, I bicycled behind the caravan, intent on witnessing what happened next: the unloading of the trucks, the cookhouse stoves being lit, the crews having their first cups of coffee, elephants being led out of their compartments, tents being spread out on the ground, huge coils of rope and long poles being put in place.

A dwarf noticed me watching. "Hey kid, wanna help?" I became part of a team of dwarves who, crouched over, ran in under the main tent, elephants having raised it a few feet off the ground, and then dragged out ropes that were attached to elephants as the poles were made vertical and the vast canvas raised to its full height. Nearly seven decades later I can still feel the rough, damp surface of the fabric that rubbed against the back of my head like sandpaper and inhale the dense smell of raw circus.

Mother and her cowboy son

Having become apprentice to the dwarf who recruited me, chore followed chore as the sky brightened until at last not only the big tent but all the smaller ones had risen like a field of colorful mushrooms. At midday I ate lunch around a picnic table with a group of men ranging in height from four to seven feet, who would soon be putting on clown makeup.

"I got something for you, Jimmy," said the dwarf who had first noticed me. I felt honored that he remembered my name. "You did a good job. Maybe you should join the circus when you're old enough." He handed me three tickets. "You earned 'em. Bring your mom, bring your brother."

Growing Up Radioactive

In the fifties one didn't have to read the daily newspapers closely to be aware that radioactive particles were in the air. Invisible debris was being carried by wind from the desert test grounds of Nevada to the far corners of the earth and being mixed with the fallout of Soviet, French, and British nuclear tests. Radioactive strontium 90 was making its way from mushroom clouds into the food chain, arriving in every bottle of milk and each inhaled breath.

I knew from close range what nuclear weapons could do to those targeted by them. It must have been in 1950 or '51 that two young Japanese women, survivors of the atom bomb that had been dropped on Nagasaki on August 9, 1945, arrived in Red Bank as house guests of Roger Squire, the town's Methodist minister, and his family. A national peace group had arranged for plastic surgeons in New York to treat some of the people who had been burned by the blasts. Thanks to our occasional attendance at Methodist church services, I saw those two very poised women sitting side by side in a pew near the front of the church, their faces hidden behind silk veils. I couldn't stop staring. I imagined their faces were partly melted. Though I had seen a few postexplosion photos of the victims and ruins of Hiroshima and Nagasaki, being in sight of these two women bought home to me in a more intimate way than photography the human dimension of war, the effects of nuclear weapons, and the fact that the victims of war were rarely those responsible for war. Their scars, though unseen, were etched into my memory, a door to the world's pain, and made me more aware of the seriousness of existence. I was also old enough to realize that taking Japanese victims of America's atom bombs into one's home was not something that all Americans would appreciate. Such hospitality required courage.

In the years following Mother's purchase of our first television set in 1951, with its tiny screen little bigger than a sardine tin, one of the occasional "news specials" allowed us to join the live audience witnessing America's open-air nuclear test explosions. Cameras, television crews, reporters, scientists, observers, and military brass were sheltered in concrete bunkers a few miles from the blast site. Views of the desert were interlaced with interviews with those in the shelter until the countdown began. Ten nine eight seven six . . . There was at last the word "zero" followed by a split second of silence, then the screen going white followed by the spectacle of a rapidly expanding globe of light and fire that stood on a seething column of smoke exploding upward, in which a conflagration never seen before 1945 was rotating within a mushroom cloud.

In the most memorable of the tests, buildings had been constructed at varying distances from ground zero, with blast-protected high-speed cameras positioned at strategic points. Soon after the test, television viewers saw in slow motion the blast's impact on houses not unlike our own. A two-story white clapboard house turned black on its blast-facing side before the shock wave struck. The structure, as if made of paper-thin glass, was in a flash torn to fragments while the splinters were catapulted away from ground zero by a wind far beyond hurricane strength.

Checking Wikipedia, I find that in 1951 there were sixteen US nuclear tests; in 1952 there were nine, and the next year eleven—thirty-six in three years, on average one per month.

While I doubt I watched all of the explosions, nuclear war was enough on my mind for me to build a foot-high model of a mushroom cloud using a cardboard tube for the upward shaft and a cardboard disk for the horizontal top layer, then applying cotton wool and spraying it with red, yellow, and orange paint. Made for the annual New Jersey Science Fair, I placed the blast model in a homemade wooden display case along with panels of text explaining the destructive effects of a nuclear explosion, augmented by extracts from John Hersey's book *Hiroshima*. My exhibit won no award—it wasn't a science experiment—but it seemed to me an achievement that my own quiet protest against nuclear war had found a place in the fair. Most fair goers stopped to study it.

The subject wouldn't go away. The sense of being condemned to die in a sooner-or-later, bound-to-happen World War III was a constant background noise that became so normal that it was always present if not always noticed. The world was not a safe place.

Discovering God

When I was a child, Mother still had several Communist books in one bookcase. Icon-like silhouettes of Karl Marx, Friedrich Engels, Vladimir Lenin, and Joseph Stalin emblazoned their covers. I have no memory of Mother ever reading any of them or even pulling them off the shelf. Once or twice I glanced inside but was put off by the absence of pictures. Sometime in the mid-fifties these volumes migrated to a box in the attic. Cleaning the attic years later, I noticed they had altogether disappeared. I never read the titles. What were those books about? I can only guess that the topic was Marxist history and doctrine. For Mother these few volumes must have been evocative of heady days in her twenties when she was one of the many who saw themselves laying the foundations of a new economic order that would scrub the world clean of injustice, greed, hunger, and war—and also of the myth of God.

It was only later in life that I learned some basics of Marxism, one key element of which is materialism, the view that nothing exists that isn't tangible and measurable—hence the absolute rejection of an intangible, immeasurable, immortal God, still less a God aware of and interested in the inhabitants of an inconsequential planet called Earth.

Materialism insists that life is an accident occurring in a mindless universe; evolution, a series of purely temporary local events with extinction and nonbeing on the last page. There are no immortal souls, and life has no ultimate meaning. While the experience of consciousness may seem to be immaterial, it has material causes. Conscience and consciousness are rooted in chemistry and DNA. The death of particular beings is as irreversible as is the eventual death of each planet and star. Sooner or later, each light goes out forever. Death wins. Belief in a life after death is a comforting fable for those unable to embrace reality.

In the meantime, thanks to science, everything can be explained, or will be explained sometime in the future.

In principle, materialist doctrine is what both my parents attempted to believe or at least, in joining the Communist Party, had assented to. But in my experience neither of them was at war with God or even the idea of God. Insofar as they were atheists, Mother was, I gradually realized, a Methodist atheist—and Dad, I discovered as I got to know him, was a Catholic atheist. In both cases, the adjective was more revealing than the noun.

As a child I once asked Mother, "Is there a God?" She paused and then replied, "I don't think so." What struck me more than her words was the sorrow in her voice. I cannot think of another occasion in childhood when the emotional climate of an answer impressed me so deeply.

Despite her efforts to be an atheist, and thus a good Communist, Mother's never-completely-lost religious faith resulted in her taking Dick and me to the Methodist church in Red Bank from time to time and never missing Christmas and Easter services. Though we sat in the balcony, once in church Mother was not a passive participant. She sang the hymns with enthusiasm and knew many of the verses by heart.

The Methodist minister, Roger Squire, became aware we were there, greeted us at the end of those services we attended, learned from Mother where we lived, and sometimes dropped by our house. It was always a delightful event for my brother and me, as he had a talent for connecting with kids. Only as an adult did it cross my mind how remarkable it was, given the chilly draft of the Cold War, that he had the courage to make pastoral calls on a Communist and her two sons who lived, quite literally, on the other side of the tracks.

I liked Roger Squire and thanks to him began to develop a serious respect for Christianity. Yet I wasn't drawn to becoming a Methodist. It wasn't that his sermons were boring—quite the opposite—but that sermons were the main event, with hymn singing a close second. Singing hymns seemed to me thin soup. Most of the hymns seemed aimed more at ourselves than at God; they were sermons made to rhyme and set to music. I wasn't certain there was a God, but if there was, did this add up to worship? In any event, thanks largely to Roger Squire, I heard enough of the gospel to form the beginnings of an image of who Jesus Christ is.

It wasn't only the Methodist church that I visited. Mother never objected to my going to other churches in the area when friends invited me, but I found myself watching the services as if from the moon. Sermon-centered services were too classroom-like. If there had been a blackboard behind the pulpit, it wouldn't have seemed out of place. I wasn't inspired to return. I had no interest in memorizing the Ten Commandments, as the local Dutch Reformed Church urged me to do, giving me the text printed on a pocket-sized card. Reading them through, I found I had no temptation to worship idols, kill anybody, nor did I covet my neighbor's wife.

My disappointment in Protestant church services did not cure me of sometimes sensing a Presence that might be what the elusive word "God" was all about. When I walked our cocker spaniel on clear nights, the stars overwhelmed me. A single pinprick of radiance flickering in the black sky, I knew from visits to the Hayden Planetarium in Manhattan, might contain an entire galaxy with countless solar systems. I was aware that in many cases I was seeing light that had traveled centuries before reaching my eyes. I was aware that the ebony blackness beyond the farthest stars had no ending and that there might be a "place" so remote from the cosmos that the entire cosmos disappeared. Compared with what I was gazing at, I was infinitely less than a mote of dust, and yet the microfilament of subdust that was me had eyes and a mind—a soul?—capable of awe and astonishment.

The year 1952, the year I turned eleven, was a big one for me. At a school friend's invitation, this was the year I first attended a service at Christ Episcopal Church in nearby Shrewsbury. It was one of the oldest buildings in the area. In 1778, the Battle of Monmouth had been fought close enough for the church to serve as a field hospital for the wounded. The church's wooden sideboards still bore the scars

Christ Church, Shrewsbury, New Jersey

of musket balls. Undisturbed by the American Revolution, a gilded crown that once represented King George III remained at the top of the steeple. Dark blotches on some of the pews were, at least in my eyes, bloodstains. It was a place that brought the past into the present.

And here I found actual worship. The eucharistic liturgy hit me with tidal force. Entering the church that first time, I found myself in a different energy field than I had ever encountered before. The altar, not the pulpit, was the center point. The church was not a classroom in disguise. Arriving a little late that first time, as I walked into church I heard the *Kyrie Eleison* being sung by the congregation, not a catchy hymn but an ageless chant. I soon learned that these two words were one of the most ancient Christian prayers, Greek for "Lord, have mercy."

I began coming every Sunday. At my own request, after a period of instruction in the course of which I learned a few more words of Greek, I was baptized on July 27, 1952, with my mother, aunt, and uncle plus a neighbor among the witnesses. Afterward I was invited to become one of the acolytes serving at the altar. As a baptismal gift, the priest of the parish, Father Theodore LaVan, gave me a thousand-year-old Byzantine coin that, on one side, bore an icon of Christ. He had found it, he told me, in Istanbul when he was a theological student. This remarkable and prophetic gift was my first encounter with the world of "Eastern" Christianity.

Why did I connect with the eucharistic liturgy so powerfully? It was as if some puzzle about my own identity had been resolved. Every action in the service was directed toward the invisible God, while the bread and wine on the altar, in a compelling but ungraspable way, became an entry point into the life, death, and resurrection of Christ.

Was there a decisive moment of coming to believe in God or affirm the Christian creed? Did I read the Bible or any religious books at the time of my baptism? Apart from using the *Book of Common Prayer* during services, not that I recall. We had two Bibles at home that had belonged to my maternal grandmother, but I was more impressed by the several peacock feathers they contained than by the words. The Old and New Testaments reached me chiefly through readings in church. I didn't read myself into belief. I found it was far easier to believe in God than not to. Not believing would have been like opting to be colorblind. That first conversion was not so much connected with doctrine or dogma than it was a movement within myself into a place of beauty. The natural world, with its green grass and wild strawberries, its sunrises and its Milky Way, was for me a vast headline proclaiming the existence of God.

Yet that first period of engagement in church didn't last long—less than a year. One Sunday morning I called the neighbor, Mr. Lawes, who provided me with my weekly ride to church, and told him I wouldn't be coming. My withdrawal may have had to do with acute embarrassment that the FBI was interviewing all our neighbors and that Mr. Lawes, who lived just down the street, was doubtless one of those who had been questioned about our family. I had never spoken to anyone about my parents being Communists.

My reading at the time was another factor. I was devouring science fiction and taking the portrayals by some of the authors of a god-free future too seriously. It seemed to be the shared view of many of the authors who engaged me that religion was an invention of prescientific humans, a relic of the superstitious past, and "God" a sort of Santa Claus figure. Smart people were not religious believers. To speak affirmatively about belief in God seemed a confession of being not too bright.

My religious life, at least in any formal sense, went into recess. I briefly tried to call myself an atheist, but attempting to glue that word to myself required a betrayal of my own experience. Instead, I called myself an agnostic because I couldn't quite dismiss the sense I had of God being real. "Agnostic" also suggested an independent state of mind. It was an appealing label and also a smart person's word. It was a mask that might fit me should anyone wish to know what my thoughts were about God. Even so I remained deeply conscious of a bottomless mystery pervading the universe. Also, like my parents, I loved nature, and nature is full of nonverbal news about God. Wherever I looked, whether at ants with a magnifying glass or at the moon with a telescope, everything in the natural order was awe inspiring, and awe is a religious state of mind. Creation made it impossible to dismiss God. But for a time it was an impersonal God—God as prime mover rather than God among us. Yet there was a sense of loss. Sundays seemed strangely empty.

Sci-Fi

As my church engagement went into recess, my main reading focus was on science fiction. The more boring sci-fi stories were simply about a future that was nothing more than a redecorated present, strong on rocket ships and firepower, interplanetary war and robot soldiers—"white men going forth to conquer the universe," as Ursula Le Guin has noted. The better authors created future worlds in which humanity faces radical challenges—the heroes are out to protect the human race while at the same time trying to decide exactly what *is* human. Robots were a frequent theme, rivaling human beings in intelligence and vying with humans for supremacy.

One of the authors I appreciated was Isaac Asimov, who foresaw the development of a universal ethical code for robots. Asimov's robots were pacifists, programmed never to kill. They couldn't become tools of war.

Me at my desk

Several sci-fi authors portrayed life among survivors of a nuclear catastrophe—books that were dark mirrors reflecting Hiroshima's shadows. One of Ray Bradbury's most haunting stories, "There Will Come Soft Rains," described an automated house whose inhabitants—truly a "nuclear family"—had been vaporized by a nuclear blast. Meanwhile, the myriad functions of the bomb-proof house keep running smoothly, the master computer unaware that the humans and the pets that once inhabited the house are no longer present. Wake-up alarms go off, meals are prepared, coffee brewed, lights turned on and off according to the hour, the thermostat adjusted, floors and counters robot-cleaned. But a gust of wind blows a branch through a broken window, spilling cleaning solvent on the stove. Fire erupts. The robot-house warns the family to get out while futilely attempting to extinguish the blaze.

"I don't try to describe the future," Bradbury commented. "I try to prevent it." In his novel *Fahrenheit 451,* his setting is a future America where the work of fire departments is no longer to extinguish fires—most buildings are fireproof—but to find books and burn them. The book's title is the combustion point of paper. In Bradbury's dystopia, possession of books has become a criminal offense. On the margins of society secret, quasi-monastic colonies have come into existence whose vocation is the preservation and memorization of books.

It was a timely novel. The smell of burning books was in the air in McCarthy's America, as it had been not many years earlier in Hitler's Germany and Stalin's Russia. Several years later, when I was a high school student living in Hollywood, I had the privilege of sitting at Bradbury's side one night while he gave a lecture on the love of books. My job was to hold a mike and run a tape recorder. One of the questions he was asked that evening was about *Fahrenheit 451.* "There are worse crimes than burning books," Bradbury said. "One of them is not reading them."

I discovered that one of the sci-fi authors whose books I read, Frederick Pohl, lived in Red Bank. I found his address in the phone book and biked out to his house, but didn't have the courage to knock on the door. I was surprised at how unpretentious a house it was, a step up from ours but not a big step. This was my first realization that even well-known authors rarely got rich.

Route 66

In 1954, when I was twelve, I somehow persuaded Mother that I was old enough to have a summer visit with my father even though this would involve a solo trip halfway across the USA. Had I a time machine, I'd love to listen to what I said that helped convince her to say yes. The result was that I was allowed to travel alone by train from New York to Chicago, change stations by taxi, then board another train that took me on to St. Louis, Missouri, where Dad was still based, though Los Angeles was about to become his home. The St. Louis–Los Angeles segment of the journey would be by car with Dad at the wheel. Then, at the end of the summer, the journey would be repeated in reverse. The train trips worked as planned, thanks no doubt to conductors keeping an unobtrusive eye on me.

Not many hours after leaving St. Louis, Dad stopped at a roadside restaurant, a big clapboard house with a screened-in porch. I don't know if I would have noticed the small black-and-white sign  tacked to the front door had Dad not pointed it out. "Colored people served in back," it read. Dad asked, "Do you think we ought to go in?" I was hungry and the food inside smelled awfully good. On the other hand, I didn't want to eat in a place that welcomed only white people. I said, "No." "Neither do I," Dad said. "Let's keep looking." We got back in the car and drove on. My perception of the world and myself was never quite the same after that. Dad hadn't told me what to do or given me a lecture about racism but had allowed me to share in a decision and, in doing so, made me more aware of what doors to go through and which ones to leave unopened. Finally we found a roadside grill that had no restrictive sign on the door. After a meal of homemade meatloaf and mashed potatoes, Dad allowed me a sip from his bottle of Pabst Blue Ribbon beer. I liked the label and was thrilled that a door into the adult world was being opened a crack, but one taste was enough. "It makes me think of horse piss," I said. "I expect you'll develop a taste for it when you get a little older," Dad replied.

Making our way along Route 66—passing through Oklahoma, Texas, New Mexico, and Arizona—we saw places that I had gazed at in the pages of *National Geographic* magazine and longed to visit. The Grand Canyon was the high-  light, but there was also a side trip to a Navajo vil- lage. Real Indians! ("Native American" had not yet entered my vocabulary.) I was impressed not only to be among people for whom Columbus was a late arrival but that Dad had such friends. We stayed the night as guests of a Navajo family who turned out to be pious Catholics, crossing them- selves as they took us into a small Catholic church that was filled with brightly painted images of Christ, Mary, and the saints—blood red, madonna blue, lemon yellow, burnt orange, moss green. I had never before entered a church of such visual intensity.

Passing through the southern tip of Nevada we made a side trip to the Hoover Dam, with its towering cascade of concrete holding back an ocean of water. In a nearby gas station, while Dad refilled the tank, I noticed a "one-armed bandit"—a slot machine—and impulsively tried my luck. In went a quarter and out came a shower of silver dollars! I quit while I was ahead and never played again.

In Arizona or California, Dad made a detour that brought us to a ridge from which we could view one of the camps that had housed Japanese American detainees during World War II. We had seen ghost towns along the way—abandoned towns with open doors and bro- ken windows and tumbleweed on the streets—but here all the empty barrack-like buildings appeared ready for use. "No Trespassing" signs studded the high fences and locked gates.

"Have you heard of the McCarran Act?" Dad asked. I hadn't. "It's a law passed by Congress a few years ago. One of its provisions is that, in case of national emergency, the president can order the detention, without trial or a hearing, of anyone regarded as a threat to national security. What it really means is locking up Communists or anyone accused of Communist sympathies." I was speechless, gazing with dread at the camp and its guard towers. I pictured both my parents, and maybe my brother and me, behind barbed wire. "The official justification," Dad explained, "is the need to lock up people who might commit actions of sabotage in a time of crisis, but in reality it means locking up dissidents. Just being regarded as suspicious is enough. All that's required is to have been put on a list by the FBI. The list of those to be arrested already exists—no doubt I'm on it." (Years later it was discovered that Catholic Worker founder Dorothy Day was among those J. Edgar Hoover had placed on the to-be-detained list.)

When at last we reached Los Angeles, I was bursting with excitement. For the first time, I would be meeting my half sister, Rosanne; her mother, Dorothy; plus Dorothy's parents and her brother, Jack Baskin; plus his wife and two daughters, Elaine and Marianne. Suddenly I had a much bigger family.

Rosanne was, for me, not half sister but simply sister. No halves. Despite the three-year gap in ages, we took to each other instantly. She was funny, playful, beautiful, and loved to tease. Thanks to Rosanne, her cousins became my cousins, her uncle and aunt mine too. But Dorothy was, and always remained, a stepmother. With her, I always felt like a visitor, not a relative.

My holiday with Dad ended with a return drive to St. Louis, where he had to hand over his responsibilities at the regional Communist Party office to his successor and clear his apartment before returning to Los Angeles. Visiting the dingy office that was his workplace, I watched one of his colleagues printing leaflets on a mimeograph machine. The headline read, "Say No to Jim Crow." "Who is Jim Crow?" I asked. "Jim Crow," Dad explained, "means racism—any law or practice that treats negroes like second-class citizens. Saying no to Jim Crow means opposing laws and customs that favor white people." He pointed to a poster tacked to the wall that had to do with a campaign to save a black man from execution who, Dad said, had been falsely accused of raping and killing a white woman and been convicted by an all-white jury. "If the man wasn't black," Dad remarked, "he wouldn't be on death row. In fact he wouldn't even have been arrested."

The summer visit had passed too quickly. During the weeks it lasted, not for a moment did I feel homesick. California was the New World, New Jersey the Old.

The Family of Man

While I came back to Red Bank with a severe case of California fever, still it was good to be home. Besides school and my paper route, there were occasional New York outings with Mother and Dick to see plays and visit museums.

The religious awakening that had ignited in me when I was eleven and twelve was briefly rekindled when I visited the Cloisters, the medieval branch of the Metropolitan Museum of Art. Here segments of ancient European monasteries and churches have been stitched into one harmonious structure. The Cloisters is a time machine. I found myself briefly inhabiting the medieval world. So much beauty: sculpture, frescos, paintings, metalwork, illuminated manuscripts, wood and ivory carvings, herbal gardens, plus the museum's celebrated unicorn tapestries. Though I wasn't nudged back to church, my idea of what Christianity was all about sailed into deeper water.

The Family of Man

Created by Edward Steichen
Prologue by Carl Sandburg
The Museum of Modern Art, New York

I was also developing an appreciation of photography set alight by an exhibition at the Museum of Modern Art. Its theme was "The Family of Man." Its curator, Edward Steichen, had assembled a vast sequence of black-and-white photos that not only asserted but demonstrated that, for all the diversity of culture, skin color, local economy and development, varieties of religion and differences of clothing, we are indeed one human family bound together in love, pain, labor, awe, anger,

49

gratitude, and grief. I bought the exhibition book and still have it, a survivor of many moves. For me, it's a Bible without words. The collection of photos has as its golden thread the *us-ness* of being. Beneath our separateness is a deeper unity.

The exhibition was also a warning. One of the images was of a Japanese boy with a charcoal-smeared face who had been far enough from the nuclear explosion at Hiroshima to survive. He stood before the photographer statue-still, eyes staring not at what he was seeing but what he had seen. I could imagine what was burned into his retinas, a lost world suddenly turned to ash.

Me in 1955, year of "The Family of Man" exhibition

Another photo was of an un-self-conscious young Indonesian woman with full, bare breasts shopping in a vegetable market. I had seen Greek and Roman statues of nude woman but not actual nudity, not bodies that breathed. The allure, beauty, and mystery of the naked human body was made more intense by her being part of a culture in which less was hidden. I knew enough of the book of Genesis to be reminded of the unembarrassed nudity of Adam and Eve before the Fall.

Such photos drew me to aspire to more than snapshot photography. Money I earned from my newspaper route was now mainly saved for a Contaflex, a German-made, single-lens reflex camera that challenged me to take photos worthy of its potential. Every week I brought a few more dollars to Dorn's Camera Store and each week caressed the camera, admiring its details and enjoying its weight in my hands. It took the better part of a year, but by Christmas I was able to walk out of the store without having to leave it behind.

My Contaflex camera is long gone, succeeded by a series of Nikons, plus, in recent years, several digital cameras and now a mobile phone, but my love of photography has never faded. *The Family of Man* remains a book I often return to. Besides its images, I've often pondered the proverbs scattered through its pages. One came from Russia: "Eat bread and salt and speak the truth."

A Transcontinental Bus Ride

I had traveled by train to St. Louis and then driven with Dad to Los Angeles for a summer visit when I was twelve. The following year I managed to talk Mother into letting me travel by Greyhound bus coast to coast to Los Angeles and back. Today it astonishes me that I was allowed to make so long and complex a journey by myself. On the one hand, it speaks of my adolescent persistence, but even more it reveals Mother's concept of parenthood. Mother provided me with a letter explaining who I was, what I was doing, that I was traveling with her permission, and how to reach her at any hour of the day or night. I also had a packet of preaddressed two-penny postcards to be mailed one by one each day. All I had to do was check off line by line a list confirming that I still had my wallet, money belt, camera, two canvas bags, telescope, and coat. After Mother's death, I found one of the cards, postmarked Memphis and dated July 11, 1955, tucked away in her desk. It's now framed and hangs in our house.

It wasn't a straight line, coast-to-coast journey. In those days one could buy a cross-country Greyhound ticket at a flat rate—I think it was $99, round trip—but take any route, with any number of stops and bus changes along the way. My ticket, a series of segments patched together by staples, stretched the length of our living room.

The route made a 3,500-mile roller-coaster-curve from its starting point in New York's Port Authority Bus Terminal, then across New Jersey before dipping southward through Pennsylvania and Virginia along the Appalachians and the Blue Ridge Mountains, then sliding westward across Tennessee through Oklahoma and Texas to New Mexico and Arizona before arriving in Los Angeles. There were at least ten bus changes just in the California-bound route.

How long was the westward ride? I am guessing about a week. I slept at least two nights in buses, which means four or five overnight

Setting off on a cross-country trip

stops outside the bus along the way. The first of these was with a relative, my elderly cousin Catherine Nesbitt, who lived in the farm country outside Memphis. She was the soul of hospitality, unhurried and warm hearted. I was startled to discover a large framed photograph of General Robert E. Lee astride his gray horse, Traveler, hanging over the living room fireplace. I had never before been in a region that had been part of the Confederacy during the Civil War, or what my Tennessee cousin referred to as "the War between the States." Had Mother placed an equivalent photo in our house, it would have been of Abraham Lincoln. I was too shy to ask about her views on slavery or race, but her kindness made me hope for the best. My favorite memory of that overnight visit was sitting on the deep porch of that old house in the afternoon sunlight turning the handle of an old-fashioned ice cream maker, then helping eat the peach ice cream that resulted. The cream came from a local cow, and the peaches had been picked that morning in the orchard behind the house.

No link on the journey was without conversations with strangers. As the bus passed though Alabama, I was amazed to discover the unshaven man sitting next to me was on his way to a job in a diamond mine. Diamonds in Alabama! I had no idea. Another temporary companion offered me a sip of whiskey from a hip flask. I said my politest "no thanks." Another man was hoping his former wife would have him back. It didn't seem likely to me.

Crossing the Texas panhandle we encountered a tornado. We had been slowly driving through waterfall-like rain until the driver, unable to see ahead, pulled the bus to a halt at the side of the highway. As we did so, the rain abruptly stopped, revealing a charcoal-black tornado that looked just like the twister I had seen in the movie version of *The Wizard of Oz*. At its base it was dragging a welter of debris across the prairie a few miles to the north. Spotting an overpass farther up the road, the driver drove ahead, sheltering there until he judged it safe to move on. As we resumed our westward route, he made the brief announcement, "That was a close one, folks!" Everyone applauded. Had houses been destroyed? Was anyone carried off to Oz? I never found out.

I must have sweated through that close encounter. That night my seatmate informed me that I was in urgent need of a shower. I checked into a hotel at the next major stop and scrubbed myself till I smelled like soap.

Carlsbad Caverns National Park in New Mexico was one of my destinations. Arriving at night in the town of Carlsbad, about twenty-five miles from the caves, I decided to stretch out on a cushioned bench in the bus terminal rather than pay for a hotel room. Here, about two in the morning, I attracted the attention of a local policeman whose flashlight awakened me. "Who are you, boy?" I told him and then presented my mother's to-whom-it-may-concern letter: "My son, James Hendrickson Forest, has my permission to be traveling by bus to visit with his father in Los Angeles, California, making several stops along the way. You may call me collect at any hour of the day or night for further information." Mother's work and home numbers followed. After talking to her by phone and being reassured that I wasn't a runaway, the policeman said that if I didn't mind being in jail, he could put me up for the rest of the night. "It's just a bench and a blanket and a thin mattress," he said, "but better than here." Thus I had my first night behind bars. The cell door was left ajar.

After that adventure, my visit to the Carlsbad Caverns was an anticlimax. I recall the lights being turned out by the park ranger in a cathedral-like section of the caves known as "the Big Room," four thousand feet long and two hundred feet high. I have never experienced so absolute a blackness or, at the same time, so deep and resonant a silence. I was both thrilled and terrified.

Arizona came next, with the Grand Canyon my principal stop. As in New Mexico, this also required a detour, changing buses in Flagstaff and heading north on a Greyhound whose route ended at the Grand Canyon's southern rim.

As so often happens to pilgrims, the most treasured memories are of hospitality along the way. When I got off the bus, the driver asked where I planned to stay. When I admitted that I hadn't yet worked that out, he invited me to use the suite at the Canyon Inn that was reserved for Greyhound drivers. While there was no spare bed, I was given use of a cushioned bench beneath a window alcove that gave a panoramic view of the canyon. The driver also arranged for me to eat my meals at the hotel restaurant "on the Greyhound tab." Or was I in fact his guest? I suspect the latter.

That afternoon I walked along the rim, watching color changes in the layered canyon walls as the light shifted, until, with the coming of sunset, the cliffs turned from a yellow-brown ocher to blood red and then purple before becoming a sea of black ink. Beauty, beauty, beauty. Earlier in the day I had overheard someone say, "This is the church for me." That rang a bell. Indeed the contemplation of beauty is a wordless revelation of the fingerprints of God.

The next morning I set out for a solo walk down to the canyon's bottom following the Bright Angel Trail. The descending journey went well. Luckily the day before I had purchased a broad-brimmed cowboy hat for sun protection as well as a canteen, having been warned about dehydration. I walked slowly and with care—the cliff-hugging trail was at some points barely wide enough for the mules that occasionally passed calmly by carrying tourists and provisions to Phantom Ranch, a small hotel at the bottom of the canyon. It was a drier, hotter walk than I had anticipated. I got no farther than a watering stop about five miles from the rim and three thousand feet down. Fortunately, common sense kept me from pressing on to the Colorado River, three miles farther and another fourteen hundred feet lower.

Now came the hard part, the upward climb. It took longer than I had estimated. Halfway up I watched the sky turning a deeper and deeper blue as the sun began setting in the west. I realized I was not going to make it to the top before sundown. As the canyon walls began to darken, I was still the better part of an hour from the trailhead. A moonless night fell like a theater curtain. There was only starlight plus a faint glow from the village above. The last half hour, I might as well have been blindfolded. Nose pressed against the cliff face I walked sideways, my hands rather than my eyes preserving my safety as the path zigzagged upward. I was no longer hot but cold, out of water, exhausted, and aware of the abyss at my back. I have rarely in my life felt such relief as when my head rose above the ledge at the trail's starting point and I could see the Canyon Inn.

Feeling like a survivor, I slept like a rag doll in the Greyhound suite and, after breakfast in the morning, continued on my way to Los

Angeles, arriving about midnight to find Dad waiting at the bus terminal, beaming like a lighthouse. Riding in his pickup truck to the house he and Dorothy rented in East Hollywood, Dad told me stories about his trip to Maine when he was a young man.

Bright Angel Trail, Grand Canyon

What I enjoyed most during those summer weeks was our combining forces with the Baskin family for a camping trip amid the redwood trees of Big Sur. The number of kids—Rosanne and I, plus our cousins Marianne and Elaine—equaled the adult populations: Dad and Dorothy, Jack and Virginia. The redwoods towered angelically above our small encampment with its several tents. With the tops of the trees disappearing overhead, I felt scaled down to squirrel size. Light filtered in soft columns. Dawn was late; night fell early. Often the breeze carried the salty smell and even the sound of the nearby Pacific Ocean which, we found, could be reached by trails that led to cliffs, at the bases of which were narrow coves. Humans were not plentiful. In 1955, it had only been a few years since electricity and phone lines had reached Paleolithic Big Sur.

The major goal of my trip had been, of course, Dad himself. When I returned to New Jersey—this time opting for a Los-Angeles-to-New-York straight run, thus maximizing my time in California—I began pressing both parents with the idea of not just having summer visits with Dad but moving into his house. My practical justification was that by the time I completed high school I would have established California residency and thus have nearly free entry to one of the state universities. This made sense, but my real agenda was to be close to Dad. I desperately wanted a full-time father, not just a vacation dad.

In September 1955, I had my first year at Red Bank High School ahead of me. Here the most important item was extracurricular—engagement in a small after-class group responsible for writing, editing, and laying out the school newspaper. We were fortunate to have the guidance of an English teacher, Mr. Falk, who had once been a reporter for the *New York Times* and who used the *Times'* style as the model for our work. Skills that I would make use of for the rest of my life owe much to Mr. Falk. I learned what a pica is as well as em-dashes. I remain ever mindful of journalism's foundational five questions: who, what, when, where, and how. "Thomas Jefferson once said," Mr. Falk told us, "that 'the man who reads nothing at all is better educated than the man who reads nothing but newspapers.' If you want to be a journalist, your job is to prove Jefferson wrong. You do that first of all by getting the facts straight—that's much harder than it sounds—and, if there are sides, fairly reporting each side's point of view." He attempted to teach us to write crisp, lean, Hemingway-like sentences: "Don't bury your reader in adjectives."

Meanwhile, with letters going back and forth between Mom and Dad, my campaign to move to Los Angeles was gaining traction. By the early spring of 1956, it had been worked out between my parents that I could not only visit in the coming summer but live with Dad and his family for the indefinite future. I was overjoyed. At the time, self-centered teenager that I was, it didn't occur to me how hard a decision it must have been on both sides—agonizing for Mother to let me leave home at age fourteen, and hard for Dad to convince his wife Dorothy to let a stepson become part of the family. Nor could I easily fit into their house. To make room, Dad had to convert a back porch into a bedroom.

After finishing my first year of high school in June 1956, I once again crossed America's four time zones, this time by train. Each westward click on the rails seeming to chant, "California, California. . . ."

Dream City

Los Angeles is a patchwork quilt of neighborhoods that, in the late fifties, were often blanketed with thick, yellowish, eye-stinging smog. I was moving into a house on the east edge of the city's most famous patch, the film factory of Hollywood. Our neighborhood was not glitzy—in fact very little of Hollywood had much sparkle. We lived in a two-story rented duplex at 1758 North Alexandria Avenue, half a block above Hollywood Boulevard and a mile east of the dream city's most famous intersection, Hollywood and Vine. To the north of our house, at the top of Mount Hollywood, was Griffith Observatory, which the previous year had served as a key location for the James Dean film *Rebel without a Cause*.

Thanks to arrangements made by Dad before I arrived, I already had a summer job working on the Paramount Movie Ranch. This was in the Santa Monica Mountains above Malibu about thirty miles northwest of Hollywood. My stepmother's brother, Jack Baskin, engineer, builder, and real estate developer, had recently purchased the ranch from Paramount. In the years since Paramount bought the property in 1927, the ranch had been used for countless films, including such classic Westerns as *The Gunfight at the OK Corral*.

In 1957 the ranch's western town set and the surrounding hills were being used to film several television serials. During free time I would sometimes watch the actors and crews at work, quickly learning that setting up a shot took most of their time, filming not much. In the movie world, I discovered, one of the essential talents is being good at waiting.

The border between reality and fantasy had become thin indeed. Since I had grown up on Westerns, day-and-night access to the actual set of a nineteenth-century western town was a daily surprise. Most of the weathered wooden buildings were only facades with ladders in back that gave access to upper floor windows, necessary for gunfight scenes. But several of the buildings were real, including the sheriff's office, with its one-cell jail, and the saloon, which had the classic long bar and was stocked with soft drinks as well as beer, for those several years older than I. There were also stables and a large barn, the latter housing various wagons plus a stagecoach that I occasionally climbed into, wondering what film stars had sat there in times past.

My job on the ranch put me in the cafeteria, serving tables and working in the kitchen. Sometimes, while waiting on tables, I tuned in on the conversations of actors and crews having their meals. The main topics were career-related gossip and irritations with directors and agents. I was disappointed that dialogue about the purpose and meaning of life wasn't part of their conversational agenda.

Hollywood High School awaited me at the summer's end. On its north side, the school faced one of Hollywood's most iconic landmarks, Grauman's Chinese Theater, often used for film premieres. Hollywood High had many famous graduates, Judy Garland among them, but was far whiter than any school I had been in up to that time. In 1957 there was only one black student—in fact his skin was a creamy brown—in a population of about two thousand.

In my social studies class one day, the teacher launched a discussion of racial integration in schools. At the time, nine black students, five of them born the same year I was, were being jeered and spat at by white students and their parents at the previously all-white Little Rock Central High School in Arkansas. National Guard troops had been called in by President Eisenhower to protect the nine and enforce the Supreme Court ruling that outlawed school segregation. White racists gathering daily at the school were displaying such signs as "Keep Our White Schools White" and "Race Mixing Is Communism." A blond classmate of mine sitting at an adjacent desk, one of our school's glamorous cheerleaders, astonished me by declaring that "the rights of white people are being attacked in Little Rock" and blaming integration efforts on "Communists and outside agitators who belong in Russia." I was shocked to find such ugly opinions wrapped in such an attractive body.

Having gotten high grades my previous year at Red Bank High, I was put into an "advanced placement" class in English and American literature, and it was within that group that I formed several friendships. One of these was with Sonia, whose father was a writer for *Gunsmoke*, a hugely popular weekly TV drama. As I wasn't allowed to make long phone calls from home, for a month or two I would call Sonia after supper from the pay phone at a nearby gas station. One night I discovered how close an eye the FBI was keeping not only on Communists in Hollywood but on their teenage kids. I picked up the receiver, put my dime in the slot, dialed Sonia's home number, and, instead of the usual ring, heard a strange click and then found myself listening to a recording of my conversation with Sonia twenty-four hours earlier. Even Dad and Dorothy, though used to being closely watched, were surprised that my use of a local pay phone had been noted and was being audited. "It makes romance a little awkward," Dad pointed out, "when Big Brother is listening in." He laughed, adding, "Maybe if you find a girlfriend whose father isn't a name in Hollywood they'll leave you alone."

Dad suggested that, if I was being treated like a Communist, perhaps I ought to know something about Communism. "Would you like to attend," he asked, "my weekly evening class in Marxism?" I agreed, more to please Dad than out of actual curiosity, and briefly joined a discussion group that met in someone's living room elsewhere in the city. I stuck it out for only a few sessions, but Marxism bored me. I was far more interested in literature and the wilderness than in Marxist economic theory or proletariat ownership of the means of production. While he never said so, Dad must have been disappointed to have a son who was allergic to a doctrine that was so illuminating to him. I was outspoken in opposing nuclear weapons and advancing civil rights, which must have pleased him, but for me such issues had to do with survival and basic human values, not with politics or ideologies.

On one occasion a Hollywood celebrity visited our home. The writer Dalton Trumbo joined us for supper one night. Before his arrival, Dad explained to me that Trumbo was one of the blacklisted "Hollywood Ten" who, in 1947, had refused to answer the questions of the notorious House Committee on Un-American Activities, for which he spent eleven months in federal prison. In 1954, Trumbo won an Oscar for a script—*Roman Holiday*—he had written under a pseudonym.

Forbidden poetry was front-page news in California in the spring, summer, and fall of 1957. Allen Ginsberg's *Howl* had been issued as a booklet by a San Francisco publisher, City Lights, and days later was banned by the state of California. The publisher, it was charged, "did willfully and lewdly print, publish, and sell obscene and indecent writings, papers, and books, to wit: *Howl and Other Poems*." The practical consequence was that *Howl* could not legally be sold in California. Both Ginsberg and Lawrence Ferlinghetti, publisher of City Lights, must have been tempted to send bouquets to the censors. Is there a better way to interest people, for example a fifteen-year-old high school student who likes to read, in a book than to ban it? God bless censors. In the blink of an eye, *Howl* became a bestseller and Ginsberg internationally famous.

I was disappointed that even the principal bookseller in Hollywood, Pickwick's, didn't dare to ignore the California ban, but the owner, Louis Epstein, kindly pointed me in the right direction—to a certain newsstand in West Hollywood. "I can't be certain," Epstein told me. "Literature is not what people go there to buy, but chances are they'll have it." He was right. *Howl* was easily the least obscene item one could purchase at that seedy location, but even there the Ginsberg poem was kept quite literally under the counter. Seventy-five cents made it mine. I hadn't yet heard the term "Beat Generation," but I was now in proud possession of one of the major works in what eventually became the Beat Canon.

My friendship with Sonia faded, and in its place I got close to a wonderful classmate named Kathy Newman. We both loved poetry, which we read aloud to each other after school while stretched out on the front lawn of her home. I don't recall any serious necking until the night we met at my house to do homework together and ended up, though fully clothed and with no buttons undone, as pressed together on the couch as two halves of a clamshell. Dad found us in this state of almost-love-making and, once Kathy was sent home, made it clear to me that this sort of thing must not happen again. Of course it did, but remained, by today's standards, remarkably chaste.

Running Away

Meanwhile, I was learning day by day how to be part of a very different family than I had belonged to in Red Bank. One element of life was the weekly family meeting at which the four of us—Rosanne and I both theoretically equal to Dad and Dorothy in this exercise in one-person-one-vote domestic democracy—discussed any practical issues and problems in home life and decided who was to do what chores and when: who would cook supper on what days, who would wash the dishes, who would vacuum the downstairs rooms and clean the bathroom, etc. A book of minutes was maintained in which all decisions were carefully noted. For two weeks I was "ostracized" (a new word for my vocabulary) from the kitchen for not doing a good enough job of washing the dishes. But I got a passing grade for one of my Saturday chores: washing Dad's pickup truck.

One of my disappointments in moving to California was that I saw much less of Dad than I had hoped—between his daytime job as superintendent at a building site and his nighttime "party work," he was often away from early morning till late at night. Perhaps I should have stuck with attending his weekly class in Marxism, dull though it was.

Having bought a bike, in the summer of 1958 I used it to pedal my way to the San Jacinto Mountains fifty miles east of Los Angeles and made it to the "mile high" town of Idyllwild, where I got a job washing dishes and assisting the short-order cook at the Koffee Kup Kafe. The owner's name, predictably, was Klyde. A local Native American who raised and stabled horses kindly gave me permission to sleep in a shed on his property, so I had a rent-free roof over my head in exchange for giving an occasional helping hand.

Besides my restaurant work, I attended a concert given by the Weavers (I had my first encounter with Pete Seeger, who it turned out knew

Dad), did some ditch-digging for a plumber, painted signs for several local shops, fell in love with a violinist who failed to fall in love with me, and for two days and nights worked around the clock providing food and coffee to firefighters when Idyllwild was threatened by a forest fire. I also managed to take a course in ecology (not a word one often heard in those days) that involved a week of camping in the surrounding forest. One happy morning I awoke to find a deer standing over me, her front legs to one side of my sleeping bag, her rear legs to the other, placidly eating leaves, no more worried about me than about the tree that was providing her breakfast.

The summer had been a prolonged experience of living on my own and earning the dollars that I needed to survive on. While I was every inch a teen-age kid, at the same time I had never felt so grown up.

When I returned home a week before school was due to start, life suddenly took a nightmarish turn. Opening the front door of our house on North Alexandria, I heard Dad and Dorothy—upstairs and unaware I was there—in the midst of a loud and bitter argument. It quickly became clear that Dad had discovered Dorothy was having an affair with a mutual friend and that separation and divorce were not far off. The day was hot, but I felt as if I had stepped into a walk-in freezer. My Los Angeles family was unraveling before my eyes. On the spur of the moment, I decided to flee. Putting my bike in the garage behind the house, I hitchhiked up the coast to San Francisco and, once there, got a ride across the Bay Bridge to Berkeley.

The whole way I was in a state of shock. While in a sense my side trip to the north was simply an extension of the independent life I had been leading for weeks at Idyllwild, now I was fueled by panic—lost, confused, and anchorless. All I had was a sleeping bag and camera plus a backpack with basic necessities and less than ten dollars in my pocket. In the hills of a park in Berkeley, I found an out-of-the-way spot hidden behind bushes where I could unroll my sleeping bag at night and hide it during the day.

What little money I had saved during the summer was quickly spent. Going to a local photography shop, I tried to sell my dearest possession, my Contaflex camera, probably worth about a hundred dollars. It was taken on consignment—if and when sold I would get 80 percent of the sales price. Looking back, it's a good guess that the shop owner must have worried that he might be selling stolen goods. What was a kid without an address doing with a camera like that?

When I was out of cash, hunger came quickly. I began stealing food—first chocolate bars, then bread, sliced meat, lettuce, and cheese from local supermarkets. After four days roughing it in Berkeley and having just been chased out of a supermarket with a bag of pilfered food in my arms, I realized I had no alternative but to return home to Los Angeles.

Despite the despair I was feeling about my crumbling California family, I collected at least two good memories. One was a conversation I had with a hospitable black jazz musician who had driven me across the Oakland Bay Bridge the day I arrived in San Francisco. He asked if I had "ever been laid." I shyly admitted that I was a virgin. "Oh boy," he assured me, "you sure have a lot to look forward to!" And there was an elderly man, a retired professor, who walked his dog every morning in the park that had become my camping place. He noticed me—a skinny kid in need of a shower and haircut—and got me talking about my troubles. His advice was simple: "Go back home. No matter what the tensions are, your family will be desperately worried." Thanks to a donation from him I returned (with my unsold camera) to Los Angeles by bus.

Back in Hollywood, Dad was both relieved and angry. "I found your bike in the garage, but no note, no phone call. Don't you think we have a right to know where you are? Have you any idea how anxious I was? We had to call the police." I had never seen him so upset. I apologized profusely but didn't tell him about the overheard argument with Dorothy that had triggered my brief exodus, nor the dread I had of my adopted household disintegrating. It wasn't that I was close to Dorothy—for me she had been the unwelcoming stepmother one meets in fairy tales. I was an unsought complication in her life, a reminder of Dad's first marriage, and was probably regarded as a bad influence on Rosanne. But if her marriage to Dad was ending, then it was a given that Rosanne would remain with her and far from clear that Dad would be able to keep me in his future home, wherever that might be.

The day after my return, school resumed. Though treading water at home, I enjoyed my classes and continued to get excellent grades. I ran for the student council and was elected. I also joined the debating club—the Forensic Society—at which I gave a lecture with the title "A Generation in the Shadow." In it I identified myself as "part of a generation growing up under a mushroom-shaped shadow that, of its nature, makes us think of ourselves and the future in more uncertain terms than any generation before us, with the possible exception of medieval populations facing the Black Plague." I asked, "When in the history of the human race have we built and possessed weapons and had them ready for use, but decided to let them rust?" I ended with a summons to find a way to get rid of nuclear weapons: "Slavery was once considered acceptable, but our ancestors finally got rid of it. Can't we do the same about an evil that threatens all our lives?" It was my first antiwar speech.

Because I showed promise as an art student, I was awarded a scholarship to take life-drawing classes Saturday mornings at the Los Angeles County School of Art (now the Otis School of Art and Design). To my disappointment the models were not nude, but it was exciting being among serious art students several hours a week. I was also appointed design editor of the Hollywood High yearbook, *The Poinsettia*.

As part of a series of profiles of high school students, a Los Angeles newspaper did an article about me in which I mentioned my current vocational ambition was to become a park ranger. "Who knows," I told the reporter, "but maybe one day I'll be a park ranger on the moon." This gave the story its headline: "Boy Maps Natural Science Career, Eyes Conquest of Moon."

Seen as a model student, I was chosen by the school principal to be interviewed on a Los Angeles television program that did its broadcasts from one of the film studios—Warner Brothers, as I recall. I remember nothing about what I said in front of the camera, only that my face was painted orange by a makeup artist—in the days of black-and-white TV, apparently orange made one's face look more natural. I had lunch in the studio cafeteria amidst actors dressed as cowboys and Indians, zombies and clowns, royalty and crooks.

For an ambitious sixteen-year-old kid, I was doing remarkably well. The only little problem was that, though I was playing the part of being happy, I wasn't happy. While I overheard no more arguments between Dad and Dorothy, there was an alarming silence at home. Dorothy was away more often. Dad was distracted and withdrawn.

Yet there were moments of dialogue. Dad worried about my ethical formation when he discovered me reading novels by Ayn Rand, first *The Fountainhead* and then *Atlas Shrugged*, both of which had been recommended by a classmate. Initially, I admired the Nietzschean supermen that Ayn Rand made into her heroes, but as I passed the halfway mark in *Atlas Shrugged* it dawned on me that Rand was less a novelist than a missionary for ruthless selfishness who opposed any social system that sought to foster the common good. To the extent that Rand had a religion, it was symbolized by the dollar sign. Both Rand paperbacks ended up in the wastepaper basket.

Dad was relieved to see me abandoning Ayn Rand, but soon after he was newly distressed when he found me reading Boris Pasternak's novel *Doctor Zhivago*, with its unromanticized description of the Russian Revolution and the civil war that followed. The book had been banned in Russia and its author expelled from the Writers' Union and forced by the Kremlin hierarchy to refuse the Nobel Prize for Literature. "But it's really a good book, Dad," I assured him, adding the question, "Don't you want to read it?" "No, but I have read a lot about it and know that it misrepresents Soviet history. And anyway I don't have the time." My guess is that the real obstacle was "party discipline." *Zhivago* was, for party members, forbidden reading.

About this time I came upon an issue of *Life*, a photo-intensive weekly magazine, that included an article on "the Beat Generation," a label used to describe a small movement of writers and poets who felt out of step with the culture of the fifties. They wanted no careers, were not chasing money, and were in combat with the ad-driven consumer society. The Beats were marching to a different drummer.

I was fascinated. While the only "Beat" text I had read was *Howl*, I linked it with Henry David Thoreau's *Walden*, which I had read for my English class and which had stirred me to imagine the possibility of a Thoreau-ish life on my own, out of both home and school, free of dependence on either parent. After all, hadn't I already lived that way for ten summer weeks?

Besides pictures of Jack Kerouac and Allen Ginsberg, the article in *Life* included a photo of a "Beat hangout," a coffee shop near the beach in Santa Monica just a few miles away. Coffee shops, said the text, were the preferred gathering places for Beats. Such havens, as I envisioned them, were populated with exiles from the cultural assembly line, reading poems to one another and talking about existentialism, which I couldn't define but which sounded like a philosophy I could embrace once I knew more about what it meant.

After supper one evening I took the bus to Santa Monica, getting off at a beach stop in sight of the coffee house shown in *Life*, a one-story building tucked into the dunes. Once inside I found I was the youngest person there by two decades or more, and that, apart from me, everyone was with someone else. In my fantasy of Beat culture, I had somehow expected that I would be noticed and made welcome— "Hey, kid, use this chair, make yourself at home"—which of course didn't happen. Instead I sat at a small square table feeling as alone as I had ever felt in my life. A waiter came up and I ordered a cup of coffee—it was, after all, a coffee house. I eavesdropped as best I could on the conversations going on around me. While I wasn't sure what "Beat" conversations would be about, in fact this was more or less what I might have heard at any diner or all-night café. No poetry was being read, nor was anyone discussing existentialism. After drinking my coffee as slowly as possible, I slipped outside, crossed the highway, and walked onto the dark beach on the other side of the road.

Next came one of the most unnerving experiences of my young life, so strange that I still don't know if it actually happened or was a hallucination brought on by my sense of home imploding. Not far down the beach were the concrete foundations of a large house. Scorch marks attested to its destruction by fire. What hadn't been destroyed in the flames had been scrubbed clean by ocean storms. A wide fireplace stood in what had once been the living room. I climbed a concrete stairway that emerged from the sand, then walked toward the fireplace. Sensing I wasn't alone, I turned around to find a slim, short male figure gazing at me. Hair, skin, feet, skin-tight clothing—all were a dull, dark, charcoal gray. He had a dancer's wiry body, hands resting on his hips. Though I heard only the sound of the Pacific surf, I sensed I was being laughed at. Insofar as the silent laughter could be translated into words, they would have been, "I own you." It was a demonic presence. I stared at the figure for several seconds, then ran back to the highway as if I were running for my life. Luckily almost immediately a bus pulled up at a nearby bus stop. I was back home at a reasonable hour.

Years passed before I began entertaining doubts about the reality of the event. Up to that evening, to the extent I had given a passing thought to demons at all, they were no more real or threatening than cartoon characters with horns. But from that night onward, stories about demons seemed credible. It was only later in life that I connected the experience in that burned-out house with the severe stress I was experiencing and which I felt unable to talk about with anyone—plus the fact that both my parents and my stepmother were Communists, which would have been impossible to leave out if I were to talk honestly about my home life. "In America the Communist Party in the fifties was all cloak and no dagger," Lucy Forest, Dad's last partner, told me not many years ago.

Aware that life in our household on North Alexandria was rapidly disintegrating, and encouraged by the self-sufficiency I had managed that summer in Idyllwild, I began to think seriously about dropping out of school, leaving Hollywood, and even leaving the United States, an outward-bound, Beat-inspired, young Thoreau. I was drawn to Canada. Studying *National Geographic* maps, I spotted a remote town, Blackwater, in the mountainous wilderness of central British Columbia. The town's main attraction was its isolated location plus the poetry of its name. For weeks, being a migrant in Canada was a vivid fantasy. I shared the vision with my classmate friend Barry Vogel, a fellow would-be Beatnik, who took seriously the possibility of crossing the border with me. But Barry came to his senses when he realized how devastated his mother would be.

Running away to Canada was, in the sense of Robert Frost's poem, a road not taken. Instead, the Christmas school holiday having just begun, I returned by train to my mother's home in Red Bank. It wasn't clear to me when I left Los Angeles that I wasn't coming back, but once in Red Bank it was obvious that it had been a one-way journey. I wasn't up to witnessing the final installments of Dad and Dorothy's marriage. Neither did I have an appetite to resume high school.

Like many teenagers before me, I began gazing at military recruiting posters. "Join the Navy and see the world" was a slogan that had immense appeal. See the world? Yes! The local recruiting office was

located in the basement of the Post Office. I went in and loaded up on colorful folders with photos of ships at sea and distant ports of call.

In April 1959, age seventeen, I joined the Navy.

In Uniform

I felt drawn to the sea, and thus to the Navy, much as had been the case with Ishmael in *Moby Dick*, who "had little or no money in my purse, and nothing particular to interest me on shore" and so sought refuge "in the watery part of the world" as a way of coping with "a damp, drizzly November in my soul."

As things turned out, I was fated to remain on dry land. While in a sailor's uniform, I never boarded a ship or submarine or even a rowboat. I had joined the Navy to see the world and instead saw a bit of Illinois, a fragment of New Jersey, and a great deal of Washington, DC.

Strangely enough, for someone who has spent his entire postmilitary life opposing militarization and war, joining the Navy was just what I needed and also excellent preparation for what was yet to come. At that point in my life, the Navy met many needs. To a major degree I was on my own, yet in a stable structure that provided for life's necessities along with many challenges and much to think about.

My first eight weeks in uniform—June 1 through August 4, 1959—were spent at the Great Lakes Naval Training Station (sometimes referred to by its graduates as Great *Mistakes* Naval Training Station) on the northern outskirts of Chicago and the western shore of Lake Michigan. My head was shaved, I learned to march, make my bed in just the right way, and to peel potatoes with assembly-line efficiency. I became adept at assembling a rifle and hitting the target, at the same time doubting I could ever shoot to kill.

While I can't claim to have enjoyed boot camp, for me it was mainly an adventure, even a time of occasional mild mischief. For many others it was harder. I recall a few recruits in my barracks who wept themselves to sleep and two sad boys who suffered breakdowns; they were given early discharges and sent home.

I quickly found myself in a slightly responsible position. Despite being a high school dropout, as a result of test scores I was appointed "intelligence officer" of my company. This meant that I had to coach the forty or so young men in the company, especially those who were failing to check the right circle in response to multiple-choice questions that were beamed on a screen in a testing room. The problem was that a number of people in my company were barely literate. In principle the illiterate never get into the Navy in the first place, but clearly some recruiters were willing to cut corners in order to meet their quotas. Ten or twelve men in my company couldn't answer the questions because they couldn't read them. Remedial education was not an option; there was no time or material for a literacy program in the evenings.

Under pressure from the first-class petty officer in charge of our company (our performance reflected on him), I came up with a Plan B. It might also have been called Plan Bilko, in honor of Sergeant Bilko, the central figure in a popular fifties TV comedy who cheerfully swindled both his senior officers as well as the Army itself. Before being marched into the room where the closely monitored tests were given, with a competing company filling alternate rows, I was able to

I'm second on the left

place myself at exactly the right spot in line to sit at a front-row-center desk from which several people seated farther back on either side of me could see how I was holding my pencil: if I held it straight up, this meant the answer was A; if I held it horizontally to the left and right, I was signaling the answer was B; if I pointed it forward, check C; while covering the pencil with both hands meant D. Several preassigned people who could see my pencil replicated the signal so that everyone in the company, no matter where they were sitting, got the message.

The only problem was that it hadn't occurred to me that the system would work as well as it did. On the first test we took using my pencil-signaling method, the entire company got a perfect score. Apparently this was unprecedented. An investigation followed. It was finally reluctantly accepted that I, as intelligence officer, had done an amazing job of tutoring the company that week.

Surviving that near disaster put me briefly under a cloud of suspicion but without punishment. I realized I had to create a credible bell curve, high enough to put us ahead of the competing companies in the same week of training, but not so high as to set off another alarm. I assigned a number of mistakes to each person in the company, with only a few getting all the answers correct and with some variation from week to week.

The result was that the competing companies won flags for marching, marksmanship, and other competitive achievements, but we got to carry the "I" flag—"I" for intelligence—as we marched down the parade field on the day of graduation while the Navy band played "Anchors Aweigh." It was our company's one and only flag, and we felt immensely proud of it even though it had been achieved by cheating. I thought to myself that all's fair in love and war, and that passing multiple-choice military tests fell under the war heading—an exercise in survival in battle. We had played and won a mouse-beats-cat, Tom-and-Jerry game. The officer in charge of our company was delighted we had played it so well.

In fact, being integrated into military life involved learning all sorts of tricks, not the least of which was applying a certain brand of under-arm deodorant pads to our shoes to obtain the mirror shine required whenever there were inspections.

Our company commander, a middle-aged chief petty officer responsible for turning us from anarchist kids off the street into spic-and-span sailors, had a way with words. During our first week of training, we stood at attention as he told us, "The Navy *owns* you. In case you didn't get that, I'll say it again. *The Navy owns you.* For the hard of hearing, let me repeat: *The United States Navy* **owns** *you.* You are the *property* of the US Navy. You are owned and operated by the Navy. Have I made myself clear? We issue the orders and you obey the orders or there will be hell to pay. Any questions?" There were no questions. It dawned on me that being in the military had a great deal in common with slavery.

True North

When I enlisted, I signed a contract that guaranteed me, once out of boot camp, a place at the Navy School of Journalism. It turned out that the promise had been a recruiter's carrot. In the latter weeks of boot camp I was told a mistake had been made—I didn't meet the journalism school's minimum-age requirement—and therefore I would have to choose a different vocational path. After spending half an hour looking through a catalog of specialized Navy schools, I opted for Weather School. This meant that I would become an "aerographer's mate" working, either on land or sea, with Navy meteorologists. Was I disappointed? Not at all. By then I had met several Navy journalists stationed at Great Lakes, and I knew that much of the work a military journalist does is filling in the blanks on boiler-plate texts sent to hometown newspapers about how sailor John Jones had been assigned to serve on the USS *Coral Sea*—basically public relations work promoting the Navy. Meteorology, on the other hand, meant engagement in an important aspect of environmental studies.

In July 1959 I arrived at the Navy Weather School, located on the grounds of the Naval Air Station in Lakehurst, New Jersey, a place best known as the site of the Hindenburg airship disaster thirty-two years earlier when a huge, swastika-decorated German zeppelin had burst into flames while landing. Thirty-six people died. The base still housed several Navy dirigibles and also served as a training center for parachutists, one of whom died during the months I was there when his chute failed to open.

Far from "seeing the world," I was less than an hour's bus ride from Red Bank. But if the location was not exactly exotic, I felt challenged by the studies that awaited me.

Our small school accommodated about forty students for an intense, five-month program. Besides learning the basics of meteorology (what constituted a warm or cold front, the types of clouds and what they indicated, how to read and draw a weather map, how to translate weather data into five-digit groups of standard code, etc.), we were trained in touch-typing and took part in occasional military drills. The day started with inspection, all of us lined up and given a quick once-over. Following breakfast, classes began.

My one and only fistfight occurred on the Lakehurst Naval Base. Early on, a fellow student had borrowed a dollar from me but, despite my sporadic requests, never got around to paying it back. He had the job of distributing the mail, a chore with an ounce of power among people starved for letters from home. Wearing his role as if it were a crown, he was not above delaying delivery of a letter addressed to anyone who annoyed him. Within weeks, everyone in our unit came to regard him with loathing.

One morning I demanded the return of my dollar. He looked at me with contempt, reached into his shirt pocket, took out a dollar bill, held it in front of my face, then let it drop to the floor. Leaving the money where it fell, I grabbed him under the arms, lifted him off the floor and hurled him against the nearest wall. It still amazes me to recall how light he felt and how easily I made his body fly across the room. He came back with his fists flying. Far from being alarmed, I rejoiced in the combat, hammering away, hardly aware of the crowd that quickly gathered around us. The fight might well have lasted until one of us had done real harm to the other, but luckily a bell summoned us to inspection. As we stood at attention outside the barracks, I remember taking great pride in his bloodied lip and bruised face. Fortunately, when the inspecting officer noticed the state of his face and asked what had happened, he told the classic prescribed lie—he had tripped on the stairs.

This battle won me a good deal of admiration from my classmates. I was immensely pleased with myself—I sensed I had successfully passed a manhood test. At the same time I was alarmed to discover what strength and deadly will I possessed when my anger was sufficiently aroused, and the exhilaration that battle can awaken. This was a side of myself that I had not previously known.

Perhaps that encounter with my own violence was a contributing factor in the spiritual awakening that occurred in that period of my life. There had been a great deal of veiled unhappiness and desperate searching that past year, much of it centered on my failed attempt to live with my father. I had dropped out of school, returned for several months to my mother's home, then—like so many confused kids down through the centuries—plunged into the military. I was now trying to make of myself both a sailor and a weatherman and doing well at both, but finding that neither role gave me a sense of real meaning. I sought deeper waters.

In this searching state of hyperalertness, that Saturday night I went to see the film that was being screened at the base theater. It happened to be *The Nun's Story*, in which Audrey Hepburn played the part of a young Belgian woman who embraced monastic life in a Flemish convent but years later, during the German occupation of Belgium, left to join the resistance movement in the uncloistered world. Between these two events the film provided a compelling portrait of a nun's rigorous religious formation, a later episode in which her obedience was abused by a superior, and a near love affair with a physician working at the same hospital where the Hepburn character was serving as a nurse. It was a complex story that took pre–Vatican II Catholic Christianity, warts as well as bells, quite seriously. Hepburn played the part of someone wholeheartedly attempting to live a Christ-inspired life. At a key moment early on in the film a Gospel text was read aloud: "If you would be perfect, go sell what you have, give it to the poor . . . and come follow me." *The Nun's Story* is about one person's struggle to translate that sentence into her own life.

It's a bit embarrassing to say one has had a mystical experience, and more embarrassing to say that what set the stage for that experience was a movie. But that's what happened. I left the theater, went for a walk, and under a clear moonless sky, thick with stars, experienced—how to put it into words?—the presence, the reality, the all-connectingness of God, a God who somehow was aware of me despite my near-nothingness. The old question "Is there a God?" evaporated. I would never again begin a prayer, "Oh God, if there is a God . . ."

Words fail—attempting to describe a mystical encounter is like putting lead boots on a ballerina. I was both absurdly happy and deeply silent. God said not a word, and yet somehow there was an overwhelming sense of being submerged in love, an intimate love and a love that excluded no one and nothing. I had never been so overwhelmed with joy. My compass had been adjusted to true north.

Well after midnight I got back in my bunk, but hardly slept. I thought more about the film and decided that the thing to do when

I got out of bed that Sunday morning was to go to Mass at the base's Catholic chapel. Mass as celebrated in a Gothic Belgian chapel had been one of the beauties of the film. I wanted to take part in the real thing. But the real thing was hugely disappointing. The base chapel resembled a shoebox. The pre–Vatican II liturgy was said by a priest whose unintelligible Latin was whispered at breakneck speed to Mass attenders, mainly women, many of whom appeared to regard Mass as a time for saying the rosary or, in the case of the men who were there, something to be stoically endured from the back of the church. I left at the end with no urge to return the following Sunday.

Yet the sparks ignited during my midnight walk were not put out by the contrast between what Mass can be in Flanders and what, on a US military base and in many parishes, it so often was in 1959.

I had a friend in my class, one of my roommates, whom I had noticed reading a Bible that he kept in his locker. He also made use of a copy of the Episcopal *Book of Common Prayer.* I told him that I had been baptized in the Episcopal Church five years earlier and was thinking about reconnecting. We talked about the film, which he also had seen. In the weeks that followed he and I managed to find time to have conversations about Christianity, to read some prayers together on a more or less daily basis, and to follow the biblical lectionary. When I told him I would love to visit a monastery, he told me about Holy Cross, a community of Episcopal monks in the Hudson Valley near West Point. Encouraged, I wrote to the prior asking if I might come for a visit at Christmas, after graduating and before reporting for my next assignment. I received a positive response.

Early in our studies we had been asked to fill out a form indicating our three preferred assignments following graduation. At the same time we were told that the better we did with our exams, the better our chance of getting one of our three choices. Hoping I might be stationed in the Mediterranean, I put the Sixth Fleet at the top of my list and studied hard to get grades that would make my wish come true. The result was that I graduated first in my class, but far from being sent to Europe, I received orders to report to a Navy unit that worked at the US Weather Bureau (today the US Weather Service) headquarters in Suitland, Maryland, just outside of Washington, DC.

I was off to meteorology's Vatican. But first came my visit to Holy Cross Monastery.

A Bus Ride up the Hudson

Fresh out of the Navy Weather School and following a brief visit with my Red Bank family, I set out to spend Christmas at Holy Cross Monastery. Not the least important part of the journey, it turned out, was waiting at the Port Authority Bus Terminal in Manhattan for a bus that would take me up the west side of the Hudson River to the town of West Park. With time on my hands, I was browsing a carousel full of paperbacks at the waiting room's newsstand and came upon a book with an odd title, *The Seven Storey Mountain,* by Thomas Merton. The author's name meant nothing to me. It was, the jacket announced, "the autobiography of a young man who led a full and worldly life and then, at the age of twenty-six, entered a Trappist monastery." There was a quotation from Evelyn Waugh, who said this book "may well prove to be of permanent interest in the history of religious experience." Another writer compared it to St. Augustine's *Confessions.* I cheerfully paid seventy-five cents for a copy.

It proved to be a can't-put-it-down read for me. In the bus going up the Hudson Valley, I recall occasionally looking up from the text to gaze out the window at the heavy snow that was falling that night. Merton's life story has ever since been linked in my mind with the silent ballet of snowflakes swirling in cones of light beneath streetlights.

While still in Lakehurst, I had been reading D. H. Lawrence's *Lady Chatterley's Lover,* which certainly held my eighteen-year-old attention—a long-suppressed book in which love-making was vividly described in almost sacramental terms. In *The Seven Storey Mountain* I was surprised to discover that Merton, when he was precisely my age and also on the road, in his case in Italy, had also been reading Lawrence. In the shadow of his father's recent death, he too was on a desperate search, while having no clear idea what it was he was seeking. It was while in Rome that a mosaic icon over an altar in one of the

75

city's oldest churches triggered in Merton an overwhelming awareness of the presence of God and even the reality of the risen Christ. "For the first time in my whole life," he wrote, "I began to find out something of who this Person was that men call Christ. It was obscure, but it was a true knowledge of Him. But it was in Rome that my conception of Christ was formed. . . . It is Christ God, Christ King."[1]

It was an experience I immediately connected with, having had an equivalent encounter not many weeks before.

Did I get as far as that passage in Merton's thick book while on the bus? I don't recall. Perhaps. Certainly I got that far and much further within a day or two of my arrival.

By the time the bus stopped at the monastery gate, the snow was deep. I crunched my way down a buried driveway to the massive oak door of a handsome stone-and-brick building that I could see was linked to a church. I rang the bell but had to wait a bit, as a service was in progress. At last the door swung open revealing an elderly monk in white robes. "Ah, you must be Jim Forest! We were a little worried. Thank heaven the snow didn't prevent your coming." Then he led me into the church to take part in what was left of Compline. The monks—there must have been twenty of them—were divided into two groups that faced each other in the choir on either side of the altar and were singing in plainchant. I was overjoyed.

The week passed quickly, during which I took part in all the services, finished reading *The Seven Storey Mountain*, and was given a rosary by the prior and taught by him how to use it. He also suggested, once I was settled in Washington, that I make contact with the rector of St. Paul's Episcopal Church.

I felt so at home at Holy Cross, and at the same time so impressed by Merton's journey to monastic life, that I began to think this might be the place to come once I was out of the Navy. The fact that it was an Episcopal rather than a Catholic monastery seemed to me of minor importance. I knew nothing about the divisions within the Episcopal Church and hadn't given any thought to the Anglican Communion's Thirty-Nine Articles and the fact that Church of England's roots were in the bedroom of King Henry VIII.

Before leaving I made arrangements to return for Easter.

---

1. Thomas Merton, *The Seven Storey Mountain* (New York: Harcourt Brace, 1948), 109.

Navy Weatherman

I never "saw the world" while in the Navy, but during the seventeen months that began in January 1960 I had the blessing of seeing a great deal of Washington, DC—its museums, libraries, and monuments, its churches and cathedrals, its cafés and bookshops, plus a few of its jazz nightclubs. I was a frequent visitor to the National Art Gallery.

I also had a fascinating job and liked the people I was working with. Within the vast building that housed the Weather Bureau, the technology was astonishing. It was as if I had stepped onto the set of a science-fiction film. Just one floor below our Navy offices a massive computer was housed within an air-conditioned glass enclosure that, using robot fingers located in an adjacent room, drew graceful isobars on large maps. It was hypnotizing to watch. Images of entire weather systems were made fuzzily visible by cameras placed on early satellites; the first weather satellite, Vanguard 2, had been launched by NASA on February 17, 1959, ten months before my arrival. (Vanguard 2 is still up there and is expected to continue functioning until 2259.) While a full decade would pass before there were photos of the entire earth, meteorologists were among the first who were privileged to see portions of our planet from above the atmosphere.

Adjacent to our suite of offices was a noisy room with sound-absorbing doors and walls in which ranks of teletype machines churned out up-to-the-minute weather data from hundreds of far-flung locations—temperature, air pressure, humidity, visibility, precipitation, type of precipitation, depth of rainfall, wind speed and direction, cloud cover, cloud types and cloud height—all the fragments of information that, when placed on a map, make possible the creation of a portrait of how things are in the atmosphere at any given moment and provide essential clues in predicting what to anticipate in the hours and days ahead.

One element of our work had an apocalyptic edge. As a training exercise in the meteorological aspects of nuclear war, each week we drew a series of maps predicting fallout patterns at twelve-hour intervals over a three-day period if a twenty-megaton nuclear weapon exploded at noon that day over the center of Washington, DC. It was clear that none of us would be among the survivors.

Despite this doomsday reminder, I enjoyed my work and did well in the Navy. Within a year and a half of enlisting, I had been promoted to third-class petty officer, the Navy equivalent of an Army sergeant. I had also gotten a high-school-equivalency diploma, doing so with such good results that I had to take the test a second time to prove I hadn't cheated the first time.

There were some funny moments. One of them happened on an overcast day at the end of January 1961 soon after the inauguration of John F. Kennedy. The Navy attaché at the White House called our unit seeking assurance that there would be no rain that afternoon as he was planning to take the president for a ride on the Potomac in an experimental open-top vehicle that floated over water on a cushion of air. The hitch was that the craft didn't function well in wet weather. Several officers gathered round what was called the Weather Table and, using the latest reports from weather stations in and around the capital, quickly agreed that there would be no rain before nightfall. With that prediction to relay, the senior officer on duty called the Navy attaché to report the good news. I was close enough to hear laughter on the other end of the line. The attaché asked, "Great! Just one thing. Have you looked out the window?" That was the one source of information that had been neglected. In fact rain was falling over both the White House and the Weather Bureau. It was a cautionary lesson about the blind spots of experts. None of us had looked out the window.

The Works of Mercy

T hat first year in Washington was a time of rapid religious evolution as I sought to find my place and direction within the complex world of Christianity.

Soon after arrival in Washington I went to St. Paul's Episcopal Church, as had been recommended by the prior of Holy Cross Monastery, introduced myself to the rector, and became active in the parish. In many ways it was similar to a Catholic parish, even having an occasional evening Benediction service for adoration of the Blessed Sacrament: a consecrated wafer set in a sun-like gold monstrance was placed on the altar while those present, on their knees, contemplated this potent sign of God's presence. Week by week, however, I became aware that, among Episcopal parishes in Washington, St. Paul's was the sole local bastion of what Episcopalians regarded, often dismissively, as "high church," in contrast to "middle church" or "low church." High church was for a minority who were drawn to elaborate eucharistic liturgies and what most Protestants viewed as "empty ritual"—incense, bells, the rosary—things regarded by iconoclastic critics as "Roman" or, still worse, as "papist."

It struck me that, no matter now hurried Mass might be in many Catholic parishes, each parish was solidly anchored in the Mass. No one spoke of a Catholic parish being "high church" or "low church." I found myself, somewhat guiltily, slipping into Catholic churches simply to pray. A hallmark of the Catholic Church was that the Blessed Sacrament—the consecrated eucharistic bread—was reserved in a small tabernacle near the altar awaiting anyone who came in. Somehow its presence helped raise the curtains that usually obscure God from consciousness. In that now distant time, during the day and often at night, the doors of Catholic churches always seemed open.

Negative events also played a part in pulling me away from the Episcopal Church. The most consequential was an experience at Holy

Cross Monastery during my second visit at Easter 1960. All went well until the last day, when one of the monks asked to see me in the visiting room. Once the door was shut, he embraced and kissed me with sexual passion, his stubbly unshaven face pressed against mine. I struggled free of his grasp, exited the room, and soon afterward left the monastery in a state of great confusion. Back in Washington, I wrote to the prior, telling him what had happened. His reply wasn't helpful. He might have pointed out that monks, like everyone else, sometimes suffer severe loneliness and have sexual longings of one sort or another that they sometimes don't manage very well. I had hoped he would say that steps were being taken to make certain that in the future similar events would not happen to guests like myself. What he wrote instead was that homosexuality was often a sign of a monastic vocation. This wasn't good news for me—my erotic fantasies were focused on women. After his letter, which said not a word about safeguarding future guests from sexual assault, I had no desire to return. Despite many positive experiences at Holy Cross and much to be thankful for, the milk had been soured. (Of course the same sort of thing could have happened in a Catholic setting, but in my case never did.)

Yet I still had hesitations about becoming Catholic, and so began to explore the varieties of Christianity in Washington, visiting various churches. Among them was a Greek Orthodox cathedral, but I sensed one had best be Greek to be made welcome there. With my positive memories of the black church near our home in Red Bank, several times I attended services at the church on the campus of Howard University, a friendly place with wonderful singing and powerful sermons, but felt that, as a white person, I would always be an outsider. Also, as much as I appreciated the spirited singing and fine preaching, it was too Protestant for me; the center point was the pulpit, not the altar.

For a time I was part of a small Bible-study group that met in the apartment of an Episcopal priest whose wife, I discovered after noticing a photo on the wall, was the daughter of Bertrand Russell, British philosopher and prominent atheist. I wondered what the father made of his daughter's Christian faith. (One of the books I was struggling with at the time was Russell's *History of Western Philosophy*.)

As the weeks went by, I came to realize that the Catholic churches in which I so often stopped to pray were places in which I always felt welcomed, both spiritually and intellectually. It was time to knock on the door. One afternoon I rang the rectory doorbell of the parish of St. Thomas Apostle, in northwest Washington, and began a series of weekly meetings with one of the priests who lived there, Father Thomas Duffy. We often had our free-wheeling conversations in a hotel coffee shop across the street. For reading, he gave me an English translation of a recently published German catechism, *Life in Christ*, which took a thematic route rather than the cut-and-dried, question-and-answer approach of *The Baltimore Catechism*—"Who made the world? God made the world." Apart from the fact that I never made sense of what were regarded as the preconditions for a sin to be mortal (does anyone ever achieve full awareness or full intentionality?), nothing we talked about stopped me in my tracks.

During those same months I had come increasingly to realize that a basic element of ordinary Christian life was practicing the works of mercy: feeding the hungry, giving drink to the thirsty, clothing the naked, providing hospitality to the homeless, caring for the sick, visiting the prisoner, and burying the dead.[1] When the opportunity arose to do some spare-time work at a home for children whose parents weren't able to function as such, I volunteered. For about half a year I helped out in a woodworking shop and sometimes took part in the sports program, fracturing my right arm during a baseball game one afternoon while sliding into home plate. On Sundays when I wasn't on duty, I often had the happy chore of accompanying the Catholic children at the institution to Mass at nearby Blessed Sacrament Church.

Blessed Sacrament was an unusual parish that had embraced what was called a "dialogue Mass." Not just the acolytes assisting the priest at the altar but everyone in the church made the required Latin responses; for example, when the priest addressed the congregation with the words *Dominus vobiscum* ("the Lord be with you"), the whole congregation responded, *Et cum Spiritu tuo* ("and with your spirit"). Nearly everyone present was engaged in saying and singing the liturgy, not just witnessing it.

The parish had a substantial library on the ground floor of a house next door. It was here, on a table by a window, that I first saw copies of the *Catholic Worker*, in fact a whole stack of them going back several years. I picked up the issue on top with a mixture of curiosity and caution—the name made me think warily of the Communist paper, the *Daily Worker*. But looking through the articles and the artwork reas-

---

1. See Matthew 25:35–40.

sured me. Here was a truly Catholic journal that wove together theology, community, and liturgy with the works of mercy, while raising urgent questions about a social order that produced so many marginalized people in desperate need of help. I borrowed the entire stack, took the issues back to my base, and read each one closely.

Several books that I found in the library helped expand my understanding of Christianity—more of Thomas Merton's writing but also G. K. Chesterton's *Orthodoxy* and *The Everlasting Man*; Dorothy Day's autobiography, *The Long Loneliness*; and Eric Gill's *Autobiography*. In combination with *The Seven Storey Mountain*, *The Long Loneliness* opened doors that have helped shape the rest of my life.

A woodcut I made of the Catholic Worker building on Chrystie Street as it was in the early sixties

The next step was a two-night visit to the Catholic Worker. Sometime in the late summer of 1960, I hitchhiked to Manhattan, at the time not an uncommon way to travel for a young man with very little money in his pocket, and made my way to the address that I had found in the paper. Spring Street turned out to be on the north edge of Little Italy in the Lower East Side, and the Catholic Worker dining room and office were located in a loft at the top of a long flight of stairs. My arrival happened to coincide with moving day—I joined a parade of people carrying boxes to the Worker's new address a few blocks to the east, a dilapidated three-story building at 175 Chrystie Street.

One of the volunteers, Jack Baker, offered me hospitality—floorspace and a thin mattress and blanket near the front window of his two-room-plus-kitchen apartment. An unframed print of a Modigliani nude was tacked on one wall, a face of Christ by Georges Rouault on another. The floor sagged, and the air in that old, neglected building left a bitter taste. Jack was part of an outer ring of people who weren't on the Worker staff but who occasionally helped out. Not long before, Jack explained, he had been a prisoner at Sing Sing Penitentiary. While "behind the walls" he had made contact with the Catholic Worker.

I was deeply impressed by the people I met and what they were doing: their community life, morning and evening pauses for prayer, meals cooked and served for men and women who lived much of their lives on the street, and occasional acts of protest against both racism and preparations for nuclear war. By now it was clear to me that a Christianity that was unresponsive to suffering and injustice was Christian in name only.

Returning to Washington, ideas about my post-Navy future had a new focus. Monastic life still beckoned, but so did the Catholic Worker.

One of my companions in my search was a member of the full-time staff at the home for children, Jim Durso, a sturdy Italian from Wilkes-Barre, Pennsylvania, who possessed a wonderful balance of common sense, good humor, a contagious enthusiasm for "the faith," a no-bullshit intellect, and an eagerness to serve the community. He had only recently left a Catholic seminary, having realized not long before ordination that the celibate life would be, for him, unbearable.

Nearly every week we managed to have a meal together at which a good deal of beer was drunk while we talked theology, the writings of various Catholic authors, monasticism, the Catholic Worker movement, the classical conditions required for a war to be regarded as just, church history, the Italian American subculture, and whatever else was on our minds. If ever I get access to a time machine, I'd love to go back and listen to one of those sessions of intense dialogue. Our guardian angels must have enjoyed our exchanges.

There was also the friendship with Father Thomas Duffy. After several months of instruction and conversation over many a cup of coffee, on November 26, 1960, he received me, by conditional baptism, into the Catholic Church. Jim Durso was my godfather.

This border-crossing moment was a joyous one for me, though it did cost me some inconvenience. The otherwise hospitable Episcopalian family with whom I had been lodging in a house not far from the National Cathedral, where my host was responsible for maintaining its magnificent organ, wanted no papists under their roof.

I was shown the door.

Conscientious Objection

Ihadn't seen it coming, but my relationship with the Navy was fast approaching a crisis. While I was no longer considering a career in uniform and devoting my professional life to meteorology, my intention was to serve out my enlistment contract in the eighteen months remaining. My work involved nothing that needed absolution. Events in Cuba changed all that.

The suite of rooms used by our Navy unit included a small television studio that was connected to the Pentagon's War Room, officially designated as the National Military Command Center. Standing before a circular, rotating map of the Northern Hemisphere, twice a day one of the officers would present an overview of world weather developments, then answer questions from those at the viewing end. During the late winter and spring of 1961, I was aware that the questions often had to do with the weather in and around Cuba. Though I had read about the recent Cuban revolution led by Fidel Castro, I gave the matter little thought.

On April 13, 1961, 1,400 paramilitaries under CIA direction set sail for Cuba. Two days later, eight CIA-supplied bombers attacked Cuban airfields. The next day the invasion force landed at Playa Girón, the Bay of Pigs. The Cuban army's counter-offensive, led by Fidel Castro, quickly resulted in a Cuban victory. On April 20, the invaders surrendered.

Only after the failed invasion did I connect the dots. Despite the immediate denial by President Kennedy that the invasion was a US undertaking—initially it was blamed on unaided Cuban exiles—I knew the Navy, and even our tiny unit, had played a role in it. It made sense—the timing of military beach landings is best planned with an eye on the weather. (To his credit, within days Kennedy reversed his initial denial, regretting what had happened and admitting that the invasion was planned, organized, and funded by the CIA with US military involvement. He lamented having given the operation its go-ahead.)

Despite my parents' left-wing views, I was profoundly naïve about America's role in the world. In that period of my life it never occurred to me that my government would seek to overthrow other governments. I knew nothing about the US role in arranging regime change in Guatemala and Iran. Back in 1952, age eleven, I had worn "I Like Ike" buttons in support of Eisenhower's presidential campaign. After Eisenhower won the election I had sent him a photo of myself proudly holding a paint-by-numbers portrait I had made of him and was thrilled to receive a note of appreciation signed by the president on White House stationery. Eight years later, in 1960, I was strongly in favor of Kennedy's election. From an apartment just a mile from the Capitol, I watched his inauguration with pride and soaring expectations. I was deeply stirred when Kennedy said, "Ask not what your country can do for you, ask what you can do for your country." For all the nation's flaws, past sins, and unsolved problems, I was passionately proud to be an American.

The culpability of the United States for the Bay of Pigs invasion hit me like a torpedo. I felt implicated in a collective sin. When I read in the *Washington Post* that a daily silent protest was taking place in front of a CIA building in southwest Washington, and that Catholic Workers were among the participants, I decided to take part. It turned out to be a life-changing event.

After work and out of uniform, I joined twenty or so people carrying placards that bore such texts as "There is no *way* to peace—peace *is* the way" and "Nonviolence or Non-survival." The climate of the silent protest was prayerful. We were on one side of a wrought-iron fence, beyond which was a wide green lawn leading up to a mansion that reminded me of the Tara plantation in *Gone with the Wind*. This wasn't the CIA's headquarters, but CIA director Allen Dulles and other senior staff had offices inside. The demonstration was sponsored by the Quaker Peace Center, the War Resisters League, and the Committee for Nonviolent Action, with Catholic Worker involvement.

I had no sense that I was putting myself or my job in the Navy at risk. As I say, I was naïve. Freedom of speech, freedom to dissent, and freedom to protest peacefully were principles at the core of American identity. I took it for granted that those rights belonged to everyone, those in military service included.

I noticed several men in suits inside the fence taking photos of us. It amused me that they were using telephoto lenses. No one in the demonstration would have objected to close-ups. Any of us would have been quite willing to identify ourselves and explain why we were there.

A few days later I was summoned to the office of our unit's commanding officer, Captain Cox, and found him so angry that his hands shook. He had a hard time assembling a sentence. On his desk were several eight-by-ten, black-and-white photos of the demonstration in which I was clearly visible. "Is this you?" "Yes." "How dare you! How dare you give support to enemies of the United States?" "I wasn't supporting any enemies," I replied, "I was protesting the invasion of Cuba." Captain Cox was speechless. Previously he and I had enjoyed an excellent relationship, but after that day the only communication we had was when he handed me a letter from the Office of Naval Intelligence ordering me to report for an interview.

In preparation for that meeting I was required to fill out a detailed security questionnaire. One of the questions was: "Are there any incidents in your life which may reflect on your suitability to perform the duties which you may be called upon to take?"

I read the question with dread, realizing that I could not find a way to answer honestly in a manner that would be acceptable to the Navy. Getting back to the base along the Potomac where I was then living, I went to the Catholic chapel to pray, read the New Testament, and think. Skipping supper, I must have remained there until midnight. For months I had been aware that the serious application of Catholicism's just-war doctrine would condemn any modern war, if only because noncombatants had become war's main casualties. Also, how could any Christian, in or out of the military, promise automatic obedience to each and every future order? I thought of the many Germans who justified their obedience to the demonic demands of the Hitler regime with the words "I was only following orders." I thought of Anne Frank and the Holocaust and all the obedient soldiers who herded captives into concentration camps and gas chambers. But at the same time I was apprehensive about what would happen to me if I failed to commit myself to unqualified obedience. What would my colleagues think? How would they treat me? I was wading in fear, struggling not to drown in it.

The simple wisdom of a Russian proverb I had encountered as a child while contemplating the *Family of Man* photo exhibition in New York came to mind: "Eat bread and salt and speak the truth." It was a relief to realize that my task was simply to tell the truth and let the consequences take care of themselves.

Finally I composed this paragraph:

> *I would have to refuse to obey any order or fulfill any duty which I considered to be immoral, contrary to my conscience or in opposition to the teaching of my Church, as a Catholic. It is highly conceivable that there are duties that would be imposed on me during war time which I could not accept. Though I would participate in the actual and just defense of our country, I would not assist in any attack or war effort which necessarily involved the death of innocent non-combatants. I would obey no order in conflict with my convictions.*

On May 11, I passed through the doors of the Naval Intelligence Service and spent most of the day in a narrow interrogation room being aggressively cross-examined by two Navy officers while magnetic tape traveled from reel to reel through a recorder. It was a scene not unlike ones I had seen in countless crime movies. There was even a large one-way observation mirror built into one wall, though whether anyone was watching from the other side I never discovered.

I was presented with two choices: "cooperate" or be sent to the brig, the Navy term for prison. "Cooperate" meant not only answering questions about the demonstration I had taken part in—I was more than willing to explain what I knew about it and why I was there—but to become active with groups that organized such protests and report what I heard and observed to the Naval Intelligence Service. My family was also on the agenda. Many of the questions put to me centered on my Communist father. The word "spy" wasn't used, but it was clear that this was what I was being invited to become. Otherwise the brig. "If it's one or the other," I said, "I'll take the brig." I was surprised how easily the declaration exited my mouth. The fear that I had been struggling to keep at bay evaporated. It helped me to recall that my father had been imprisoned and not only survived the experience but enjoyed telling stories about it.

Only later did I realize that what exactly I would be charged with wasn't explained. In fact, so far as I was aware, there were no Navy regulations that I had violated, nor was I told of any. Nevertheless, I took their threats seriously, having no idea what might be possible. My attempt to explain my religious motives and Catholic teaching regarding war seemed to baffle the interrogators, who may well have been Catholic themselves. They seemed convinced that only those driven by left-wing ideology would take part in such activities. "Can you name one Catholic bishop who agrees with you?" they asked. "Any bishop," I replied, "can tell you about the church's just-war requirements."

All in all it was a nightmarish encounter, but at the end of the day, having rejected their proposal "to cooperate," I told them I would apply for an early discharge as a conscientious objector. I was asked to put in writing what I had said and agreed to do so, as long as I could make a carbon. I still have my copy, all twelve pages. I left the Naval Intelligence Service building feeling stronger and freer than when I had walked in.

I was amazingly fortunate. The next morning I discovered that the director of a Quaker-linked group called the Central Committee for Conscientious Objectors, George Willoughby, was speaking that night at the Quaker Meeting House in Washington. I attended his lecture and talked with him afterward. He told me chapter and verse what the Navy's regulations were regarding early discharge for conscientious objectors. My parish priest, Father Thomas Duffy, a graduate of the Vatican's prestigious North American College in Rome, wrote a letter testifying that I was active in his parish, was a member of the parish choir, and affirming that one could be both a faithful Catholic and a conscientious objector. On a visit to the Catholic Worker in New York, I had learned from Dorothy Day that there was a theologian on the faculty of Catholic University in Washington, Father Robert Hovda, who had himself been a conscientious objector before entering the seminary. Using university stationery, Father Hovda wrote a supportive letter for inclusion with my application for discharge. He also loaned me several books that treated war from a theological perspective. Even my military chaplain, though bewildered that I had such "an unusual conscience," backed me up, crediting his support to a street-corner encounter he had had many years earlier with Catholic Worker cofounder Peter Maurin.

Significant support also came from within my unit, most notably from my executive officer, Commander John Marabito, a devout Catholic who had almost been ordained a priest but instead opted for marriage and ended up with a career in the Navy. "Jim, I know you're sincere," he told me, "but I have to tell you I never heard a word about conscientious objection during the years I was in seminary. Can you give me anything to read that would help me understand your views from a Catholic point of view?" Providentially, I had with me one of the books Father Robert Hovda had loaned me, *War and Christianity Today*, and gave it to him, explaining that the author, Franziscus Stratmann, was a German Dominican priest who had been condemned to death by Hitler's regime for his antiwar activity but managed to escape into Switzerland and survived the Nazi period.

Cdr. John Marabito

The next morning, while having a quick breakfast in the Weather Bureau cafeteria, I noticed Commander Marabito approaching my table, a broad smile on his face and his right hand extended. He shook my hand vigorously while saying, "Jim, I read the book last night and I just want you to know I'm proud of you, very proud, and I will back you up." Which he did. Given the ire of Captain Cox, who regarded me as having betrayed both him personally as well as the nation, I've often wondered if Commander Marabito sacrificed promotion to captain as a result of his support. Captain Cox may have seen to it that his executive officer paid a higher price than I did.

Originally worried about the possible hostility I might face within my unit, I was astonished at how much support I received from my colleagues. While a few superficial relationships went into the deep-freeze, the rest of my co-workers remained friendly. Working one night in the enclosure where our unit received and sent weather data, Captain Cox paid an unexpected visit. As he stepped into the code room, he found all four or five of us singing the black spiritual "Ain't Gonna Study War No More." We stopped instantly but there was no taking back what he had heard.

There was one other official expression of military backing for my discharge, though its author was hostile to my views. I was sent to the Pentagon for an interview with a Navy psychiatrist. Arriving at his office, instead of saluting him I made the mistake of reaching out to shake his hand. He refused a handshake—the border between officer and enlisted man had to be maintained. The meeting that followed was chilly. All I can now recall about it are two sentences from the report he filed: "Forest admits to having had nightmares as a child. . . . It is recommended that he be discharged from the Navy as expeditiously as possible."

In June the discharge was approved. Within a day of permission being given, I was "processed out" and was on my way, at Dorothy Day's invitation, to become part of the Catholic Worker community at St. Joseph's House of Hospitality in New York.

Dorothy Day picketing for peace

Getting to Know
Dorothy Day

While still in the Navy, in the late summer of 1960, I had my first glimpse of Dorothy Day, though I didn't have the nerve to speak to her. The occasion was a Friday night "meeting for the clarification of thought," a phrase Catholic Worker cofounder Peter Maurin had coined back in the movement's first year, 1933, for the Worker's once-a-week evening gatherings for dialogue. A lecture or reading was the main event, followed by a lively discussion, whose forty or so participants ranged from the very sane to the mildly insane, the pious to the irreverent. There were university students, a few seminarians, a sprinkling of scholars, bohemians, socialists and anarchists, plus staff and a few members of "the family"—people who had entered the Catholic Worker through the soup line and had become embedded members of the household.

Dorothy was sitting in the front row jotting in a reporter's notebook. Taking notes was, I soon discovered, one of her most ingrained activities, a discipline that must have taken root during her early days as a young journalist.

By happy chance Allen Ginsberg was the guest speaker that night. My attention drifted back and forth between Ginsberg, who had become one of my heroes ever since my reading of *Howl* while in high school, and Dorothy. I was astonished to find Ginsberg reciting and discussing his poetry at the Catholic Worker. His text was "Kaddish," a long poem of memory and mourning about his paranoid schizophrenic mother, Naomi, who had died four years earlier after long periods in mental hospitals. The text includes a vision of God that Naomi Ginsberg had experienced:

"Yesterday I saw God. What did he look like? Well, in the afternoon I climbed up a ladder—he has a cheap cabin in the country, like Monroe, New York—the chicken farms in the wood. He was a lonely old man with a white beard.

"I cooked supper for him. I made him a nice supper—lentil soup, vegetables, bread & butter—miltz—he sat down at the table, he was sad.

"I told him, Look at all those fightings and killings down there. What's the matter? Why don't you put a stop to it?

"I try, he said. That's all he could do. He looked tired. He's a bachelor so long, and he likes lentil soup."[1]

That Dorothy Day and Allen Ginsberg were together in the same room expanded my idea of both of them. From reading *The Long Loneliness*, I knew Dorothy's Catholicism was fervent, but I didn't know what open borders it had. Ginsberg, whose poems revealed him to be a Buddhist-flavored Jew with a warm heart for Jesus, had religious depths I hadn't fully appreciated in earlier readings of *Howl*.

I stayed two nights at the Catholic Worker on that visit. Once again Jack Baker offered me sleeping space on the floor of his apartment on Spring Street.

Sharing Jack's apartment at the time was Ammon Hennacy, a lanky man of sixty-seven with a lion's mane of graying hair. Ammon had gravitated to the Catholic Worker despite his searing critique of hierarchies in general and the Catholic Church in particular, finally becoming a Catholic chiefly thanks to his ardent devotion to Dorothy. He had been imprisoned during the First World War for his refusal to submit to conscription and—thanks to a Bible in his cell—been converted by the Sermon on the Mount to nonchurch Christianity. An anarchist whose sentences rarely ended in question marks, Ammon saw himself as an icon of what others should become. He was, he declared, "a one-man revolution."

Ammon Hennacy

---

1. Allen Ginsberg, *Kaddish and Other Poems* (San Francisco: City Lights Books, 1961), 23.

When I told Ammon that I was in the Navy, his eyebrows flew upward and the corners of his mouth fell downward. "As long as you put on a uniform and obey orders, you're a yellow-bellied chicken," Ammon informed me before setting off to sell copies of the *Catholic Worker*. A corner on Wall Street was one of his regular locations; the entrance to Fordham University in the Bronx another. By biting my tongue, I managed to get along with Ammon but made no attempt to win his seal of approval.

The next day, entrusted with the delivery of a bag of mail addressed to Dorothy, I joined another Catholic Worker, Ralph Madden, on a

visit to the Peter Maurin Farm, the community's rural outpost on Staten Island. It was the latest of several farms that had been inspired by Catholic Worker cofounder Peter Maurin's conviction that urbanization and industrialism were a dead-end street—the direction for society to take was back to the land. Peter agreed with Dorothy that unions might improve the working situation in factories and on assembly lines (a forty-hour work week instead of sixty, better pay, safer working conditions), but of its nature all robot-like work was dehumanizing. Thus farms, or "agronomic universities" as Peter christened them, were a key element of the Catholic Worker program.

Crossing New York Harbor by the Staten Island Ferry, we continued by bus until we were in walking distance of an old farmhouse on a rural road near Pleasant Plains close to the island's southern tip. Once inside, I found half a dozen people, Dorothy among them, gathered around a pot of tea at one end of a large table in the dining room.

At the time, Dorothy was only sixty-three, though to my eighteen-year-old eyes she seemed old enough to have been acquainted with Adam and Eve. For the first time I was seeing her close up. What an impressive woman! Her face was long, with high, prominent cheekbones underlining large, quick eyes, deep blue and almond-shaped, that could be teasing one moment, laughing the next, then turn grave an instant later. Her hair, parted in the middle, was braided and circled the back of her head like a garland of silver flowers. She had a fresh, scrubbed look with no trace of cosmetics. The suit she wore was sober, well tailored, and of good quality.

I gave Dorothy the bag of letters that had been received in Manhattan. None had been opened—Dorothy wanted to be the first reader of any mail addressed to her. She began reading the letters aloud and commenting on them. It was my first experience of a Dorothy Day ritual, a kind of spontaneous seminar attended by whoever happened to be present, in which Dorothy wove together stories about the letter writers along with elements of history, theology, and literature.

The only letter I still recall from that day's reading was one from Thomas Merton. Based on what he had written in *The Seven Storey Mountain* about Trappist limits on correspondence, I had assumed that he wrote to no one outside his immediate family, or what fragments remained of it—his mother, father, grandparents, and brother all had died. The Merton I imagined had left the world and padlocked the door, yet here he was in correspondence with Dorothy Day, someone who was not only in the thick of the world but one of its more engaged and controversial figures.

Merton at that time was not a controversial figure. His books were everywhere: in churches, drugstores, and train and bus terminals. Each bore the *Imprimatur* ("let it be printed," a bishop's certification that the book was without theological error). Yet here he was, writing to the leader of the Catholic Worker community, taking its work seriously, and even encouraging those aspects of its work that were the most provocative.

In that letter, Merton told Dorothy about his visit the day before with the Little Sisters of the Poor in Louisville, a community that reminded him of the Catholic Worker:

> *I realized that it is in these beautiful, beat, wrecked, almost helpless old people [living with the sisters] that Christ lives and works most. And in the hurt people who are bitter and say they have lost their faith. We (society at large) have lost our sense of values and our vision. We despise everything that Christ loves, everything marked with His compassion. We love fatness health bursting smiles the radiance of satisfied bodies all properly fed and rested and sated and washed and perfumed and sexually relieved. [Merton skipped the commas.] Anything else is a horror and a scandal to us. How sad. It makes me more and more sad*

and ashamed, for I am part of the society which has these values and I
can't help sharing its guilt, its illusions.

His note of distress was amplified in what he saw wrong with his
own monastery and his role in it:

Whether I like it or not I help perpetuate [through my writing] the
illusion in one way or other—by a kind of illusion of spirituality which
tends to justify the other and make it more smug on the rebound. And
I am not poor here.[2]

Merton was one of countless people drawn to Dorothy and influenced by her. She had a great gift for making those who encountered
her, even if only through letters or her published writings, look at
themselves in a new light, questioning previously held ideas, alle-
giances, and choices. I was another of those whose life was shifting
direction thanks to her.

I was back at the Catholic Worker in the fall and again at Christmas,
on both occasions having opportunities for conversation with Dorothy.
She was, it seemed, as interested in me as I was in her. I quickly discovered that she was one of the few people with whom I could talk openly
and without embarrassment about my family background. Indeed she
had known at least one prominent Communist whom I knew for certain was a friend of my father: Elizabeth Gurley Flynn.

"Gurley Flynn," Dorothy told me, "was a young labor organizer
when I first heard her speak. I was very young myself, a journalist
about your age who had gotten a job on a socialist daily, *The Call.*
Flynn had come to New York to raise money for the relief of striking
miners' families in Minnesota. One night I heard her speak and was so
moved I gave everything I had down to the last penny. I had to borrow
the fare back to the office and went without lunch for days afterwards.
In those days Gurley Flynn was a Wobbly [a member of the IWW—
Industrial Workers of the World]. Later on she was among the founders
of the American Communist Party."

I told Dorothy about meeting Flynn one evening in my father's home
when I was a high-school student, an event I had never dared mention

---

2. Letter of Thomas Merton dated August 17, 1960, included in a collection
of his letters; see Thomas Merton, *The Hidden Ground of Love* (New York: Farrar
Straus & Giroux, 1985), 138.

to anyone else. (When Flynn died in 1964, she left her household furnishings to the Catholic Worker. Dorothy passed Flynn's rocking chair on to me.) "I could never agree with Elizabeth Gurley Flynn about Communism," Dorothy said, "except in the sense that it is practiced in monasteries. Nor could I see Russia, where so many had been martyred, as a paradise. Gurley Flynn saw it through rose-colored glasses. But I have never stopped admiring her courage and her dedication to the poor. I used to visit her during the two years she was in prison under the Smith Act."

"My father was charged under the Smith Act and also imprisoned," I responded. "Goodness! What does he think of you becoming Catholic?" Dorothy asked. "I think it puzzles him but he's never tried to change my mind. He had been a fervent Catholic himself as a boy. At one point he wanted to become a priest." "The bottle always smells of the whiskey it once held," Dorothy said with a laugh. It was a paraphrase of a sentence from St. Augustine's *Confessions*.

Back at the Worker for Christmas, I told Dorothy of the tension I was increasingly feeling about being in the military, employment that had nothing to do with the works of mercy. "Ammon Hennessey," I said, "told me I should take off my uniform, refuse to obey orders, and go to prison, but I hope that's not necessary. My work doesn't involve weapons. Do you think I should follow Ammon's advice?" "Ammon has a gift for making everyone, especially men, feel guilty if not cowardly," Dorothy responded. Then she told me about Martin of Tours, a saint of the fourth century who became a Christian while in the army and only stopped obeying orders when a battle was due to commence the next day, saying to Julian (not Julius) Caesar, "I am a soldier of Christ. To kill is not permitted to me." When the battle failed to happen, the emperor saw it as a sign from the gods and gave Martin his discharge. He went on to be one of the great missionaries of European history. I took Dorothy's telling the Martin story as meaning I could continue in uniform until events forced me to withdraw my obedience.

"What do you want to do," Dorothy asked, "when you leave the Navy?" "I'm thinking of entering a Benedictine or Trappist monastery." Dorothy told me a number of Catholic Workers had ultimately become monks or nuns and suggested I might consider working with the Catholic Worker as an in-between step. "You would be welcome here." She added, "You will know your vocation by the joy that it brings you."

Books, Borscht, and Icons

Having gotten an early discharge, I went directly to St. Joseph's House in Manhattan. By chance Dorothy was present to welcome me that day. Aware I was coming, she had arranged for me to share an apartment with Stuart Sandberg, a Catholic Worker volunteer who had recently graduated from Cornell University.

At the time, St. Joseph's House was a three-story brick building on Chrystie Street. It consisted, on the ground floor, of a dining area and kitchen plus a small, one-desk office on one side of the front door. One floor up, in the back, were two rickety enclosures for the distribution of clothing—one for men, one for women. I was shown the men's department by Arthur J. Lacey, who described himself as "the archbishop and haberdasher of the Bowery." In the front of the second floor was an area with several ancient couches and hand-me-down armchairs, an improvisational living room. One flight up, on the top floor, was an office area with half a dozen desks and an equal number of typewriters, none of which was remotely new. One of the staff, Walter Kerrell, had put several horseshoe crab shells on the wall over his desk, each painted as a mask.

It was so small and cramped a building that only one person actually lived there, a rarely seen hermit named Keith, who had a room that none of us ever visited in a fenced-off area behind the office. (Some months after joining the staff, I had a brief encounter with Keith. One night when the building was otherwise vacant, Keith caught me necking with a female friend. He chased us out the front door. My imagined future as a celibate monk was being vigorously tested.)

Other than Keith, all of us lived in nearby $25-a-month, cold-water, two-room apartments, usually shared by two people. Dorothy's room was on the sixth floor of a Spring Street tenement. Stuart and I were next door. There were four small apartments per floor, each with a tub whose tabletop cover could be raised when baths were taken. The one toilet on each floor was in a dark, broom-closet-sized space in the hallway. I often heard rats scrabbling along the pressed-tin ceiling of our apartment but never actually saw one. This may have been because there was rarely any food in the apartment. I used to bang the ceiling with a broom handle if the rats were too active, and for a while they would run somewhere else. At night armies of cockroaches came out in force, parading on the walls in battalions.

Ever aware that death by nuclear war was more than likely and probably not far off, I placed a cover of *Liberation* magazine on the wall that was emblazoned, in Kenneth Patchen's brush-stroke calligraphy, with just four words: *Get ready to die.* The text was the verbal equivalent of having, like a medieval monk, a skull close at hand that silently sang out the ascetic message, *Memento mori.*

A day at the Catholic Worker was shaped by prayer and the preparation and serving of meals. Several people would arrive early and say Matins, using booklets that had been given to us by a Benedictine monastery in Minnesota. A few, like Dorothy, would already have attended morning Mass. When I got up early enough, I followed their example, normally going to nearby Old St. Patrick's on Mulberry Street, an exceptionally ugly church that had been New York's cathedral before the construction of neo-Gothic St. Patrick's uptown on Fifth Avenue. At Old St. Pat's, a glass topped model of Purgatory—a sea of red, orange, and yellow plaster-of-Paris flames crowded with little pink naked figures—was just inside the entrance. It was worth a visit just to catch a glimpse of it. I suspect it's now in the church's attic.

Each morning, a line formed at St. Joseph's awaiting the opening of the door. Three long tables between the front door and the kitchen area were repeatedly filled to capacity at each meal. Three times a day, coffee was made and water boiled for tea. A normal breakfast was oatmeal and bread with jam. Soup and bread were the mainstays of lunch, often spaghetti or beans for supper. In the mid-afternoon there was a pause to pray the rosary for those so inclined. There were specified days and times when clothing was distributed. In the late afternoon came Vespers. After the kitchen was tidied up, the day ended with Compline. On Friday evenings there was a public lecture and discussion at which home-brewed sassafras tea was served.

Much time was spent in conversation with guests and visitors. No one was better than Dorothy at drawing out life stories from people who were not used to being listened to. "We never ask people why

they are here," Dorothy remarked.
"They just come in from the streets
to eat, to wait, to find some place for
themselves, to have someone to talk
to, someone with whom to share and
so lighten their troubles."

Each of us had at least one ongoing major chore—helping in the
kitchen, obtaining food, cleaning, dishwashing, maintaining the mailing list (a big job as the paper had 75,000 subscribers), answering letters,
managing the paper, sending out thank-you cards to each donor no
matter how small the gift.

Much of the food we needed was begged, the rest purchased. We
were well known at wholesale markets in lower Manhattan, where
vegetables no longer in prime condition were set aside for the Catholic Worker by some of the stallholders. When we had no money, we
bought the food on interest-free credit. Sooner or later, they knew, we
paid our bills.

Apart from the fact that our rent was paid by the Catholic Worker,
no one received a salary. The voluntary poverty that Dorothy stressed
as a principal Christian discipline was quite real. Charles Butterworth,
our business manager in the period I was on staff, carefully dispensed
small amounts of money as needed for subway and bus fares and other
minor expenses. He also distributed small sacks of loose-leaf tobacco—
Bull Durham—to those for whom cigarettes were essential.

During my first months at St. Joseph's House I had no need to ask
for any money as I had saved several hundred dollars while in the
Navy. It was spent little by little on transportation, beer and orange
juice, and the occasional loaf of Italian bread from the bakery across the
street. From time to time I bought a book either from the Paraclete on
East Seventy-Third Street or the Gotham Book Mart on West Forty-
Seventh.

Mindful of the alcoholics who were members of the household, beer
and wine had been banned by Dorothy from Catholic Worker apartments, but the ban was not always observed. One night my co-worker
Bob Kaye discovered Charles Butterworth standing vigil outside our
door, as he rightly suspected Bob and I were in possession of an open
bottle of beer. On a more-or-less daily basis we bought a quart of lager.

Early on I started selling the *Catholic Worker* on street corners in
Greenwich Village. I turned out to have a talent for it, coming up

with an exuberant street-market chant that went something like this: *"Catholic Worker! Penny a copy! Best newspaper in New York City! Catholic Worker! Penny a copy! Read all about it! Catholic Worker! Penny a copy! Free if a penny's too much, a dollar if it's your lucky day! Catholic Worker! Penny a copy! Five dollars if you won the lottery! Catholic Worker! Penny a copy!"* I improvised, sometimes announcing an author's name or a headline in the current issue. When I was selling the October 1961 issue my chant included, *"Thomas Merton says the root of war is fear!"* I had been a newspaper boy not many years earlier but had never enjoyed selling newspapers so much or done it so audibly. Setting out before sunset on Saturdays with a thick stack of the current issue, I stayed on the street until the last copy was sold or the weather turned hostile. Few paid the penny cover price. Even nickels were unusual. A dime or a quarter was common, while many gave a dollar or five dollars, sometimes even ten or twenty. Many had a vague idea of what the Catholic Worker was all about and were happy to make a donation. I invited anyone interested to come to Chrystie Street "for a bowl of the finest Catholic Worker soup." By the time I had sold the last copy, one of my co-workers compared my coin-filled pockets to the breasts of Marilyn Monroe. Back in my apartment, I counted what the night's donations added up to—the total was rarely less than a hundred dollars, a lot of money in the early sixties. (The buying power of a hundred dollars in 1961 would be more than $800 today.) It was an excellent way to make the Catholic Worker and what it stood for better known, and at the same time a splendid way to raise money. And every penny was needed—the Catholic Worker bank account was almost always nearly empty.

Dorothy seldom indulged herself, though at times she accused herself of being self-indulgent, as she did one summer afternoon when she and I had gone for a walk in the neighborhood. I don't recall our goal, only that it was an oven-like day. Passing a small kosher restaurant at a corner somewhere along Ridge Street, Dorothy suggested we stop for a glass of cold borscht with a spoonful of sour cream. We sat at the counter. Once it had been served, Dorothy was slightly scandalized at herself—"Borscht with sour cream! What luxury! This isn't voluntary poverty." The last sentence was said with a mischievous smile. The voluptuous treat was five cents a glass.

One didn't have to live long with Dorothy to realize she had very little sense of ownership. What she had was often given away or, in the case of especially beloved books, loaned with faint hope of return. A friend complained that none of the sweaters she had knitted for Dorothy remained with her for long—sooner or later, each was given away.

Dorothy, who never seemed overly anxious about how little money there was in the community bank account, tended to pass on gifts as quickly as possible. In one memorable instance, a well-dressed woman visiting the Worker house gave Dorothy a diamond ring. With no fuss at all, Dorothy thanked the visitor and slipped the ring into her pocket. Later in the day she gave it to Catherine Tarengal, a complainer second to none who was known within the community as "the weasel." She lived nearby with her handicapped son and often ate meals at St. Joseph's. We paid her rent each month. One of the staff—I fear it was me—suggested to Dorothy that the ring might better have been sold at the Diamond Exchange on West 47th Street and the money used for Catherine's rent. Dorothy replied that Catherine had her dignity and could do as she liked with the ring. "She can sell the ring and buy whatever she wants," Dorothy remarked, "or she can take a trip to the Bahamas, or she can enjoy having a diamond ring on her hand just like the woman who gave it to the Worker. Do you suppose God created diamonds only for the rich?"

While Dorothy was an enthusiastic and unapologetic borrower of other people's ideas and sayings, tirelessly reciting passages from favorite saints and writers, her way of seeing was very much her own. I think of what happened one day when my roommate Stuart and I were cleaning a small apartment in a cold-water tenement on Ridge Street. Dorothy had been having trouble managing the climb to her sixth-floor apartment on Spring Street. These two rooms were just one floor up, but the apartment was in a state of near ruin. A great deal of rubbish plus layers of linoleum and wallpaper had to be removed before white paint could be applied to the walls. Stuart and I dragged box after box of debris down to the street, including a hideous—so it seemed to me—painting of the Holy Family. Mary, Joseph, and Jesus had been painted on a piece of plywood in a few bright colors against a battleship gray background. We shook our heads, deposited it in the trash along the curb, and went back to work. Not long afterward Dorothy arrived carrying the rejected painting. "Look what I found! The Holy Family! It's a providential sign, a blessing." She put it on the mantle of the apartment's extinct fireplace. I looked at it again and this time saw it was a work of love and faith, however crudely rendered. While no masterpiece of iconography, it had its own unpolished beauty, but I wouldn't have thought so if Dorothy hadn't seen it first.

When Dorothy was present at St. Joseph's House, she was completely present, but often she was away writing at her beach cottage on Staten Island, spending a day or two at the Peter Maurin Farm, visiting other Catholic Worker houses in distant places, speaking at churches and colleges that might be several time zones distant, or visiting her daughter, Tamar, and her grandchildren in Vermont. Her periods away left a hole that no one else could fill. In Dorothy's absence, no one was in a position to make a significant decision that everyone else would accept. Dorothy alone could lay down the law. She was, said Arthur Lacey, "the abbess."

Being part of the Catholic Worker in New York City in those days was a major blessing, but not an easy blessing—exhilarating and draining, inspiring and discouraging. In the early sixties, the New York house probably was one of the least happy communities in the widespread Catholic Worker movement. In fact we were hardly a community at all. We had no community meetings. Not all of us got along with one another.

In 1961 there was one short period of serious friction. In Dorothy's absence a decision was made by our two-person kitchen crew that treats donated to the house—the occasional pound of butter, box of eggs, slab of bacon—would henceforth go to those on "the line" rather than to "the family." This change in custom, they argued, was in line with the Gospel verse, "The last shall be first." "The line" referred to those people who turned up for meals but whose names were unknown to most of us. "The family" was the much smaller group of people who over the years had become part of the household, were living in apartments rented by the Catholic Worker, and had various chores to do within the household. Each family member was known by name, or nickname: Smokey Joe, Missouri Marie, Indian Pete, Mad Paul, Charley O'Keefe, Italian Mike, Russian Mike, St. Louie Marie. . . . The family ate after the line. Traditionally, anything special that turned up in small quantities was saved for them.

As a result of this alteration in policy, members of the family, who had seen many volunteers come and go, were outraged, and the core staff—eight or ten people at the time—was itself divided. Conflicting quotations from Dorothy's writings began to appear on the community bulletin board, each faction hurling fragments of Dorothy's writings at the other. On the one hand there might be a quotation from Dorothy declaring that we must be ready to roll up in old newspapers and sleep on the floor, giving our beds to those who most needed them; and, on the other hand, a few sentences in which Dorothy humbly reflected that voluntary poverty sometimes meant accepting one's limitations.

Dorothy soon returned from her travels. Without bothering to explicate the contradictions in her writings, she said that the butter and eggs were to go, as before, to the family. Two people resigned, angry that Dorothy had failed to live up to some of her own declarations.

I continued to see the Catholic Worker as a way station to the monastery and was alert to discover where that monastery might be. So long as one's chores were covered by others, one could arrange free time off—a half day, a full day, a weekend, or even longer. Late that summer I took off a week to visit St. Joseph's Trappist monastery in Spencer, Massachusetts. I traveled by borrowed bike, sleeping in orchards for two nights along the way. Luckily there was no rain. Though unexpected at the abbey, I was made welcome and given use of a cot in the guesthouse attic. The celebration of Mass and the singing of monastic offices at various times during the day deeply impressed me.

On my third day I met the director of vocations. Might I join the community as an apprentice monk? I asked. He was quite encouraging until he learned I had left the Navy as a conscientious objector, at which point there was a change of expression—disappointment, regret—on his previously welcoming face. "Sorry, Jim," he said, "but I don't think this is the place for you. We find that people who didn't do well in the military tend not to do well in monastic life." (Five years later, when I was secretary of the Catholic Peace Fellowship, he wrote a letter of apology and expressed his gratitude for the work CPF was doing in encouraging conscientious objection to the Vietnam War. A check from the monastery was enclosed. Before becoming a monk, he added, he had been an Air Force chaplain. "I've come a long way," he said.)

A monk whom I was helping in the guesthouse kitchen was alarmed at my enthusiasm for the books of Thomas Merton. "Some people," he warned me, "regard him as a heretic."

Returning to New York, I told Dorothy about my conversations at St. Joseph's Abbey. "Don't be discouraged," she advised. "Merton is certainly not a heretic! And there are many other monastic doors to knock on." She told me about a Catholic Worker, Jack English, who had become a Trappist at Merton's monastery in Kentucky.

Working with Dorothy

It was in the aftermath of the butter blow-up that Dorothy appointed me managing editor of the paper. She had to find someone—one of the two people who resigned was my predecessor. Not yet twenty, I was the youngest person ever to have held that post, and also the least qualified, but I had an enthusiasm for the paper and had learned the basics of journalism in high school from a professional. Dorothy, of course, was and remained the editor-in-chief.

A more competent mentor than Dorothy Day I could not have had. She had been working as a journalist for nearly half a century, since she was nineteen—my age! I found myself cutting up the long galley proofs made from trays of freshly set type and laying out pages, deciding what articles to put where, what graphics to use, and where to place them, and where cuts were needed if an article was too long for the available space. There was also the task of writing headlines and the adventure of going with Dorothy to the printing plant in the Bronx. There we worked side by side with one of the men who had long been convert-

Dorothy Day in 1961

ing our paste-up layouts into columns of gorgeous metal type, "putting the paper to bed," as it was called. It was very traditional work in a gray-and-black factory environment that smelled of printer's ink and molten zinc. Gutenberg would have felt at home, readily understanding changes that had occurred in the world of metal type in the five centuries that had passed since he printed his first Bible. The technology had evolved but was fundamentally similar. What would completely bewilder him, were he to visit today, is the digital, cold-type, computer-driven, post-industrial publication technology of the twenty-first century. I was lucky to participate in hot type's last act.

I had my first article in the *Catholic Worker* that December, a piece Dorothy had asked me to write. It was published under the headline "Advent and the McCarren Act":

> *"An injury to one is an injury to all," goes the old Wobbly saying. As we are members in Christ's Mystical Body, to which all are called, this should be especially meaningful to us, making us particularly aware of the basic demands of justice which are a prerequisite to love. But it has even added significance at this moment in the liturgical year as we are now entering into the season of preparation for Christ's coming, Advent, which reminds us that we must be doing just that—preparing for Christ, building His Kingdom.*
>
> *In June of this year, in a tight five-to-four decision, the Supreme Court upheld the McCarran Act. This law requires groups labeled by the government's Subversive Activities Control Board as "subversive," to register as such, identify all their mail and literature as "subversive" and face fines up to $10,000 and five years in jail for each day of non-compliance.[1]*
>
> *We are hearing more and more about the Communist threat, the war threat, military preparedness, "first strikes" and Communist gains, and we can expect, too, to hear more justifications for limiting basic freedoms only to those who are "on our side" or "who agree with us." The same logic used in the McCarran Act says, "If you want peace, prepare for war." It hasn't worked yet. To that is now added, "If you want freedom, prepare for fascism."*
>
> *As members of the Mystical Body the only answer we can give is the witness of Christ's Life in our own. In our witness we build the Kingdom which on that last day will be ours for eternity; our tools, the Works of Mercy on which we will be judged.*

It was a young writer's awkward first attempt to link liturgical life with the pressing issues of the day, the aspect of the Catholic Worker

---

1. A few years later, in 1965, the Supreme Court adopted a more critical approach toward the McCarran Act. The court voted 8–0 to invalidate the act's requirement that members of the Communist Party had to register with the government as foreign agents. Another part of the act was later repealed for violating the First Amendment.

movement that made our work so controversial. We were out of step with the Cold War, out of step with racism, out of step with dominant economic structures. "Our troubles are rooted," Dorothy bluntly remarked, "in our acceptance of this filthy rotten system." If we had only limited ourselves to the works of mercy, we would have been widely praised, but we insisted on criticizing a social order that resulted in great suffering and the premature death of millions. As the Brazilian archbishop Dom Helder Camara put it, "If I feed the hungry I am called a saint, but if I ask why so many are hungry I am called a Communist."

At a time of well-tended walls between churches, one of Dorothy's striking qualities was her engagement with Christians of other churches, most notably those in the Orthodox Church. What was at the root of Dorothy's affinity to Orthodoxy, I'm not certain, but a major factor must have been her friendships with various Russians living in and near New York and the special role, beginning in her teens, that Dostoevsky's novels had played in the formation of her concept of Christianity. There were passages from *The Brothers Karamazov* that she knew by heart and often recited, most notably, "Love in practice is a harsh and dreadful thing compared to love in dreams." She all but ordered me to read Dostoevsky.

For some mysterious reason Dorothy drew me into the Russian Orthodox side of her life, though I had no interest in Christianity's Eastern half. Dorothy decided it was an awareness I needed to develop. The first time I visited an Orthodox church it was with Dorothy, and the first time I attended Orthodox Vespers it was with her as well. In the early sixties, she had become acquainted with Father Matvei Stadniuk, a priest from Moscow serving as dean of the Russian Orthodox cathedral on East 97th Street in Manhattan. One day she brought me with her when she went to visit him.

Dorothy's longing for the healing of the centuries-old schism dividing Eastern and Western Christianity drew her into the Third Hour group, founded by a Russian friend, Helene Iswolsky, whose father had been the last ambassador of czarist Russia to France. The family was living in Paris when the Bolshevik revolution occurred in November 1917 and never returned home. The Third Hour was one of the few groups in which people of various churches who shared a deep respect for Orthodox Christianity came together.

One evening Dorothy brought me with her to a Third Hour meeting. Among those present, besides Helene Iswolsky, were the poet W. H. Auden and the Orthodox theologian Alexander Schmemann. Also in the room was Alexander Kerensky, who, nearly half a century earlier, in the period between the last czar's abdication and the Bolshevik takeover, had been prime minister of a short-lived democratic Russia. Kerensky was fortunate to have survived.

Trying to make sense of Russian and Slavonic words and phrases that others were using so comfortably, I was the most silent person in the room. Two Slavonic words stood out, *sobornost* and *dukhovnost*. *Sobornost*, I came to understand, meant conciliarity and was at the center of Orthodox process, while *sobor* alone meant a principal church or cathedral. Guided by the principle of *sobornost*, key decisions were not made by a ruling bishop or a dominant individual but by councils meeting in a *sobor*. *Dukhovnost* meant "quality of spirit." It is normally translated as "spirituality," but the English word is usually understood to mean a private relationship between the individual and God, while *dukhovnost* suggests moral capacity, courage, wisdom, mercy, social responsibility, a readiness to forgive, a way of life centered in love.

On another occasion Dorothy brought me with her for a meeting with the Jesuit priest Daniel Berrigan. Dan had come down from Le Moyne, a Jesuit college in Syracuse, New York. We gathered at a high-rise apartment on the west edge of Harlem, our host being William Robert Miller, jazz critic as well as editor of the Fellowship of Reconciliation's magazine, *Fellowship*. Dan, the guest of honor, was a lean man with short cropped hair, wearing tailored clericals and a Roman collar. He was introduced to us as a poet who had won the Lamott Poetry Prize, a prestigious award. He also had founded an international house at Le Moyne where students lived in community while preparing for service work in Latin America. Miller remarked on the ecclesiastical thaw that was astonishing the world as Pope John XXIII began proving to be something more than a pope between popes.

Once the introductions were over, I recall Dan pulling a sheaf of paper from a jacket pocket and proceeding to read aloud the text, an analysis of Catholic social teaching. Undoubtedly, it was an excellent essay, even suggestive, in style and content, of all that would become so widely appreciated in Dan in the coming years. For better or worse, however, honesty requires my admission of boredom. I must have had little sleep the night before. Dorothy, however, was less bored than annoyed. "Just like a priest!" she snapped as we began making our way back to the Lower East Side. "He didn't leave room for anyone else to talk!" But the next day, in a more placid mood, she asked me to write "Father Berrigan"—she never referred to priests informally—and request a copy of his paper. "I want to read it again. It might be something for us to publish." This was a pattern I gradually came to anticipate in Dorothy, snappish one day with more positive second thoughts the next.

Dorothy's devotion to the Catholic Church was rock solid though not without its sharp edges. She often quoted a sentence from Romano Guardini: "The Church is the cross on which Christ was crucified." The "church" in this case was its human, institutional component, the self-serving, clerical institution, not the mystical body of Christ.

Dorothy had no interest in altering basic church dogma. One of the very few times I was aware of Dorothy taking a degree of distance from Catholic doctrine had to do with indulgences—the obscure teaching that the pope "can remit temporal punishment in purgatory still due for sins after absolution." (I am quoting a definition in a Catholic dictionary.) She wasn't pleased when I included in the paper a brief report that Pope John XXIII had authorized, under certain conditions, a plenary indulgence to laborers. "It shows the respect the pope has for workers," she remarked, "but indulgences are not something all our readers understand." I admitted that I didn't understand indulgences either.

The only doctrine she actually challenged—a doctrine that was not a matter of dogma—was the just-war theory, a concept that had its roots in the fourth-century writings of St. Augustine. Dorothy stood for the sacredness of life at every stage of development, from the womb to the death bed; she opposed all killing, whether in war, abortion, euthanasia, or capital punishment. "Our manifesto," she declared countless times, "is the Sermon on the Mount and the works of mercy." The opposite of the works of mercy, she pointed out, "are the works of war—starving the hungry, depriving the thirsty of drink, the destruction of homes." For Dorothy, hospitality and mercy could be—should be—a way of life for every Christian. "We are here to celebrate Christ," she said, "through the works of mercy."

Hospitality of the Face

Besides the work of cooking and serving meals and the distribution of clothing, social protest was also an integral part of Catholic Worker life.

Solidarity with the civil rights struggle was a priority. A Ku Klux Klan bullet had just missed Dorothy during a visit to Georgia. Once a week several of us went to the nearest Woolworth's department store to take part in a picket line protesting the segregation of Woolworth lunch counters in the Deep South. At the time civil rights activists, mainly students, were being badly beaten for taking part in interracial sit-ins.

In that same period the Catholic Worker was campaigning against fallout shelters and what was called "civil defense," a cosmetic phrase that we saw as promoting the illusion that nuclear war was survivable and even winnable. At the sound of a siren, signaling the onset of a nuclear attack, residents were required by law to take cover indoors or in designated underground shelters. Beginning in 1955, Dorothy and several other members of the community had been jailed repeatedly for refusing to take shelter during nuclear attack drills. In 1960 so many people joined in refusing to take part that afterward the annual drill was abandoned, but even then several of us would go uptown once a week to distribute leaflets challenging the illusions of civil defense. For an hour at midday we would stand on the four corners of a Lexington Avenue intersection near the city's civil defense headquarters. The message of the leaflets we handed out was that you are not likely to survive nuclear war by taking shelter in the subways, hiding under your desk, creating a shelter in your cellar, or building one under your backyard, but if by any chance you did survive, you would find yourself in a world so devastated that you would envy the dead.

One of the most valued lessons I learned at the Catholic Worker was the result of distributing leaflets to people hurrying along the busy sidewalks of Manhattan. New York's street grid and light system being what it is, people walk the avenues and cross the streets in waves. I quickly learned that the response of the first person in each wave (a male more than 95 percent of the time) almost always determined the response of everyone who happened to be following him, even though they were strangers to one another. Not a word was said, not a glance was exchanged—the process was unconscious. This meant that I had to do my very best to get the man in front to take the leaflet. If I succeeded, some of those behind him were likely to follow his example. If he refused, I became an invisible man. If he balled up the leaflet and threw it on the ground, some of those following him were likely to do the same. My best hope was to make sympathetic eye contact with the front runner. This requires what a nun friend of mine, Sister Mary Evelyn Jegen, has called "hospitality of the face."

What I learned on Lexington Avenue is that we're as linked together as those varieties of fish who travel in schools. It's a human tendency to shape our lives, activities, opinions, and even our vocabularies according to what is more or less "normal" among the people we happen to be living and working with or wish to be accepted by. With rare exceptions, we adjust ourselves, even our understanding—and religious life, if any—to fit within the political and economic norms of the society we happen to belong to. Thus, I realized, if I had been living in Germany in the 1930s and didn't have well-formed convictions that put me on guard about the true nature of Nazism, the chances are I would have joined in shouting *Heil Hitler* when it was required and perhaps become a card-carrying Nazi. Or if I had grown up in a racist milieu, it would be remarkable if I hadn't become a racist myself. If everyone in the neighborhood puts the national flag by their front door, would I dare to isolate myself by not doing the same? If the group that surrounds me is prowar, chances are I will be too and will play a supportive and, if pressed, an active role in war.

I learned at the Catholic Worker that it takes courage and a carefully formed conscience for your thoughts, words, and actions not to be shaped by whatever social group you happen to be part of. We are obliged to wear quite uncomfortable masks and finally think of the masks as our actual faces. We're no different than the trees growing in a perennially windy place that are shaped by the prevailing winds.

Mail from Merton

In July 1961, Dorothy astonished me by handing me a just-delivered letter from Thomas Merton and asking me to answer it. Looking back, little in my experience of Dorothy impresses me so much as her willingness to share a relationship, in this case handing over to a young volunteer a letter from so important a correspondent as Merton, and entrusting him with the response. Perhaps it was her way of encouraging my interest in a monastic vocation plus her awareness of my appreciation of Merton's books.

The letter accompanied a poem about Auschwitz and the Holocaust—"Chant to Be Used in Processions around a Site with Furnaces"[1]—which Merton had written during the trial in Jerusalem of Adolf Eichmann, chief bureaucrat of the Holocaust. In his letter to Dorothy, Merton described the poem as a "gruesome" work. Written in the staccato voice of Rudolf Höss, the commandant of Auschwitz catalogued the many efficiencies he had introduced so that the concentration camp could more seamlessly produce its quota of dead bodies. A key line in the poem read, "All the while I had obeyed perfectly." In its final sentence, the mass murderer's gaze turns from himself to the reader: "Do not think yourself better because you burn up friends and enemies with long-range missiles without ever seeing what you have done."

In 1961, when at least one American monastery had built a fallout shelter to retreat to in case of nuclear war, I expected to be blasted to radioactive particles every time I heard the city's air raid sirens being tested. The sirens would begin their coordinated howling, the islands of shrill sound being punctuated by silences so severe New York suddenly seemed desert-like in stillness. Stunned, momentarily paralyzed

---

1. Thomas Merton, *In the Dark before Dawn: New Selected Poems of Thomas Merton*, ed. Lynn Szabo (New York: New Directions, 2005), 119–22.

111

by the significance of the noise, I would stop whatever I was doing and stand at the Catholic Worker's office front window, gathering a final view of our battered neighborhood with its few scarred trees struggling for light and air—even here, a kind of beauty. Shortly it would all be consumed by fire. No need to think about a hiding place. Even if there were a massive barrier against the blast and radiation, the firestorm would consume all the oxygen. Last moments are too important to be wasted on panic. In our Catholic Worker way, we had done our best to take Jesus and his assurances at his word. If our faith seemed insane to many others, it gave these moments a certain tranquility. But each time the sirens ended their apocalyptic shrieks, with no sudden explosive radiance brighter than a thousand suns, I felt like an airline passenger setting shaking feet upon the ground after a no-wheels landing in a carpet of foam spread out across the runway.

With such thoughts in mind, I wrote to tell Merton of our appreciation of the poem and said we would gladly publish it. It would serve, I said, as our response to the Eichmann trial. The poem posed the question, What was the value of being horrified at Hitler's crimes if we were doing nothing to prevent a nuclear holocaust?

Thomas Merton in his writing shed

Not many days later I had a response—a letter to Jim Forest from Thomas Merton! I would not have felt more elated had I been a ten-year-old boy who had just been handed a lifetime pass to Disneyland.

Merton's letter was brief. The key sentence noted that we live in a time of war and need "to shut up and be humble and stay put and trust in God and hope for a peace that we can use for the good of our souls."

In September Dorothy handed me another packet from Merton, this time containing a chapter, "The Root of War Is Fear," from his forthcoming book, *New Seeds of Contemplation*. Merton had added to it several pages especially written for the *Catholic Worker*. Once again, Dorothy asked me to thank Merton and

THE

CATHOLIC ✠ WORKER

Vol. XXVIII No. 3   October, 1961   Subscriptions 25c Per Year   Price 1c

THE WORKER PRIESTS

By Anne Taillefer

"Man is a living paradox and the Incarnation—the Word made flesh—is the greatest paradox of all" (Henri de Lubac). Thus vocation, the call of the supernatural to the natural, the message of the Lord, when utterly pure and obediently heard is apt to surprise us shatteringly. Of all the strange vocations that of worker-priest may be among the most dispossessed.

The present Anglican bishop of Tanganyka, who was then Father Trevor Huddleston, one of the great fighters against apartheid in South Africa, once said: "the trial of the worker-priests is that of Joan of Arc". Strangely enough his words are echoed in a letter written by an eminent ecclesiastic, years ago, to Father Godin, one of the founders of the movement: "It is doubtful if the Catholic Church, the Catholic hierarchy, by itself would have the courage to operate this reform. God will have to help or to constrain it to do so."

In another letter the same ecclesiastic who may or may not have been Cardinal Suhard says: "The rechristianization of France and above all of its workers demands, to begin with, a radical reform of our society. The form of slavery called proletarial must first be abolished totally . . . The

THE ROOT OF WAR

By Thomas Merton

The present war crisis is something we have made entirely for and by ourselves. There is in reality not the slightest logical reason for war, and yet the whole world is plunging headlong into frightful destruction, and doing so with the purpose of avoiding war and preserving peace! This is a true war-madness, an illness of the mind and the spirit that is spreading with a furious and subtle contagion all over the world. Of all the countries that are sick, America is perhaps the most grievously afflicted. On all sides we have people building bomb shelters where, in case of nuclear war, they will simply bake slowly instead of burning up quickly or being blown out of existence in a flash. And they are prepared to sit in these shelters with machine guns with which to prevent their neighbor from entering. This in a nation that claims to be fighting for religious truth along with freedom and other values of the spirit. Truly we have entered the "post-Christian era" with a vengeance. Whether we are destroyed or whether we survive, the future is awful to contemplate.

The Christian

What is the place of the Christian in all this? Is he simply to fold his hands and resign himself—

let him know we would be publishing his essay in the next issue. She instructed me to insert subheads and get the pages marked up for the typesetter. I also had to decide whether the several added pages should run at the beginning or the end of his essay—Merton had left it to us to decide. I put the added text up front.

"The Root of War Is Fear" was published on page one of the October issue, side by side with a drawing of St. Francis of Assisi. It was an essay that got Merton into a great deal of trouble. At the heart of the expanded Catholic Worker version was a challenge: "The duty of the Christian in this crisis [in which nuclear war becomes increasingly thinkable and likely] is to strive with all his power and intelligence . . . to do the one task which God has imposed upon us in the world today. That task is to work for the total abolition of war." Unless war is abolished, Merton continued, "the world will remain constantly in a state of madness and desperation, always on the verge of catastrophe." Unless we set ourselves to this task, "we tend by our very passivity and fatalism to cooperate with the destructive forces that are leading inexorably to war."[2]

---

2. The full text of the additional material can be found in my biography of

Merton's essay was widely read and discussed. Doing my best to make it known beyond our own readership, I wrote and mailed out a press release to a wide range of newspapers, magazines, and wire services.

From that point on, Merton and I began a frequent correspondence that lasted until his death in 1968,[3] averaging a letter per month from Merton.

One of the people to whom I sent a copy was my father. He responded with an appreciative letter in which he said it was encouraging to see a writer of Merton's stature writing for the *Catholic Worker*, that he agreed with much of it, but that he had to disagree with the idea that the root of war is fear. "The root of war," Dad wrote, "is bad economics." Of course this was basic Marxism. But Merton's essay continued to bubble in his thoughts for a long time afterward. Several years later Dad wrote to tell me that he had come to realize that "the root of bad economics is fear."

Soon after we published Merton's "Root of War" essay, I received a letter from John Heidbrink, Church Work Secretary of the Fellowship of Reconciliation. The FOR was the oldest peace organization in the United States, founded in 1914. One of the conditions for membership was the refusal "to sanction or participate in war in any form." In those days it was almost solidly Protestant in staff and membership. A number of denominational peace fellowships were associated with the FOR—Methodist, Episcopal, Presbyterian, Baptist, Lutheran, and others. Deeply impressed by Pope John XXIII and the Catholic Worker's history of war resistance, the thought had arisen in Heidbrink's mind that the time might be ripe to found a Catholic Peace Fellowship (CPF). John was a Presbyterian minister who was more taken with Francis of Assisi, Dorothy Day, and Thomas Merton than with Jean Calvin, Martin Luther, or Paul Tillich. He proposed that the CPF launch itself with the publication of a booklet containing Merton's *Catholic Worker* article, "The Root of War Is Fear." The FOR would pay for the booklet's publication and also cover the cost of mailing it

---

Merton; see James H. Forest, *Living with Wisdom: A Life of Thomas Merton*, rev. ed. (Maryknoll, NY: Orbis Books, 2008), 152–54.

3. Merton's letters to me are published in *The Hidden Ground of Love*, 254–308. They also are the core of my book *The Root of War Is Fear: Thomas Merton's Advice to Peacemakers* (Maryknoll, NY: Orbis Books, 2016).

out, he said, along with a letter introducing CPF to Catholic bishops, priests, nuns, and lay people all over the country.

I read Heidbrink's letter aloud over lunch to see how the idea struck the rest of the Catholic Worker staff. Dorothy's initial response was negative—"Those Protestants just want to use you," she said rather grumpily. But the next day she remembered things she respected about the FOR and could see that there was peace work to be done for which the Catholic Worker had neither the staff nor the resources. All we could do on our own was publish the paper and carry on the demanding work of maintaining a house of hospitality. We were ill equipped to counsel Catholic conscientious objectors or do the sort of organizing work that was desperately needed if the Catholic community was to rediscover certain submerged elements in its own tradition, particularly as regards conscience and peacemaking—the Gospel of the Beatitudes.

In November, Heidbrink and I met for a meal at Ratner's, a nearby kosher dairy restaurant whose waiters presided like doctors over their customers' diets. Nourished by borscht and blintzes, the Catholic Peace Fellowship had its first faint beginnings in a milieu as Jewish as a yeshiva in Jerusalem. I signed up as an FOR member and agreed to set up a meeting to discuss the FOR proposal with others who might take an interest. I also wrote to Merton to let him know what we were up to.

A meeting was convened at the apartment of Eileen Egan, a friend of Dorothy's and a senior staff member of Catholic Relief Services. To my disappointment, it quickly became clear that a Catholic peace group linked to a mainly Protestant organization would too easily be dismissed by most Catholic bishops and clergy—such was the anti-ecumenical climate that prevailed at the time. The wall dividing Catholics and Protestants was as hard to cross as the wall then dividing Berlin. Instead, participants in the meeting decided to establish an American sister group of a British Catholic peace association, the Pax Society. In time it evolved into the US chapter of Pax Christi International.

Hitchhiking to Gethsemani

In December 1961, Merton suggested that I come for a visit. There was no question in my mind about accepting, but first there was an issue of the *Catholic Worker* with another Merton essay to get to press and a weekly night class in English Literature at Hunter College, for which I had a paper to write on William Blake. I was able to leave for Kentucky toward the end of January 1962. Poet friend and fellow Catholic Worker Bob Kaye joined me. Bringing along a few loaves of still-warm bread from a Spring Street Italian bakery plus two small rucksacks of clothing, we traveled by thumb.

It was an exhausting three-day pilgrimage—long waits in remote places in inhospitable weather. As we stood on the roadside with our frozen thumbs in the air, armies of dashboard statues of Jesus of the Sacred Heart, his plastic arms spread wide, blurred by us. The image of Christ's compassion and mercy influenced few of the drivers. One of our hosts along the way was a drunk driver who, playing tag with death, miraculously brought us unharmed through a blizzard as Bob and I prayed our way to the Abbey of Gethsemani. "I would rather die in a warm car," I said to Bob, "than freeze to death on the edge of the interstate." The third night, miraculously ignored by police, we had a few hours of uncomfortable sleep on benches in the Indianapolis bus station.

When at last we arrived, we discovered the monastery was mainly made up of weathered, ramshackle buildings, with the oldest a structure dating back about a hundred years. The rolling hills of rural Kentucky were wrapped around the abbey on every side. The gatehouse was located under an archway on which were painted the Latin words *Pax Intrantibus*—"Peace to all who enter." An elderly monk led the way to the guesthouse, where we were given adjacent rooms. Bob collapsed on his bed while I found my way through a connecting passageway to a balcony in the back of the monastery church. Having survived the trip, a prayer of thanksgiving came easily but didn't last

long. The church's silence was broken
by distant laughter so pervasive that I
couldn't fail to be drawn to it. I wasn't
in fact certain it was laughter, which
seemed an improbable sound for a
sober Trappist abbey. The source, I
quickly discovered, was Bob's room.
"Well, that's the difference between
Bob and me," I thought. "I pray, and
he gives way to laughter. God probably prefers the laughter." I pushed
open the door, and indeed Bob was

laughing, but the sound mainly came from a black-and-white-robed
monk lying on the floor, knees in the air, face bright red, hands clutch-
ing his belly. He was more like Robin Hood's well-fed Friar Tuck than
the fast-chastened Trappist monk I had imagined, but who else could
this be than Thomas Merton, the author of so many books about such
serious subjects, laughing himself half to death on the floor?

And laughing about what? While Bob must have told a funny story
or two about our thousand-mile journey, the most compelling answer
was in the air. After three days of rough travel without a change of
socks, Bob had just taken off his shoes. The room smelled like the
Fulton Fish Market in a heat wave—a breathable translation of the
Catholic Worker's reading of the gospel. It made Merton laugh until
the necessity of inhaling took precedence. Then there was a shaking of
hands and a more traditional welcome.

Merton was still smiling as he left, telling us when we could get
together later. As we parted I realized why his face, never seen before,
since none of his books in those days carried the usual author photo,
was nonetheless familiar. It was like Picasso's, as I had seen it in a
book by photographer David Duncan. Both faces were similar in their
expressiveness—eyes bright, quick and sure, suggesting mischief one
moment and wisdom the next. His features were unremarkable on
their own, but so animated in dialogue. I was also impressed by his
voice. Far from being pretentious or academic or piety personified, he
reminded me of the kind of cheerful truck drivers who had sometimes
given us rides on the way to Kentucky.

Later that day I had my first glimpse of Merton's ongoing dialogue
with non-Christians. There was a knock on the door of my room in the

guesthouse. Merton was standing there, but in a hurry. He handed me a folder of papers that turned out to be a collection of Jewish Hasidic stories that a visiting rabbi, Zalman Schachter, had left with him a few days before. "Read this—these are great!" And off he hurried without further explanation, leaving me with a collection of amazing tales of mystical Polish rabbis with souls on fire who had lived generations before the Holocaust.

The abbot, Dom James Fox, though a most hospitable man, was not initially quite so positive as Merton about a visit from two shaggy young Catholic Workers. In those days most American men had frequent haircuts, but haircuts seemed to Bob and me a massive waste of money. The morning of the second day Merton apologetically explained that our unshorn hair did not please Dom James. If we were to stay on at the abbey, we had to submit to haircuts. Merton hoped we wouldn't object. A little while later Bob and I took turns sitting in a barber chair in the basement room where the novices changed into their blue denim work clothes. While the novices stood in a circle laughing, our hair fell to the concrete floor. Going from one extreme to the other, I suddenly found myself as bald as I had been on my first day at boot camp.

After the haircut, Merton took me to the abbot's office. On Dom James's desk was a copy of the latest *Catholic Worker* as well as several issues of the *Wall Street Journal*, not a combination one often encounters. He asked about Dorothy Day and community life at the Catholic Worker and what events had led me to the Catholic Church. I will never forget the solemn blessing Dom James gave me at the end of our conversation. "Would you like me to give you a blessing?" he asked. Readily assenting, I knelt on the floor near his desk while he grasped my skull while praying over me in Latin. He had a steel grip—I wouldn't be surprised if his fingerprints remain on my scalp. There was no doubt in my mind I had been seriously blessed. I have ever since had a warm spot in my heart for Dom James, a man who has occasionally been maligned by Merton biographers, assigned the role of Darth Vader to Merton's Luke Skywalker. It was obvious that, whatever tensions might have existed in his relationship with Merton, he had immense respect for him.

One monk who had little sympathy for Merton was the abbey's other noted author, Father Raymond Flanagan, whose books were well known to Catholics at the time, though they never reached Merton's wide audience. I almost met Father Raymond one afternoon when

Merton and I were walking down a basement corridor that linked the guest house kitchen to the basement of the main monastery building. There was a point in the corridor where it made a turn. Standing there, next to a large garbage container, was an older monk who was not so much reading as glaring at the latest *Catholic Worker*. He held it open, at arm's length, as if the paper had an unpleasant smell. Father Raymond looked up, saw us coming, balled the paper up in his fist, hurled it into the garbage container, and strode away without a word. I was amazed.

Merton explained that Father Raymond had rarely had a high opinion of his writings and often reported Merton's faults at the community's chapter meetings, at which infractions of the Benedictine Rule and Cistercian Usages were confessed by each or revealed by a fellow monk. "When I first came here," Merton told me, "Father Raymond used to denounce me during the Chapter of Faults for being too hung up with contemplation and not concerned enough with the world. Now he denounces me for being too hung up with the world and not concerned enough with contemplation." (The tension between Merton and Father Raymond never abated. In March 1968, just eight months before his death, Merton reported in his journal a furious verbal assault by Father Raymond, enraged with Merton's opposition to the war in Vietnam.)

Shortly before Vespers one day, Merton came to my door to collect me. He had on the white woolen robe the choir monks wore during winter months while in church. It was an impressive hooded garment, all the more striking at close range. I reached out to feel its thickness and density. In a flash Merton slid out of it and placed it over my head. I was unprepared for how heavy it was! The robe met a practical need, he explained. In winter it was hardly warmer in the church than it was outside. The chapel stove was lit only after a layer of ice had formed on the inside of the windows. "If we wore only our black and white robes, on days like this we would freeze to death," Merton remarked.

At the time of the visit Merton was novice master, the person responsible for the education and spiritual formation of the novices, of which there were at least twenty. Bob and I were invited to sit in with the novices in the classroom where Merton lectured and entered into discussion with the young monks. The topic at the time was contemplative theology. "I remember Merton's depth and his earthiness," Bob recalled in a recent letter. "He was erudite, playful, elemental, matter of fact—a very, very practical man who, even if given to moments of poetry and lyrical beauty, spoke like a stevedore. Common sense: 'This is what these guys [the church fathers] say, this is the story, this is how we use it to sharpen our wits and soften our souls to the truth, this is how we stay sane. This is how you lay the brick.' He didn't use language carelessly or frivolously. There was no embroidery there."

At one class Merton wore a peace button that I had given him. He proceeded to explain the symbol to the novices—a circle bisected by a vertical line with two diagonal lines descending from the midpoint in opposing directions. It was a design that superimposed the semaphore signals for N and D—nuclear disarmament. "It's an elegant design with a simple message," Merton pointed out. "Good for any monk to wear. We generally try to prevent mass murder." The novices laughed and Merton with them.

The guest master, Father Francis, knew I was at the monastery at Merton's invitation and thought I might be able to answer a question that puzzled him and no doubt many of the monks: "How does Father Louis [Merton's monastic name] write all those books?" Of course I had no idea, but I got a glimpse of an answer before my stay was over. A friend who sometimes volunteered at the Catholic Worker, Allen Hoffman, had sent a letter to Merton in my care. Allen, though not Catholic, admired Merton's antiwar writings but hadn't a clue as to why he would "imprison" himself in a monastery that itself was part of a church that was in such need of reform. He urged Merton to leave and do something "more relevant," such as join a Catholic Worker community and take part in campaigning on the streets for nuclear disarmament.

What was most impressive to me about this particular letter was less the content of Merton's response than the experience of watching Merton write. He had a small office just outside the novitiate classroom. On his desk was a large gray Royal typewriter. He inserted a piece of monastery stationery and wrote a reply at lightning speed. I had never seen anyone write so quickly. You might sometimes see a skilled stenographer type at such speed when copying a text, but even in a city newsroom of that period one rarely saw anyone writing at a similar pace. The sheet of paper was in danger of bursting into flame.

I wish I had made a copy of his response. Allen died young, and the letter was lost. I recall Merton readily admitted that there was much to reform both in monasteries and in the Catholic Church. He also said that monastic life was not a vocation to which God often called his children. Yet he gave an explanation of why he thought the monastic life was nonetheless an authentic Christian vocation and how crucial it was for him to remain faithful to what God had called him to. It was a solid, carefully reasoned letter filling one side of a sheet of paper and was written in just a few minutes.

I wasn't aware of it at the time, but for years Merton had been campaigning for greater solitude. In 1960, nearly a year before our visit, plans were made by Dom

Merton's hermitage

James for the construction of a small cinder block building on the edge of the woods about a mile north of the monastery. Merton had lit the first blaze in the fireplace on December 26, not many weeks before our arrival. There was a bedroom behind the main room, its narrow bed covered by a patchwork quilt. Merton occasionally had permission to stay overnight, but it would not be until the summer of 1965 that it became his full-time dwelling. At that point he became the abbey's first Trappist hermit.

The hermitage already had a lived-in look when Bob and I visited. It was winter, so there was no sitting on the porch, but we stood there for a time gazing into the wet distance. Merton broke the silence to say, "God is raining." Once inside, Merton got a blaze going in the fireplace, the only source of heat. A supply of split logs was kept in a large basket on the left side of the hearth. A Japanese calendar hung on one wall with a Zen brush drawing for every month of the year, though the page being shown was long past. Also on the wall was a black-on-black painting by his friend from Columbia days, Ad Reinhart. If looked at carefully, it revealed a cross. Three side-by-side windows provided a panoramic view of fields and distant hills. A long table behind the windows served as a desk. A bookcase stood next to it. On Merton's worktable was a Swiss-made Hermes portable typewriter. On the lawn, a tall timber cross had been erected that had an iron-rimmed wagon wheel leaning against it. Off to one side of the hermitage was an outhouse that Merton shared with a black snake, a harmless but impressive creature. As yet, the hermitage had no kitchen or chapel and no running water or electricity—these were added several years later. There was a shallow closet in the bedroom. Merton opened the door to reveal on its inner side a papal blessing made out to "the hermit Thomas Merton."

In response to a question Bob had asked about the Mass while we sat talking in the hermitage, Merton spoke of the eucharistic liturgy being a kind of ritual dance at the crossroads, a place of encounter for every condition of person and every degree of faith, and also an intersection linking time and eternity.

Walking with him to the hermitage a day or two later, on this occasion just the two of us, I asked Merton to hear my confession, in the course of which I talked with him about a question that had been haunting me for many months: should I "try my vocation" (the phrase Catholics used in those days) as a monk—and, if so, did he think I should do it at the Abbey of Gethsemani? I told him of the negative advice I had been given at St. Joseph's Abbey in Massachusetts, and of a similar response I had gotten by letter from a Benedictine monk at St. John's Abbey in Minnesota. In both cases the fact of my having left the military as a conscientious objector was seen as an indication that I would not be a good fit. Merton smiled. "In some monasteries they might elect you abbot for the same reason, but not in America. You would think it would be a good sign if an applicant was opposed to war! There was a time when you couldn't get baptized unless you promised not to kill people. Well, you are certainly welcome to come here and enter the novitiate and see if you are cut out for Trappist life, but somehow I think the path you are already on may be where God intends you to be. Right now the church needs people working for peace in a way that's impossible here—the kind of things you're doing at the Catholic Worker. If you want to try the life, it's possible, and I would be glad to have you. But wait a while. I think the Holy Spirit has other things in mind."

Dorothy Day University

When I started coming to the Catholic Worker, the capital "S" Sixties was just getting under way, the now legendary decade of long hair, free love, rock-and-roll, marijuana and LSD, counterculture, dissent and protest, of Vietnam and Selma, assassinations and riots, of Joan Baez, Bob Dylan, and the Beatles, of Martin Luther King Jr. and Malcolm X, of the March on Washington, and the music festival at Woodstock.

Not only did the Sixties come to the Catholic Worker, but some of the decade's countercultural inventors belonged to the community or were near at hand. Dorothy didn't welcome the cultural shift. The times reminded her of the countercultural world she had been part of in her youth, just before America's entry into World War I and the decade following. For Dorothy, there was the bitter memory of her love affair with journalist Lionel Moise and the abortion that followed, an event too painful for her to even hint at in her autobiography.[1]

Her second sexual relationship, in the 1920s, had been with Forster Batterham, the father of her only child, Tamar. To her great disappointment Forster had refused to legalize their informal affiliation—he was a conscientious objector to the bonds of marriage. They had lived together without license or vows for a relatively short period. Dorothy's conversion to Catholicism led to their parting. By the time she founded the Catholic Worker in 1933, a major element of Dorothy's voluntary poverty was sleeping alone. There was no legal or ecclesiastical impediment to Dorothy's marrying, if she wished to, but for the rest of her life she regarded herself as having been married, and in some sense still being married, to Forster. She was a reluctant celibate. It was part of her long loneliness.

---

1. For details about that period of Dorothy's life see my biography of her, *All Is Grace: A Biography of Dorothy Day* (Maryknoll, NY: Orbis Books, 2017), 39–55.

I admired Dorothy for her example, her disciplined witness to celibacy, and aspired to celibacy myself, but practicing celibacy was, I discovered, a battle against powerful tides even for a would-be monk. One night a fellow Catholic Worker volunteer and I ended up in bed together. It was just that once but a major border had been crossed—I was no longer a virgin. Going to confession the following Saturday night, I reported this event to the priest on the other side of the curtain, but timidly added it last, as if it were a postscript. Annoyed at my incorrect ordering of culpable actions, he admonished me in a voice that could have been heard a block away, "Mortal sins first!"

One of the people we saw at occasional evening get-togethers was Ed Sanders, later a major countercultural figure but then a student at New York University who was also deeply engaged in antiwar activity. He and I became involved in preparing a sit-in before the entrance of the Atomic Energy Commission in the event that the United States resumed testing nuclear weapons. Ed appreciated the protest side of Catholic Worker while dismissing Catholic teaching in general as bizarre if not, when it came to sex, repressive and harmful. A prankster, he enjoyed being outrageous. One evening I had heard Ed mention his idea of starting a poetry journal; it would be called, he said, *Fuck You: A Magazine of the Arts*, but I assumed he was joking and joined in the laughter. At the time the journal's rude title was an unprintable phrase—in most social contexts even unsayable. But it turned out Ed was serious. The first issue, published by mimeograph in January 1962, included the claim that it had been edited and produced at the Catholic Worker. In fact the only actual link was that two or three of the poets represented in the first issue were younger members of the Catholic Worker staff.

At the time it was being printed, I was far from New York, a guest of Thomas Merton at the Abbey of Gethsemani in Kentucky. Having gotten a telegram from St. Joseph's House letting me know that President Kennedy had announced a series of nuclear tests, I called the Worker to let the staff know I would be leaving for New York by bus the next day in order to take part in the protest action. Dorothy rarely answered the phone but did so on this occasion. I immediately discovered that she was in a state of rage. Not many minutes before, someone had shown her Ed Sanders's magazine. "Did you have anything to do with this," she asked. Her voice was far from friendly. I had no idea what she was talking about. "With what, Dorothy?" With distaste she managed to pronounce the journal's name. I assured her I hadn't.

Dorothy was seldom outraged, but when it happened she was volcanic. It must have crossed her mind that, should a copy of Sanders's journal find its way into the hands of the archbishop of New York, Cardinal Spellman, it would ignite dynamite. He might well demand that the Catholic Worker no longer describe itself or its publication as Catholic. Spellman had picketed the theater screening the film *Lolita* and was a champion of the Legion of Decency. Explaining to the cardinal that this magazine was an ill-considered student prank that had nothing whatsoever to do with the Catholic Worker movement would not necessarily make him change his mind. The scandal might be ruinous. Decades of work by herself and others would be discredited. (Luckily, the cardinal apparently never saw Ed Sanders's journal.) Dorothy's response was to demand that anyone in the community who had been involved with the publication must leave immediately. They were not welcome at St. Joseph's House nor would their rents be paid by the Catholic Worker.

I too became a casualty of Dorothy's distress. I was leaving the Abbey of Gethsemani earlier than planned. Dorothy, wanting to delay my return, insisting that I go instead to Tennessee and write about a civil rights project she admired. I reminded her that, having been one of the organizers of the upcoming sit-in in New York, I couldn't back out. I would gladly go to Tennessee afterward. But Dorothy was on the boil—with Ed Sanders's magazine in her hand, it wasn't a good moment to work out a compromise. She gave me an ultimatum: "Either go to Tennessee or you are no longer part of this community." At the time, I felt I had no option but to join in what I had helped organize. From Dorothy's point of view on that short-tempered day, I was simply being willful.

A few days later, back in New York, I was one of about fifty people blocking access to the main entrance of the Atomic Energy Commission at its building on Hudson Street in Manhattan. Merton had a part in our sit-in. A letter from him, sent care of the Catholic Worker, was hand delivered to me as I sat on the subzero pavement during the hour or two we awaited arrest. It began, "If you are not in jail. . . ." Wearing handcuffs and with his letter tucked into my shirt pocket, I was soon on my way to a Manhattan jail known to New Yorkers as The Tombs.

Thanks to my Gethsemani haircut, a photo of me being carried to the police van was striking enough to be placed on the front page of one of New York's newspapers the next day.

Our trial didn't take long. Singling Ed Sanders and me out as the ringleaders of the protest, which in fact we were, an irritated judge sent us to Hart Island Prison for fifteen days.

Hart Island is in the Long Island Sound between the Bronx and Queens. Its use as a prison began when Confederate soldiers were housed there during the Civil War. It also has served as a potter's field, where New York City's unclaimed dead are buried in numbered trenches. Ed and I shared a bunk bed in a dormitory in which we were the only white prisoners. We were warmly received, though there was some laughter about our mild sentence. "Fifteen-day sentence! That's what you get if you're white! Fifteen years if you're black," as a prisoner named Leon put it. "But you did good! Away with them atom bombs! They ain't good for nobody's health, no sir!" Like many others in the dorm, Leon was doing time for selling drugs.

Ed and I were fascinated by the subculture of poetry that came to life after lights were turned off. One prisoner would recite a narrative poem in rhymed couplets about urban street life, and then another would carry it on until a third and fourth took their turns. It was a poem evolving night by night that had multiple authors, no written

existence, nor any end in sight. At least in that dormitory, Hart Island was a haven of poetry.

A television was in each dorm. One night the guard was kind enough to allow us to watch a Cuban fighter named Bennie Paret trade punches with Emile Griffith in a fight for the welterweight world boxing championship. The televised battle was witnessed in silence with no cheers for either side. Gradually it became obvious that the combat between these two men was very personal. Griffith backed an exhausted Paret into a corner and kept slamming his face. Paret seemed to have passed out, but the attack didn't stop until, too late, the referee at last cried "hold it" and restrained Griffin, but by then Paret was in a coma. Last rites were given. He died soon afterward. "Hey, man," Leon said, looking toward Ed and me, "good thing those guys had no atom bombs in their gloves."

Once released from prison I didn't attempt to return to the Catholic Worker, a decision I have ever since looked back on with sorrow and regret. Only later in life, having gone through the white water of parenthood—I have six children and ten grandchildren—did I realize that, had I come back to Chrystie Street once released from jail, no one would have been happier to see me than Dorothy. But I was too young to comprehend the about-faces adults can make when the lava cools. It took me months to renew my relationship with Dorothy. She took the first step, sending me a letter congratulating me for my stay on Hart Island. "Visiting the prisoner," she reminded me, "is a work of mercy." She asked my forgiveness. Her big sins, she confessed, were anger, impatience, and self-righteousness and the harm she sometimes did to those she cared about most.

Arrested at the Atomic Energy Commission in New York, February 1962

Dorothy often described the Catholic Worker as a school. To this day I sometimes joke about being one of the older undergraduates at Dorothy Day University. It certainly has been a school for me, even if occasionally I have been expelled by its headmaster.

Among the things I learned in that year of my life is that the poverty-stricken, the homeless, the jobless, the afflicted and abused, the addicted and mentally ill, the unfortunate—the people for whom houses of hospitality exist—were at times easier to live with, more patient and compassionate, than those who had come to serve them. Yet for all our shortcomings, irritations, and conflicts, we managed to get a great deal done: food begged or purchased, meals prepared and served, clothing received and given away, dishes washed, floors scrubbed, sheets laundered, the paper edited and mailed out, those with medical needs assisted, hospital patients visited, and thank-you notes sent out to each and every donor, acts of love and protest carried out—all that and much more, with many pauses for prayer.

I also learned that saints are not always saintly. While I have no doubt that Dorothy Day warrants inclusion in the church calendar as a model of sanctity, it was not just to pass the time of day that she went to confession every Saturday night.

A Derailed Train

My return from that first meeting with Merton, plus the arrest and stay in jail that followed, marked both an end point and a beginning—the end of my time as part of the New York Catholic Worker's core community and the beginning of a period of my life that included marriage and parenthood plus a search for a way to make a living that combined peace work and journalism, or at least work that didn't burden my conscience.

I felt like a derailed train. As I think back on that period, I realize I wasn't far from a nervous breakdown. I was homeless, unemployed, and just out of jail. I felt uncertain about where I stood in the Catholic Church. Was I still in the church? Did I want to be? Past thoughts of becoming a monk vanished like a puff of smoke in a gale. As for a possible return to the Catholic Worker, I had as yet no idea how my relationship with Dorothy was to be repaired or even if it was reparable. If not the Catholic Worker and not a monastery, then what next? I had no idea. The stress was considerable.

One of the several people Dorothy had expelled was Jean Morton, some of whose poetry had been published in Ed Sanders's magazine. Jean had come to the Catholic Worker, as had I, out of the military, in her case with an early discharge from the Air Force. No romantic sparks had been struck between us. When we were together, I felt not just slightly younger (she was sixteen months my senior) but years her junior. I recall one evening Jean giving me a poem in which she described me as "healthy"—a nice word, but in the context of the poem the word "healthy" really meant *too* healthy. Jean made me feel naïve and embarrassingly innocent. For my part, I was impressed by her forthright, unjudgmental manner, her sense of humor, her laughter, her care with words, her vigorous poetry, and her Brooklyn working-class accent.

We were friends and had been co-workers but hadn't been close until we became Catholic Worker exiles. For a short time we were two of the four people temporarily sharing a two-room apartment in a tenement on Spring Street. Then one night, awash with beer and feeling sorry for ourselves, we became too close. Within weeks the consequence became evident—Jean was pregnant. The ultimate result, our son Benedict, was born nine months later. But neither of us was at all prepared for marriage, still less for parenthood. Suddenly, with no focused sense of future and both of us very much at sea, Jean and I were a couple living together. Thank heaven abortion never crossed our minds.

Meanwhile there was the urgent matter of finding a place to live and making a living. At the time Jean was in a very shaky state and not up to job hunting.[1] While at the Catholic Worker I had become involved with the Committee for Nonviolent Action (CNVA), a pacifist group with an office on Grand Street that organized demonstrations and acts of civil disobedience protesting nuclear weapons plus the missiles, planes, and submarines that were their delivery vehicles. I was offered a job working with the CNVA publications program. The salary was minuscule but enough to cover rent and groceries.

Then I was asked if I would go to Tennessee and do some preparatory work for a CNVA project, an interracial walk for nuclear disarmament that would start in Nashville and end in Washington, DC. My task was to seek local cooperation and arrange hospitality and places for public meetings. Inexperienced though I was for such an assignment, I was willing to try, but Jean panicked at the prospect of being left on her own. When she asked me if she could come with me to Tennessee, I said yes.

We went by bus. A couple who taught at Fisk University (one of the first colleges founded for black students) had agreed to act as host, expecting just one person. They opened their door and found the two of us. Having as guests an unmarried couple sharing a bed was not what they envisioned or were comfortable with. A day or two later I received a phone call from one of the CNVA staff in New York informing me that there had been a meeting at which it was decided that either Jean should return or we had to marry. When I told Jean,

---

1. Later Jean became a skilled therapist, an ardent feminist, and a human rights activist.

she said, "Okay, let's marry. Why not?" Two days later, we were officially declared man and wife. It was a marriage without a courtship, rings, or anyone saying "I love you."

We were an odd couple—not well matched to each other and also not well matched to the work we were attempting to do. Meeting with clergy and educators many years older than we were, inviting them to play host to people who perhaps would prove to be even odder than we were—not surprisingly we had little success. On our way east to the next stop along the route the march was planned to take, we found ourselves being followed by the Tennessee State Police. We stayed that night at a five-dollar-a-night motel. Unable to cope with the pressure and in a state of profound exhaustion, the next morning I woke gazing at a moldy ceiling and too exhausted to move. The motel owner got me to a hospital. I ended up spending two days with an IV in my arm while Jean stayed nearby with the family of a local minister. Someone older and more experienced was dispatched from CNVA to take my place while Jean and I returned to New York by bus.

Back in the city, I now had a huge responsibility coming my way—a small human being to care for. I realized it was time to live in a less improvisational way. Our precipitous marriage had better work. We found a cold-water flat not far from the Catholic Worker. I wrote Merton to explain what had happened and soon had a long response that began with a blessing for the marriage and also an appreciation of Jean's writing—"I think she is a good poet," he wrote. I reestablished contact with Dorothy, met Jean's parents, and obtained Jean's reluctant agreement to marry sacramentally in a nearby Catholic parish—not an easy decision for Jean, an early feminist, as she was estranged from the church, its clericalism, and its all-male hierarchy. (The fact that it was a marriage carried out in violation of her conscience would, many years later, be a factor in its annulment by the Vatican.)

Merton worried about me, and not without good reason. "It seems everything is happening at once in your life," he wrote, "jail, marriage, peace walk, eviction, and what else? Don't let it become an avalanche. You want to keep your footing and be able to look about you and see what you are doing. The trouble with movements is that they sweep you off your feet and carry you away with the tide of activism and then you become another kind of mass man. . . ."[2]

---

2. Letter dated April 29, 1962, Merton, *The Hidden Ground of Love.*

Jim and Jean, December 1962

Eileen Egan, a close friend of Dorothy, found me a desk job with Catholic Relief Services in their offices just behind St. Patrick's Cathedral. With a decent paycheck coming in, within a few months we were able to move to Staten Island and rent a larger apartment—hot water, shower and bathtub, even a spare room for guests.

Several months later I landed a job as a writer for a business journal whose offices were on Madison Avenue. The work wasn't inspiring, but it paid well. At the same time I was learning new aspects of journalism. I was also learning a great deal about what goes on behind the curtains in a consumer economy, not least the intense and costly research and testing that lie behind the labeling and packaging of food, drugs, and soft drinks.

Despite her being out of sync with many aspects of Catholicism, Jean had formed a bond with several of the nuns of Regina Laudis in Bethlehem, Connecticut, a Benedictine monastery that had links with the Catholic Worker. Though these black-clad women were as Catholic as the pope, their deeply rooted contemplative life plus their good humor, candor, and common sense made Jean feel at home. While we were visiting the monastery at Christmas 1962, Jean seemed to be starting labor. It proved a false alarm, but our son's near arrival among the Benedictines at Regina Laudis gave Benedict his name when he was born on Staten Island the last day of the year.

The guest of honor at Ben's baptism two weeks later on Staten Island was Dorothy Day.

I felt re-anchored in the Church.

Liberation

After half a year of business journalism on Madison Avenue, the best part of which was lunching with the seals, polar bears, and other captive animals at nearby Central Park Zoo, along came a job offer that seemed a perfect fit. In March 1963, I was hired as managing editor of *Liberation*, a monthly journal closely linked with the peace and civil rights movements.

Liberation sublet space from the War Resisters League, whose suite of offices at 5 Beekman Street was on the top floor of an eight-story, turn-of-the-century building a block east of City Hall. Among *Liberation*'s authors were Martin Luther King, Nelson Mandela, James Baldwin, Bertrand Russell, Kay Boyle, artist Kenneth Patchen, and poet Gary Snyder. While I was on the staff, Thomas Merton was added to the list. Among the magazine's editors as well as its frequent contributors were A. J. Muste, Bayard Rustin, Barbara Deming, Dave Dellinger, and Paul Goodman. In that prefeminist period, though the theme was liberation, only a handful of women were involved. The magazine's blending of firsthand reportage, essays, poetry, and art was reminiscent of *Masses*, a radical monthly that had been suppressed by the government in 1917 when the editors were charged with sedition for their opposition to World War I. Just before its closing Dorothy Day had been on its staff.

Liberation wasn't only a publication of ideas but of action. The magazine's first issue, published in 1956, had declared that the journal would "seek to inspire its readers not only to fresh thinking but to **action now**—refusal to run away or to conform, concrete resistance in the communities in which we live to all the ways in which human beings are regimented and corrupted, dehumanized and deprived of their freedom."

And action there was. During my first months on staff, Bayard Rustin, whose office was across the hall from mine, was first envision-

133

ing and then organizing the March on Washington at which Martin Luther King would deliver his "I Have a Dream" oration.

Liberation was the first journal to publish an English-language translation of Albert Camus's essay "Neither Victims nor Executioners," which served as a kind of manifesto for the magazine. Camus concluded:

> *All I ask is that, in the midst of a murderous world, we agree to reflect on murder and to make a choice. After all, we can distinguish those who accept the consequences of being murderers themselves or the accomplices of murderers, and those who refuse to do so with all their force and being. Since the terrible dividing line does actually exist, it will be a gain if it is clearly marked.*

A. J. Muste—A. J. for Abraham Johannes—was the journal's guiding light and became one of my mentors. Over several decades, he had played a Gandhi-like role in developing nonviolence in the United States as a tool for promoting civil rights, demilitarization, and disarmament.

A. J. had come to America from Holland in 1891 when he was six. He grew up to become a Dutch Reformed minister but lost his pulpit due to his opposition to World War I. Later he became a leader of a major textile workers' strike in Lawrence, Massachusetts; then, director of a labor school. For years he had been a prominent figure on the Left and was briefly associated with Leon Trotsky, but in 1937 his estrangement from Christianity ended abruptly when he was knocked free of atheist ideology by a mystical experience. This happened while he was visiting a Catholic church in Paris, perhaps the least likely place for a former Calvinist pastor with an ingrained distaste for Catholicism to be overwhelmed by the awareness of God's presence.

Returning to Christian ministry, in 1940 he was appointed executive secretary of the Fellowship of Reconciliation, America's principal and oldest pacifist organization. When A. J. retired from the FOR in 1953, age sixty-eight, he helped found the Committee for Nonviolent Action and himself took part in various acts of civil disobedience at locations linked to nuclear weapons. In 1955 he had been arrested, side by side with Dorothy Day, for sitting in front of City Hall rather than taking part, as required by law, in civil defense exercises. The following year, with Dave Dellinger, he cofounded *Liberation*.

By the time I became a co-worker, not even A. J. was sure how many times he had been arrested or how many nights he had spent in jail. "Not enough," he remarked when I asked. He was a compelling writer. Words he translated into English from a sermon by a French colleague, André Trocmé, have since become firmly attached to A. J.'s name: "There is no *way* to peace—peace *is* the way." If nuclear disarmament is ever achieved, perhaps his craggy face and large ears will grace a US postage stamp, as has happened with such other practitioners of civil disobedience as Henry David Thoreau.

A. J. loved poetry, often reciting favorite texts from memory. One of the joys of editorial meetings was hearing A. J. read poetry submissions aloud. Music was also important in his life. One day a package arrived for A. J. from composer Benjamin Britten in England containing disks of his newly recorded *War Requiem*.

There were at least two occasions when our editorial meetings were interrupted by urgent phone calls from Martin Luther King, one having to do with the campaign King was then leading in Birmingham, Alabama, the other concerning the impending March on Washington. It was King's decision that the text of his classic defense of civil disobedience, "Letter from Birmingham Jail," first be published in *Liberation*.

I learned from Bayard Rustin that it was thanks to a lecture given by A. J. at Crozer Theological Seminary in 1950 that King, then a twenty-one-year-old student, was first exposed to the methods of Mahatma Gandhi. At the time A. J. was in his eleventh year as executive secretary of the Fellowship of Reconciliation. Later on, when King was a young Baptist pastor who had taken up leadership of the Montgomery bus boycott, it was Muste who sent Bayard and another FOR staff member, Glenn Smiley, to assist King in developing nonviolent strategy. After A. J.'s death in 1967, King said that without A. J.'s behind-the-scenes role in fostering nonviolence in the civil rights movement "the American Negro might never have caught the meaning of true love for humanity."

While ascetic in most regards, A. J. was a jellybean addict. Throughout 1963, it was one of my chores to make an occasional jellybean run on his behalf to a nearby candy store. At editorial board meetings of *Liberation*, A. J. would sit on a folding chair looking very bony in his baggy trousers and rolled-up short sleeves, and reach out for the occasional jellybean while taking part in discussion of the strengths and weaknesses of whatever submission was under consideration. (When

Ronald Reagan became president in 1981, one of the things that helped me keep him on my list of fellow human beings was the discovery that Reagan had to have a jar of jellybeans on his desk in the Oval Office.)

Anyone working with A. J. found him exceptionally attentive and caring. One such colleague was his longtime secretary, Edith Snyder. She had found her way into the peace movement by a misunderstanding. An employment agency through which she was hunting for work had told her that "the head of a marriage bureau called the Fellowship of Reconciliation" needed a secretary. Edith was hired and remained A. J.'s devoted assistant for ten years. "But so far I've never reconciled any marriages," Edie lamented. "Not one!"

Working with *Liberation*'s editorial board was the perfect job for me in many respects, but not in all.

One drawback was a member of the editorial board, Paul Goodman, whose book, *Growing Up Absurd*, was all but required reading on many campuses. Paul was intellectually stimulating but friendship became problematic after he made it all too clear that he thought I would make a pleasant bedmate. Riding an elevator with him one afternoon, suddenly his hand was on my crotch. On another occasion he literally pursued me around the couch in A. J.'s apartment while we were awaiting A. J.'s return from a doctor's appointment. Being treated like a sexual dessert was an experience women were all too familiar with, I realized, but new to me. What do you do when a famous person wants to bed you? My words weren't working, and knocking him down didn't seem to be a Gandhian solution. Luckily A. J. and Bayard arrived before I resorted to force.

Another part of the problem was that my responsibilities didn't fit into a nine-to-five, five-day work week. The strain for Jean and me was great, and it wasn't only economic. Both of us were novice parents, and Ben was new at being a baby. I was away in Manhattan much of the day while Jean, on Staten Island, tried to practice motherhood, not a role she had ever aspired to. I was under intense pressure from my fellow editors to work longer hours and under equally intense pressure from Jean to work fewer. One evening that December, on my way back to Staten Island, I threw up over the side of the ferry, not because of a disagreeable meal but because I was beyond my limit. I spoke with A. J. the next day and received his reluctant blessing to look for a job that "wouldn't be so hard on Jean, Ben and yourself." By then Ben was almost a year old.

The Night Side

R esponding to an ad, I applied for a reporting job with the borough's daily newspaper, the *Staten Island Advance*. On my way to the newspaper offices for an interview with the editor, I had a lucky break. I happened to witness an accident—a car drove into the back of the bus I was riding in and the car's driver was slightly injured. I got names and took notes, then told the paper's editor what had happened. "Write it up," the editor said, directing me to a vacant desk and typewriter. The editor was pleased with the results and hired me on the spot. I was placed on the newspaper's "night side," a Monday-through-Friday shift that normally started at 4 p.m. and ended at midnight, though occasionally there were assignments earlier in the day.

Working for a daily newspaper put me in a milieu I loved. As a boy I had delivered newspapers door to door and spent many hours hanging around the *Red Bank Register*, been involved in high school journalism, and more recently had laid out and helped edit the *Catholic Worker*, worked for a business magazine and then for *Liberation*. Now I was involved in classic reporting in a newsroom environment of dense cigarette smoke, the banging of typewriter keys, and the cacophony of ringing phones.

A good half of what the paper printed had to with daily life in New York City's least populated borough, at that time accessible from Manhattan only by ferry. But Staten Island's isolation was soon to end—the Verrazano-Narrows Bridge, under construction when I got the job, opened eleven months later, in November 1964. The bridge was, for many years, the longest suspension bridge in the world. That year, nearly every issue of the *Advance* had at least one bridge-related story either about construction work or the builders, from the chief engineer down to the riveters, one of whom, Phil Harvey, was a neighbor who had also been active with the Catholic Worker.

One basic element of newspaper life was writing obituaries—interviewing a family member in mourning and putting together a compact portrait of someone who had died that day. This put me in touch with many tears. I also wrote countless reports of mundane social news—often as simple as such-and-such a group had a gathering at fill-in-the-address, at which Mrs. John Jones spoke about next year's fund-raising campaign, and Mrs. Ronald Rogers poured the tea. It was ironclad style at the time when a married woman was identified by her husband's first name. Front-page stories occasionally came my way, typically a report of a speech by a local politician or congressman. It wasn't unusual to rush out with a staff photographer to the horrific scene of a fatal accident.

My specialty became writing profiles of some of the more remarkable people living on Staten Island. These were often placed on page one of the second section. The first of my profiles involved a lengthy visit with a noted artist, John Noble, who did magnificent black-and-gray lithographs of harbor activity. Would that I had the money to buy a print! In another it was a Coast Guard officer who had just been involved in a high-risk rescue operation of the crew of a sinking fishing boat. One profile was of a Russian-born photographer whose bread-and-butter work was marriage albums, but whose hobby was making studio portraits of the down-and-out—men with battered faces and crumpled fedoras who would have been well known in the local bars.

All in all it was wonderful job. It meant talking with and getting to know lots of local folk, left and right (more the latter) and from every economic strata and line of work.

On one occasion that year the similarity of my name to that of my father put both me and my employer in an uncomfortable spotlight. A locally published ultra-right-wing journal, the *Herald of Freedom*, edited by Frank Capell, featured a story charging the *Advance* with having a notorious Communist on its staff, namely me. The activities of my father, James F. Forest, his imprisonments and views, were made my own—in those days I used James H. Forest as my byline. The *Advance* was charged with harboring a traitor. I took pleasure in sending a letter to Capell pointing that I was born several decades too late to be my father. He grudgingly published a correction but never apologized.

Among the benefits of my work with the *Advance* was that normally it was a forty-hour week (at *Liberation* it had tended toward fifty or more), with the additional plus that it involved much less travel time than had the daily commute to Manhattan. As a result I was able to bear much more of the work of parenthood, a relief for Jean. It wasn't a stressless life for either of us, but more manageable. My increased salary made it possible to move from our narrow apartment over a bar near the ferry terminal to the second floor of a large house just a short bus ride away from the *Staten Island Advance*. The owners, living downstairs, were the Rosens, a Jewish family. In the summer the house smelled of fermenting grapes—the Rosens made their own wine. A teenage daughter was sometimes available for babysitting. Jean was able to leave Ben in my care or the neighbor's part of the day and travel into the city fairly often, though there was the frustration for her of often being cut off from the city's countercultural nightlife, the poetry readings and theater,

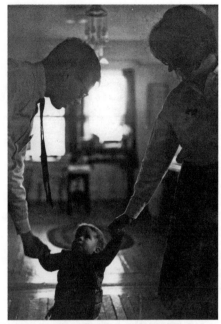

Jean and I when Ben was learning to walk, fall 1964

that she was increasingly gravitating toward and which marriage, motherhood, my work schedule, and being on Staten Island militated against.

Staten Island had its own counterculture. I designed the poster for a local production of Arthur Miller's *The Crucible*, and Jean was one of the cast. Through its re-creation of the witch hunts and executions in seventeenth-century New Salem, Massachusetts, the play provided a dark mirror of our own times in which those critical of the social order were seen as pawns, if not of Satan, then of demonic Moscow.

There was a local branch of the Congress of Racial Equality (CORE) in which Jean and I and several friends were active. Aware the group was financially hard pressed, I suggested we ask Bob Dylan if he would do a benefit concert for us—his "Blowin' in the Wind" had become a nationwide hit thanks to a recording by Peter, Paul and Mary. With help from a mutual friend, I got Dylan's phone number, called him, and he readily agreed. But a week later, after the chairwoman of our CORE group had listened to Dylan's first album, I had to uninvite him. I don't recall what reason I gave him, but it wasn't the truth—that the leader of our group couldn't stand his voice. "That man," she said, "sounds like a dying alley cat."

The Catholic Peace Fellowship

Working for the *Advance*, I sometimes had a spare hour or two late at night for my own projects. Much of that time went into fresh efforts to launch the Catholic Peace Fellowship. The idea had fizzled in 1962, but 1964 seemed more promising. The Pax group exhibited few vital life signs; its main achievement was an annual conference. Pope John's 1963 encyclical, *Pacem in Terris*, with its condemnation of war and its endorsement of conscientious objection, brought into the mainstream the hitherto marginal view that peacemaking was an integral element of Christian life and that Christians could, even should, withhold their obedience to war makers.

The CPF took shape that summer, cheered along by John Heidbrink, Church Work Secretary of the Fellowship of Reconciliation. Heidbrink had received a donation from Hermene Evans, one of the few Catholic members of FOR at that time, to cover the costs of several Catholics—Dan Berrigan, Jim Douglass, and myself—to participate in a traveling ecumenical seminar in Europe that was to begin in France in mid-June and to go on from there to Rome and then Prague, where we would take part in an East-West Christian peace conference.

Dan Berrigan, then on sabbatical leave in France, joined our group on its arrival in Paris. When I had last seen him, two years earlier in Manhattan, he was every inch a model Jesuit in tailor-made clerical attire. Now the Roman collar was gone. He wore a black cotton turtleneck, trim black chino slacks, a faded green windbreaker, and a suede leather tote bag slung over his shoulder, his mobile library and wine cellar combined. The transformation of clothing was less striking than his face. Now his face seemed blizzard-worn, the pink blown away.

What had brought him, I asked, from Le Moyne College to Paris? It was due, he replied, to his liturgical innovations—saying the Mass in English well before such usage was officially authorized—and his engagement in the local civil rights movement, jeopardizing contributions to the university. After six years teaching theology at Le Moyne, Dan had been given a year-long sabbatical in France. I asked, "Was this meant as a sugar-coated exile?" "Very likely," Dan responded, "but what a place to be!"

Our three-day Parisian stay included street searching, river walking, bread buying and wine

Taken in 1965 when I was living on Ridge Street

sipping, plus meetings with several remarkable people, one of whom was Jean Daniélou, Dan's fellow Jesuit and an eminent scholar of the early church. Daniélou spoke to us about theologians of the first centuries of the Christian era, such saints as Gregory of Nyssa and his brother Basil the Great, who, using a modern term, could be described as pacifists: people for whom killing other human beings for any reason was a rejection of Christ and his gospel.

Dan also introduced us to two worker priests, both Dominicans. That they were priests caught me by complete surprise. We met them at the Grail house, a community of Catholic laywomen. The smell of paint in the building had led me to assume that these two men were painters who happened to be taking a break in the room into which we had been ushered. One of them was brawny, with a butcher's arms and back, the other lean and quick, with a knife-fighter's tense alertness. Both were formidable. It required Dan's introduction for me to absorb the notion that they were priests, but I was again in for a surprise, as I assumed, gruff men that they appeared to be, that they would talk in a gruff way. Instead they were very much like Dan—and, again, like Dan, they shattered stereotypes. I had never imagined such a nonclerical priesthood, never thought such a worker-scholar synthesis (to use a Catholic Worker phrase) could bridge the lay–clerical divide. These plain-clothes priests, working in factories, were attempting to connect the Catholic Church in France with the post-Christian working class, who viewed the church as an ally of the comfortable, affluent class.

On our last morning, led by Dan, we trooped into the thirteenth-century church of St. Severin in the Latin Quarter near Notre Dame and, with Dan presiding, proceeded to celebrate a Mass in English, my first such experience. Presbyterian John Heidbrink read the Gospel, and everyone—Protestant, Quaker, Catholic—joined in sharing the consecrated bread and wine, "the living bread which has come down from heaven," as Dan announced with a joyous face. "Taste and see how good the Lord is."

Jim Douglass, a theological advisor to several of the bishops taking part in the Second Vatican Council, joined us once we arrived in Rome. He had arranged hospitality for us with a community of Dutch nuns living in a splendid baroque palace near Bernini's Fountain of the Four Rivers on the Piazza Navona.

Among meetings Jim had scheduled was one with Cardinal Augustin Bea, to whom Pope John had given the task of heading the newly created Vatican Secretariat for the Promotion of Christian Unity. Bea, a German Jesuit and biblical scholar, was one of the bishops most closely linked with Pope John's aspirations for the Vatican Council. Welcoming our small group, he made clear how pleased he was to see Catholics and Protestants collaborating for peace. Responding to questions about the Vatican Council, he remarked on the intense debate going on among the bishops regarding the proposed condemnation of war fought with weapons of mass destruction and the recognition of the right to refuse participation in war in any form—topics that were to be addressed in the council document on the Church in the Modern World, then known as Schema 13, still in the draft stage. "There is resistance among some members of the American hierarchy to the council taking a new direction in these matters," said Bea. The several Catholics at the meeting laughed at his diplomatic understatement. "Your efforts are needed," Bea added, raising his hands and eyes toward heaven.

A few days later, having crossed what then was called "the Iron Curtain," the all-but-actual barrier dividing Europe, we were in Prague. So arctic was the Cold War at the time, I felt like I had not just crossed a border but had arrived on another planet far from the sun.

"Our stay here began bleakly," I wrote to Merton, "but little by little a more hidden city revealed itself. We arrived, tired from traveling, having had little sleep and no time to unpack more than toothbrushes. Even the sun seemed gray. The Soviet-style hotel, built by forced labor we were told by our hosts, was unpleasant. But each day, quietly and in small ways, we discovered how wrong first impressions can be. Self-effacing Prague is a city of hidden virtues."

In 1964 Czechoslovakia (today divided into two states, the Czech Republic and Slovakia) was experiencing a share of de-Stalinization. Our hosts proudly showed us a vacant pedestal from which a giant statue of Stalin had lately been removed. (Four years later the Czech experiment with "socialism with a human face" would be crushed by Soviet tanks.)

The formal part of the conference was boring. Much of the content of what was said by Eastern Europeans in front of conference microphones was monotonously similar to Soviet propaganda, but what we learned in informal conversations with Eastern participants made us more aware than ever of how close we were to nuclear war and how important it was to create doors and windows in the Iron Curtain. "We are Christians first," said one Czech theologian, "and bearers of a national identity only second. We are responsible for each other's lives. The pity is we have so little face-to-face contact. It is harder to kill people you know by name."

The bloodshed in Vietnam was much more often on page one in the European press than in our own. The Catholics in our group became increasingly aware of the need to put together some effort among American Catholics to challenge the US-sponsored war in Southeast Asia. While having a meal one evening under gothic arches in a medieval cellar, Dan, Jim Douglass, and I resolved to launch the Catholic Peace Fellowship on our return to the United States. We talked about what CPF's focus should be and what we had to do to make its work possible. Our main goals were to organize Catholic opposition to the Vietnam War—at the time there were sixteen thousand American soldiers in Southeast Asia, but one didn't have to be a prophet to guess the number would expand exponentially—and to make known the fact that conscientious objection to war was an option not only for those in pacifist churches such as Quakers and Mennonites but for Catholics as well. We envisioned setting up a speakers' bureau and developing study kits for use in schools, universities, and seminaries. The only problem was that we had no staff, no office, and no money.

In July I was back in New York working nights at the *Advance* and putting whatever time I could call my own into laying the groundwork for CPF. Tom Cornell, my close friend and another former managing editor of the *Catholic Worker*, quickly became a partner in the work. Together we drafted a statement of purpose and rented a post office box. Marty Corbin, the current *Catholic Worker* managing editor, became CPF cochairman along with Father Philip Berrigan, Dan's brother. Merton agreed to be on the CPF's board of sponsors, as did a dozen other respected people, including Dorothy Day and Archbishop Thomas Roberts, a Jesuit who had led the diocese of Bombay in India. With the help of friends, an address list began to take shape. Merton sent a packet of his abstract calligraphies, suggesting we sell them for ten dollars each to raise a little money.

Rooted as it was in the Catholic Worker, the Catholic Peace Fellowship took a pacifist stand, emphasizing in its membership brochure the sweeping rejections of war made by Popes John and Paul, but leaving the door open for those who based their objections to war on the fact that the conditions specified in Catholic just-war doctrine could no longer be met.

For weeks, my main spare-time writing project was an article for the *Catholic Worker* on the background of the war in Vietnam. The trigger for the project was the passage in August 1964 of the Gulf of Tonkin Resolution, by which Congress authorized a rapid escalation of US military involvement in South Vietnam and open warfare against North Vietnam. The research was challenging. I was dismayed to discover how little historical material about Vietnam was readily available even in the New York Public Library. For most Americans Vietnam was *terra incognita*. I doubt one out of a hundred of my neighbors on Staten Island could have found Vietnam on a world map even if rewarded with a twenty-dollar bill. Sending a draft of my Vietnam paper to Merton, I commented that "it should have been written at least a year ago—in fact we should have been on the rooftops protesting a year ago—but here we are fighting a fire blindfolded." Responding, Merton commented that the situation in Vietnam

> *is completely poisonous. In a way it makes me much more disgusted and depressed than the [nuclear] tests . . . because here the folly of it is spelled out . . . in so much more human detail. . . . The whole thing stinks to heaven. . . .*

In another letter he remarked:

> *Because a few people in America want power and wealth, a lot of Vietnamese . . . and Americans have been and will be sacrificed.*

Merton near his hermitage

The Spiritual Roots of Protest

Moving toward the Catholic Peace Fellowship's formal launching, in late November, fourteen CPF- and FOR-related individuals arrived at Merton's monastery for a three-day retreat to consider "the spiritual roots of protest."[1]

Merton had envisioned the retreat as unstructured. "Let's make it purposeless and freewheeling and a vacation for all," he wrote to Dan Berrigan, "and let the Holy Spirit suggest anything that needs to be suggested." In a letter to John Heidbrink, he wrote: "The great thing we can all try to do is get to those spiritual roots. My part is to offer whatever the silence can give." He proposed the retreatants attend the monastic offices of sung prayer as "Gregorian [chant] is good and it heals."

Revisiting the abbey, this time I noticed that the wind brought an occasional whiff of whiskey from distilleries in nearby Bardstown. The bourbon-scented air was damp and chilly, the sky mainly overcast, with occasional rain.

This was my second face-to-face meeting with Merton. Once again there was laughter, but less of it. The times were deadly serious—in addition to the fast-expanding war in Vietnam, we had come close to nuclear war over Cuba. The assassination of President Kennedy the year before was still a painful memory. Merton spoke in earnest, listened with a quick and critical ear, and was more a fellow retreatant than the person in charge. As he prepared to speak to the group at the one session he led, I watched him pace back and forth in front of his hermitage in a state of absorption so complete and compelling that it brought home to me the gravity of what he was going to say even more than the words themselves.

---

1. For a detailed account of the retreat, see Gordon Oyer, *Pursuing the Spiritual Roots of Protest* (Eugene, OR: Cascade Books, 2014).

Dan and Merton during the 1964 retreat

Due to the wet weather, there were only two sessions at Merton's hermitage. Perhaps to give the theme of the retreat a silent symbol, Merton had placed upturned, weathered roots from several trees on the porch. Our other meetings were held in a room in the gatehouse normally used by families visiting monks. Whether in the gatehouse or the hermitage, it was a squeeze fitting all of us into the available space. At each four-hour session one of the participants made a presentation about an hour long, at the end of which there was a free-wheeling discussion.

One of the remarkable aspects of the retreat was that not all those taking part were Catholic, unsurprising today but almost unheard of in Catholic institutions in 1964. The most senior retreat participant was seventy-nine-year-old A. J. Muste, a former Calvinist who had come to identify himself as a Quaker. There was John Howard Yoder, a Mennonite scholar; eight years later he would publish *The Politics of Jesus*, a book still widely read. W. H. Ferry, vice president of the Center for the Study of Democratic Institutions in California, was a Unitarian at the time who, later in life, described himself simply as a Christian. Elbert Jean was a Methodist minister from Nashville, Tennessee, who was deeply immersed in the civil rights movement. Presbyterian

John Oliver Nelson, a Yale professor, was chairman of the Fellowship of Reconciliation. There were nine Catholics. Tony Walsh, a friend of Dan Berrigan's, was founder of a Catholic Worker–like house of hospitality in Montreal. John Peter Grady, another friend of Dan, was at the time business manager of *Jubilee*, a Catholic monthly magazine with which Merton was closely associated. Bob Cunnane was a Boston priest whose work included developing dialogue between Protestants and Catholics, Christians and Jews. Also present was another priest, Charles Ring, who worked closely with Cunnane in Boston. Finally there was Dan Berrigan and his brother Phil plus Tom Cornell and myself. In the end, John Heidbrink was unable to attend due to urgent back surgery. Nearly everyone in the group was an FOR member; most of the Catholics were involved in getting the Catholic Peace Fellowship off the ground. That the group was made up entirely of men reflected the male tilt that still marked even groups working for radical social change. It wouldn't be until 1989 that renovations of the monastery guesthouse provided accommodation for women. Thus among those missing from the retreat was Dorothy Day.

Three Latin words were cited by Merton the first day: *Domine ut videam*—"Lord, that I might see." This verse, from St. Jerome's Latin translation of Mark's Gospel, is the appeal that Bartimaeus made to Jesus to heal his blind eyes. It was a prayer at the heart of our retreat. I've been haunted by those words ever since. They opened the door to realizing that peacemaking begins with seeing, seeing what is really going on around us, seeing ourselves in relation to the world we are part of, seeing our lives in the light of the kingdom of God, seeing those who suffer, and seeing the image of God not only in friends but in enemies, seeing how interconnected we are. What we see and what we fail to see defines who we are and how we live our lives. The day-to-day challenge is to be aware of the divine presence in the other, struggling not to be blinded by fear.

The theme of seeing was made all the more real by the presence of A. J. Muste, who had recently undergone successful surgery to remove cataracts from both eyes. A. J. was in a constant state of amazement. No leaf or flash of color went unappreciated. I have never seen anyone look at the world around him more attentively, so full of awe and gratitude. He helped all of us open our eyes a little wider.

Another Latin phrase that Merton used was *quo warranto?*—by what right? In the context of the retreat this became, "By what right do we protest?" It wasn't a question I had ever before considered. Coming from a family in which protest was a normal activity—protest against injustice, protest against racism, protest against cruelty—nothing was more normal than protest. While not by nature a person drawn to protest, and shy of all crowds, as a young adult I found myself seeing protest as an unfortunate and uncomfortable obligation. How could I watch preparations for war and fail to raise an opposing voice? How could I watch black people being beaten and murdered and be passive?

"The grace to protest," Merton had written in his notes for the retreat, "is a special gift of God requiring fidelity and purity of heart." The goal is not to humiliate an opponent but to assist him seeing the world in a new light. Far from seeing an adversary merely as an obstacle, one wishes for him or her "a better situation in which oppression no longer exists." Ideally, protest aims at changes that benefit everyone.

In raising the "by what right" question, Merton forced us to consider that protest, if it is to have any hope of constructive impact on others, has to be undertaken not only for good reason but with great care for those who feel accused and judged by acts of protest. What is needed, Merton argued, was genuine sympathy and compassion for those who don't understand or who object to one's protest, who feel threatened and angered by it, who even regard the protester as a traitor. After all, what protest at its best aims at is not just to make a dissenting noise but to help others think freshly about our social order and the self-destructive direction in which we are going. The protester needs to remember that no one is converted by anger, self-righteousness, contempt, or hatred. This means that one has to use the hammer of protest carefully. Protest can backfire, hardening people in their opposition, bringing out the worst in the other. If it is to be transformative, protest needs to be animated by love, not love in the sentimental sense but in the sober biblical sense of the word. Hence Christ's insistence on love of enemies. "Until we love our enemies," Merton said, "we're not yet Christians."

Merton saw monasticism, in its origins in the fourth century, as a protest movement, and the early generations of monks as escapees from a post-Constantinian world in which becoming a Christian, far from being the path to martyrdom, was an excellent career choice. Like sailors abandoning a sinking ship, the pioneers of monasticism fled to the desert fringes rather than be part of a newly Christianized mainstream society. Even today, in Merton's view, a monk—however unconsciously—is a person whose life is an act of protest, refusing economic gain, refusing to be a consumer, refusing war. Due to the nature of monastic life, every monk lives a life of deep nonviolence. A genuine monk, Merton said, is cloistered not by monastic architecture or special clothing but by a cloistered heart. He gave as an example St. John Gaulbert who, before becoming a Benedictine, forgave the man whom he had intended to kill, the murderer of his brother, instead throwing his sword into the river and embracing his would-be victim.

One of the issues Merton raised was how untroubled most Christians were by the militarization of life and the blurring together of national and religious identity. Summoned to war, few say no or even imagine saying no. Merton saw this as a problem not only in America but wherever nationalism is the primary shaper of one's identity.

By way of contrast, Merton reminded us of the life of Franz Jägerstätter, a name familiar to the Catholic retreatants but otherwise generally unknown at the time. Jägerstätter was an Austrian Catholic farmer, husband, father, and church sexton who, for his refusal to serve in the army of the Third Reich, was beheaded in Berlin on August 9, 1943. Despite his modest education, Jägerstätter had seen with amazing clarity what was going on around him, spoken out clearly and without fear to both neighbors and strangers about the hell Hitler's movement was creating, and finally—ignoring the advice of his bishop to take the military oath—paid for his obedience to conscience with his life.

Why, Merton asked, has Christianity produced so many who fight in manifestly unjust wars and so few, like Jägerstätter, who say no? "If the church," said Merton, "could make its teachings alive to the laity, future Franz Jägerstätters would no longer give their witness in solitude but would be the church as a whole reasserting the primacy of the spiritual." (Little by little, Franz Jägerstätter has come to be widely known. An Austrian postage stamp bears his portrait. His story played a part in shaping what the Second Vatican Council had to say about conscientious objection, the limits of obedience, and, under some circumstances, the duty of disobedience.[2] In 2007, Jägerstätter was beati-

---

2. The council declaration on conscience: "In the depths of his conscience, man detects a law which he does not impose upon himself, but which holds him to obedience. Always summoning him to love good and avoid evil, the voice of conscience when necessary speaks to his heart: do this, shun that. For man has in his heart a law written by God; to obey it is the very dignity of man; according to it he will be judged. Conscience is the most secret core and sanctuary of man.

Austrian martyr
Franz Jägerstätter

fied at the cathedral in Linz, Austria. Blessed Franz is today recognized as a patron saint of conscientious objectors.)

In a talk given on the second day, Dan Berrigan returned to the witness of Franz Jägerstätter and the questions raised by his life, emphasizing Jägerstätter's pained awareness that Christians were willing to yield virtually anything the Nazi regime demanded of them. Such a pattern of church surrender to political demands, Berrigan noted, wasn't new to the Hitler period nor unfamiliar in the postwar period—churches tend to preach and act within borders drawn by the state. "What American bishop," Dan asked, "objects to making, testing, and even using nuclear weapons or objects to the Vietnam War?"

"Our only rightness is in our humility," Muste commented. "We must begin with the realization that there is no *way* to peace but that peace—the way of nonviolence—*is* the way." Developing the theme, Merton added, "Humility is vital in dealing with dissent. Who is the 'I' who [like Jägerstätter] can say 'no' to something? Don't think it's a matter of me versus society. In the broader world, the principalities have a corner on reality, and I must overcome the identity they project on me."

Our three days together ended too quickly. Many questions had been raised, few resolved, but I'm certain all of us were haunted long afterward by the exchange we had shared in. Perhaps Merton's main contribution was to impress on us the timeliness of holy disobedience,

---

There he is alone with God, whose voice echoes in his depths. In a wonderful manner conscience reveals that law which is fulfilled by love of God and neighbor. In fidelity to conscience, Christians are joined with the rest of men in the search for truth, and for the genuine solution to the numerous problems which arise in the life of individuals and from social relationships. Hence, the more right conscience holds sway, the more persons and groups turn aside from blind choice and strive to be guided by the objective norms of morality. Conscience frequently errs from invincible ignorance without losing its dignity. The same cannot be said for a man who cares but little for truth and goodness, or for a conscience which by degrees grows practically sightless as a result of habitual sin" (Second Vatican Council, Pastoral Constitution on the Church in the Modern World, sec. 16).

such as exemplified by Franz Jägerstätter—a costly nonviolent protest that reaches beyond slogans to the deepest roots of one's faith. It was in part thanks to the retreat that, in the years that followed, CPF did so much to promote awareness of the Jägerstätter story.

Back in New York in time to celebrate Thanksgiving, Tom and I learned that the War Resisters League had a room available. The location was excellent—5 Beekman Street, where I had previously worked with *Liberation* magazine. Rent for the narrow, two-window room was $25 a month, "our special rate for Catholic pacifists," said WRL office manager Ralph Digia. Taking a leap of faith that was buoyed by a thousand-dollar donation from Hermene Evans, we paid a hundred dollars in advance and signed up for a phone line. Leaving my job with the *Advance*, on New Year's Day 1965 Tom and I put up a hand-lettered sign on the door that read CATHOLIC PEACE FELLOWSHIP.

With Tom Cornell in the office of the Catholic Peace Fellowship on Beekman Street

Loneliness, the Sixties, and War

The same year the Catholic Peace Fellowship was taking wing, my marriage to Jean was crashing to earth.

Influenced by the example of Dorothy Day, I had been doing my best to be a faithful Catholic. One major aspect of this was that I had managed to convince Jean, when she was pregnant with Ben, to take part in a Catholic wedding service, an event that had given me hope of deepening our relationship but only made Jean more aware of how alienated she was from institutional Catholicism.

Thanks to financial help from my mother, Jean had begun seeing a psychologist once a week while we were on Staten Island and continued doing so after we moved to an apartment in Manhattan's Lower East Side. The counseling was helpful, but the more capable Jean became of functioning on her own, the unhappier she found herself in the role of wife and mother. She recalled one day, standing in a supermarket checkout line on Staten Island, experiencing a palpable sense of intense alienation that she had no words for. By the middle of 1965, halfway into our fourth year together, Jean and I were no longer husband and wife in any meaningful sense but two friends whose main link was that we were the parents of Ben. Our principal joint activity was working out details of care for our son. There was no shouting or hostility. In fact we felt real affection for each other—our friendship lasted until Jean's death in 2014. But Jean longed to live an independent life rooted in New York City's artistic counterculture. In addition to poetry she was experimenting with drama. One of her plays, *Archbishop X*, was about a prelate whom many people thought of as a model of saintly asceticism and prayer, but who, when on his knees in what others took to be mystical devotion, was in fact engaged in silent dialogue with a dead lover.

153

I was increasingly depressed, yet oddly enough wasn't critical of Catholicism's rigid stance on marriage—that would come later. Mainly I felt gratitude for the church, which had made such a difference in how I saw my life, the world, and the cosmos. To be a Catholic, I knew, meant accepting Catholic teaching. Among other things this meant one, and only one, church-sanctioned marriage. If you failed in that marriage, you were required to remain celibate the rest of your life. Yes, there was the possibility of some marriages being annulled by the Vatican, as in fact happened many years later with my marriage to Jean, but at the time that seemed as remote a prospect as travel to Mars. In fact I didn't disagree with the church. I could easily see that one marriage was the ideal and that those who married should work hard to preserve their bond for their own sakes and for the sake of their children. I knew all too well how painful it was to grow up in a one-parent home, no matter how outstanding that single parent was. But the reality was our marriage was dead. Jean got a job and rented her own flat. I saw a very lonely future coming my way and felt devastated.

Dan Berrigan at the CPF's first "meal of reconciliation"

One of the things that kept me going in that dark night were several deepening friendships, Merton by letter and Dan Berrigan face to face. Back from his sabbatical, Dan had been assigned to the staff of *Jesuit Missions* magazine and given a room at a Jesuit residence in midtown Manhattan. Once a week Tom Cornell and I subwayed uptown from the CPF office for a midday meeting with Dan. He lived in a room that had been a maid's sleeping space in an earlier era. It contained a narrow bed, a small desk with an electric typewriter, a filing cabinet, and a shelf or two of books; yet it was large enough to be stamped with Dan's style, every available bit of wall being used for a shifting collage of signs, posters, found objects, photos, and postcards, a delicately balanced kaleidoscope that was a form of self-portraiture.

Putting first things first, each time we met, Dan celebrated a simple liturgy. A prayer for forgiveness was followed by intercession for friends who were ill or in difficulty. We took turns reading the appointed Old and New Testament texts for the day plus a supplementary reading from a modern author. After the readings, silence. Then some reflection, usually initiated by Dan. More silence. Then a simple canon prayer from the *Bible Missal*, a Mass book widely used at the time. More silence. Finally, after the unspectacular miracle of consecration, came the sharing in that quiet wonder, and more silence, and an embrace at the end.

Apparently a follow-the-rules fellow Jesuit kept a stethoscope to the wall during these liturgical celebrations for the day came when we arrived to find Dan in considerable distress. Hours before he had been told our informal eucharists were absolutely forbidden. So we sat forlorn, trying to talk about those things that would have come later on. No sandwiches were assembled—we had no appetite. In the midst of a half-hearted sentence, Dan stood up abruptly, went downstairs and returned with a slice of rye bread. From its usual place in the file cabinet a bottle of wine and a water glass were removed, books and papers on the desk pushed aside, the bread and wine put in place, the Bible taken up. Perhaps there was some dialogue about the readings. At last the bread on its plate was taken in one hand, and the glass with its red wine in the other, prolonged silence where a canon prayer would ordinarily have been spoken, until a few quiet words from Dan, "Let the Lord make of this what he will." And so we ate and drank with profound reverence.

Afterward we had lunch, sorted through letters, reading the more important ones aloud, considered how best to respond, and discussed ideas for CPF's work. Many of the letters we discussed came from young men urgently wanting to know if, as Catholics, they could be recognized as conscientious objectors, and, if so, how to go about it. The war in Vietnam dominated our conversations—"the Land of Burning Children," as Dan would rename that country.

A Round of Irish Whiskey

Dan's brother Phil was also deeply involved with the work of the Catholic Peace Fellowship.

Phil had first entered my life in November 1961 with the delivery to the Catholic Worker of a thick manila envelope postmarked New Orleans. Inside was an essay on Christianity and racism written by Philip Berrigan, a name not yet familiar to me. Affixed to his name were the initials SSJ—the Society of St. Joseph. At the time, Phil was a Josephite priest teaching at a black New Orleans Catholic high school. Dorothy read the essay, then asked me to prepare it for publication in the December issue. I sent Phil a letter of acceptance.

In the summer of 1964, soon after my return from Europe, Tom and I received an invitation to have supper with Phil, currently in New York. I was surprised by his appearance—no resemblance to Dan. Phil was a tall, blue-eyed man with a powerful, calm handshake, a John Wayne grin, a soldier's posture, close-cropped silver hair, looking years older than Dan rather than the kid brother he was. In terms of Hollywood typecasting, Phil could have played the stoic town marshal in an episode of *Gunsmoke* or the tough, secretly pious football coach at Notre Dame or a downed pilot working with the French Resistance.

Due to his civil rights activism, Phil had proved to be too hot a potato for his superiors in New Orleans. He had been sent north to the Josephite seminary in Newburgh, New York, stopping on the way to help at a parish in the Bronx. We met in a high-ceilinged rectory with portraits of Roman pontiffs on the walls. In contrast to the spic-and-span order elsewhere in the house, Phil's room was cluttered. There were mountain ranges of books, newspapers, and magazines—issues of the *New York Times,* the *Wall Street Journal,* the *Washington Post, I. F. Stone's Weekly, The Nation, Commonweal.* Exclamation marks were noticeable in margins, whole paragraphs underlined. It was my first glimpse of Phil's hunger for data and analysis. Tom Cornell commented on leaving, "Now there is someone who does his homework!"

In war no one is unwounded. Phil bore invisible scars. In all the years I knew Phil, I rarely heard him say a word about what he had done and witnessed while in the Army during World War II. It was from Dan, not Phil, that I learned the details. Initially, while stationed in England, Phil had been assigned to a company search-ing for salvageable equipment in the blitzed cities of London, Coventry, Birmingham, and Sheffield. His work put him face to face with the merciless reality of war—children suffocated in the rubble, people burned to death in firestorms, survivors crippled for life. His artillery unit was next dispatched to the continent—first France, then Holland, finally Germany. Phil was fortunate to survive the intense combat he took part in. One day, while guarding German prisoners, he decided to sign up for Officer's Candidate School. He graduated from the ninety-day program as a second lieutenant and was posted as a platoon leader to an infantry division based outside Münster. It was a high-risk assignment—platoon leaders tended to die within two months. Suddenly the war in Europe was over, but there was still death to inhale for soldiers like Phil patrolling the devastated city: "A sweet stench hung over Münster," Phil remembered, "a vast accidental cemetery where people rotted where the explosives had caught them."[1]

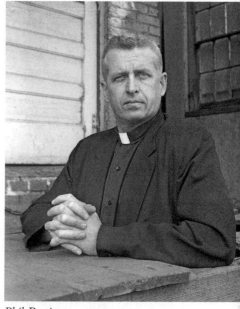

Phil Berrigan

Soon after that first encounter with Phil, Tom and I wrote to him with the proposal that he serve as the Catholic Peace Fellowship's chair-man. His response was immediate and positive, but he proposed a mod-ification: "It would be good to have a layman in charge—it may be something of an education to clerics in general." We ended up with a cochairmanship: Phil plus Marty Corbin, then managing editor of the

---

1. Murray Polner and Jim O'Grady, *Disarmed and Dangerous: The Radical Lives and Times of Daniel and Philip Berrigan* (New York: Basic Books, 1997), 78.

Catholic Worker. Dan was put on the sponsors list rather than being made another cochairman, not because he was less active in CPF than Phil but because it seemed peculiar to have two Berrigans—neither of them yet widely known—jostling each other at the top of the letterhead.

Not long afterward came a meeting with Phil that rerouted my life. Both he and Dan had been pressing me to give up my professional livelihood, journalism, in order to turn the Catholic Peace Fellowship into a full-time staffed organization. In fact I was willing to do so but only for eight months—January through August 1965. I had been offered a full-tuition scholarship by Berea College in Kentucky that would also have provided food and housing for me and Ben and, if she wished, Jean. My days as a high school dropout at last seemed numbered.

Not at all enthused by this plan, Phil called with the proposal that we meet in midtown Manhattan the following afternoon. We walked for a bit, settled in at an Irish bar, ordered some whiskey, and began to argue.

"Formal education," Phil declared, "might be the standard track for many, but a better education is available, for those willing to do their homework, in the peace movement—indeed, only in that fray can there be a meaningful linking up of the data and speculation of study with the overwhelming fact of needless human suffering and waste— and only in such a context can hope have any substance. . . . You've got more education already than you'll ever get in school, and you're getting more daily. Those certifications aren't worth the paper they're printed on. Get in the movement, stay in the movement, stick with it."

I was by no means without sensible replies. Considering the lilies of the field, I said, sounded good as an ideal but didn't seem a solid way to plan for the future. Also I was excited by the thought of four years of study at Berea, a unique academic institution that, since 1855, has provided many of its students, black and white, with full-tuition scholarships, plus room and board for those who needed it. Berea's slogan is the declaration that "God has made of one blood all peoples of the earth." Phil was not only determined but persuasive. My final consent to an open-ended commitment as CPF secretary resulted in considerable Berrigan joy, signaled by a solid whack on his leg and an exclamation of "that's the spirit, man!" Phil ordered another round of Irish whiskey.

Providing more than verbal support, both Berrigans took a practical interest in the work Tom and I were doing. They knew that CPF finances were precarious. Sixty-five dollars a week had been budgeted for the salaries of both Tom and myself, but weeks went by when there wasn't enough in the CPF bank account for me to write Tom's check or Tom to write mine. In July, Dan and Phil Berrigan came to our homes for a meeting—we were living in adjacent apartments in the same building on the Lower East Side. During deliberations about the dismal state of CPF income, Phil discretely looked into my refrigerator and Dan into the Cornell's. "In toto," Tom recalls, "they found two quarts of milk, a block of Velveeta cheese, and two half loaves of bread." Dan endorsed a substantial check he had just received for giving a lecture. We were solvent again.

Me in the early days of CPF

Draft Cards on Fire

March 1965 saw a major escalation of the war in Vietnam—the initiation of Operation Rolling Thunder, a campaign of sustained bombing of North Vietnam by the United States.

Part of our work in the weeks following was to find signers for a "declaration of conscience" pledging "to encourage those who can conscientiously do so to refuse to serve in the Armed Forces." The declaration urged others "to refuse . . . to take part in the manufacture or transportation of military equipment, or to work in the fields of military research and weapons development." The signers stated, "We shall encourage the development of nonviolent acts, including acts which involve civil disobedience, in order to stop the flow of American soldiers and munitions to Vietnam." Dan was one of the signers, Phil another.

In the summer of 1965, *Life* magazine published a spread of photos of war protesters. Most had been taken in Washington at the Assembly of Unrepresented People, an event organized by the Student Nonviolent Coordinating Committee, the Committee for Nonviolent Action, and Students for a Democratic Society. A. J. Muste was among the leaders. One photo showed the Catholic Worker's Christopher Kearns burning his draft card in front of the White House. Draft cards had often been burned by protesters as far back as World War II, but in the past no one had paid much attention. In this case the picture caught a few congressmen's eyes. A bill was quickly passed that specifically forbade the willful destruction of draft cards. The punishment for violators: imprisonment for up to five years—a heavy penalty for a tiny document worth less than a penny.

On October 16, David Miller, a former Le Moyne student of Dan's who had since become part of the New York Catholic Worker community, searched for and found his draft card. Standing on a truck in front of the Whitehall Street Induction Center in lower Manhattan, David held up his card and turned it to flame and ash. The next morning photos of David and his burning draft card were front-page news in America and many other countries. David, the antithesis of the familiar editorial-page cartoon of the long-haired, unwashed, drug-dazed protester, became the embodiment of a slogan of that time, "Not with my body you don't!" Arrested, tried, and convicted, David served two years in a federal penitentiary.

Three weeks later, on November 6, Tom Cornell plus four antiwar friends decided to replicate David's action with the intention of arguing in court that such a gesture was a form of free speech, thus protected by the Constitution. Tom also reasoned the new law was a form of idolatry, treating as sacred a scrap of paper that in reality was simply an easily replicated government form of no intrinsic value.

The event took place on a colonnaded stone platform at the north end of Union Square in Manhattan. Dressed in my best, I served as press secretary. A crowd of about a thousand people watched, including a group of outraged counterprotesters who chanted, "Burn yourselves, not your draft cards." Dorothy Day and A. J. Muste spoke in support of the action, claiming co-responsibility. "I speak as one who is old," Dorothy said, "to endorse

Five protestors burn their draft cards in Union Square. Tom Cornell of the CPF is on the left. A. J. Muste looks on.

the courage of the young who themselves are willing to give up their freedom. I speak as one whose whole lifetime has seen the cruelty and hysteria of war. I wish to place myself beside A. J. Muste to show my solidarity of purpose with these young men and point out that we, too, are breaking the law, committing civil disobedience."

In his statement, Tom outlined the failure of protests that fell short of civil disobedience to bring politicians to seek peace:

Protests against the United States involvement in the war in Vietnam have been carried out with increasing intensity in recent months, dramatically disproving President Johnson's claim for consensus for his foreign policy. Still the war continues to escalate. Each day innocent peasants are being burned to death with napalm, their crops destroyed and their hopes dashed. American men are giving their lives. American families are being shattered to pursue a war that cannot be won, a war it was shameful of us to enter, a war we must all use our moral energy to halt so that we might set about building the conditions of peace.

Americans have written to their congressmen. They have marched upon our nation's capital. . . . As conscientious objectors they have refused to serve in the armed forces. They have demanded that our nation address itself to the real problems that beset critical areas. Yet the war in Vietnam rages on and the seeds of war continue to proliferate and grow in Latin America and elsewhere.

To intimidate and stifle the expression of protest and dissent, Congress passed a bill . . . making it a criminal offense to burn one's draft card. . . . The grave crime, we are told, is not the destruction of life but the destruction of a piece of paper.

We cannot let this draconian law stand. Not only is the penalty provided outrageously disproportionate, but the very concept of the law indicates that the United States government, albeit accidentally and in a moment of frenzy, has taken upon itself the power to consecrate a piece of paper, invest it with a quality it cannot have, and then exact obeisance for that piece of paper. I can no longer carry that card.[1]

I handled press for the Union Square protest. A. J. Muste and Dorothy Day both spoke.

---

1. The full text of Tom Cornell's statement is included in Forest, *The Root of*

Each of the five made a statement, then set his card ablaze. War opponents cheered; war supporters jeered. Police made a corridor through the crowd and guided the five to a patrol car. "As the car pulled away," Tom recalls, "one cop said, 'Now you're safe!' Apparently the police knew there had been a threat of violence—this explained why there had been so many of them."

Days later the chant "burn yourselves, not your draft card" came true. Before dawn on November 10, Roger LaPorte, a student and volunteer at the Catholic Worker who had witnessed the draft card burnings, sat down on the avenue facing the United Nations, poured kerosene over himself and struck a match. His action replicated similar self-immolations committed by Buddhist monks in Vietnam. Roger died two days later. Though

Tom and I had never met him, we were hard hit. None of us had imagined war protest taking such a form in the United States, and certainly not by a Catholic Worker. Dorothy Day was so shaken that all she was up to doing that day was to pray—pray for Roger and pray that others would not follow his example. Refusing to talk with reporters, she asked Tom and me to take on that task.

Merton too was stunned and briefly considered withdrawing from the CPF advisory board. "The spirit of this country at the present moment is to me terribly disturbing," he wrote me.

War Is Fear, 216–18. Tom was tried, found guilty, and sentenced to federal prison for six months.

> *It is not quite like Nazi Germany, certainly not like Soviet Russia, it is like nothing on earth I ever heard of before. This whole atmosphere is crazy, not just the peace movement, everybody. There is in it such an air of absurdity and moral void, even where conscience and morality are invoked (as they are by everyone). The joint is going into a slow frenzy. The country is nuts.[2]*

Wanting to reassure Merton that CPF wasn't part of the general madness, I sent him a letter providing a tour of my desk as 1965 drew to a close: a membership application from a Benedictine monk with a letter describing the use his community was making of the CPF's folder on conscientious objection with draft-age men staying at their guest house; a pair of letters, one from a Navy lieutenant, the other from a Marine reservist, asking for information about how to apply for conscientious objector discharges from the military; a packet from the editor of a French Catholic journal containing recent declarations made during Vatican Council discussions of conscience and war-related topics; numerous appreciative letters commenting on an article about Roger LaPorte that I had written for *Ave Maria*, a popular Catholic magazine; a letter from a Catholic college in Los Angeles inviting a CPF speaker to give a lecture; several similar requests; a donation of $3,000 and a pledge of $2,000. I added that the demand for our folder on conscientious objection necessitated a new printing; only a few of the first printing of eight thousand copies were still on hand, while work on a more substantial booklet was under way.

Merton was reassured.

---

2. Letter to Jim Forest, November 11, 1965, in Merton, *The Hidden Ground of Love*, 285-86. For a fuller account of Merton's response to Roger LaPorte's self-immolation, see Forest, *The Root of War Is Fear*, 130–39.

Dan in Exile

During those same days, a new interfaith peace group was in formation—Clergy Concerned about Vietnam (later Clergy and Laity Concerned about Vietnam)—with Dan Berrigan, Rabbi Abraham Heschel, and Lutheran minister Richard John Neuhaus as cochairmen. Its first public meeting was scheduled to take place on November 30, 1965, at a Protestant church in Manhattan.

Two weeks before the event, on November 16, Dan's immediate superior, Father James Cotter, walked into Dan's room saying, "The fat's in the fire." Dan responded, "I haven't got much fat and where's the fire?" "You've got to go on a trip." He was being sent in haste to Latin America on a trip that included no return date.

Dan called me at the CPF office, voice choked, and asked me to come up immediately. There were but two options to consider, whether to accept the departure order or to refuse it. Were he to refuse, Dan might well be thrown overboard by the Jesuits. "After all, we do have to get along with the cardinal," one Jesuit reminded Dan. "The cardinal" was Cardinal Spellman, an outspoken supporter of the Vietnam War.

I urged Dan to obey—little could be gained by resisting the order except controversy regarding the limits of authority in an order that stressed obedience. The issue that preoccupied us—nonviolent resistance to the war—would be largely ignored. Obeying while at the same time publicizing the situation, on the other hand, still allowed the issue of abuse of authority to be raised, and with it that of conscience, while keeping Dan from being expelled from the Society of Jesus. I pointed out that there might even be some providence in going south of the border for a while. "When Br'er Fox hurled Br'er Rabbit into the briar patch," I reminded Dan, "it was Br'er Rabbit who had the last laugh."[1]

---

1. Br'er Fox and Br'er Rabbit are main actors in Joel Chandler Harris's Uncle Remus stories. Crafty Br'er Rabbit has to find new ways to keep out of Br'er

As some Jesuits were calling for Dan's expulsion from the Society, Dan arranged for me to meet his provincial to present reasons why he ought not to become an ex-Jesuit. I recall meeting the provincial in his spacious office at Fordham University and reviewing damage that would be done to many Catholics—and scandal to non-Catholics—were war opponents like Dan driven out of the Society of Jesus while war supporters remained welcome.

At the Clergy Concerned meeting on November 30, an empty chair on the stage had a sign on it reading "Father Daniel Berrigan, S.J." On December 5, a full-page ad with a long list of prestigious signers appeared in the *New York Times* blasting Dan's removal. Editorials criticizing the transfer action appeared in *Commonweal* and other periodicals. The following day, the New York chancery office was picketed with such signs as, "St. Paul Was a Rebel Too," "Jesus Was Arrested for Stirring Up the People," "Free the Church from Stalinism," and "Merry Christmas, Father Dan, Wherever You Are."

On December 7, Dan wrote me from Mexico that

letters coming in here, phone calls, and, yesterday, the copy of the National Catholic Reporter make it clear that great things are in the wind. And yet with their cost too. Phil wrote that Tom [Cornell] had been beaten after the Washington [antiwar] march. . . . This is a terrible cost to pay for being a peacemaker, and one never gets to the point of not being appalled by the violence against those he loves. . . . I am going along from day to day here, marveling at the strange ways of Providence. . . . There is nothing to be worried over on my score.

From Chile, February 17, as protests regarding Dan's exile continued, Dan wrote, "A letter from my Provincial assures me I will be welcome back to New

---

Fox's stewing pot. In one story, having been captured, Br'er Rabbit begs not to be thrown into the briar patch, which in fact is Br'er Rabbit's safe haven.

York for my work—that was a great relief indeed. I think all the fuss has helped some anchorites come to a better mind and brought a breath of freedom to more priests and laymen. Is this so?"

After a four-month, ten-country journey, Dan returned to New York on March 8. To welcome him home, Tom and I arranged a press conference at which Dan made clear that he would not be trimming his sails. "Our presence in Southeast Asia," he said, "represents a contempt for the rights of innocent individuals and constitutes a continuing divergence for the purposes of destruction of resources that are badly needed in other parts of the world. . . . When I left in November, everything seemed so closed. Now the peace movement has grown in numbers and quality."

Wasting no time in putting his body where his words were, on March 30 Dan was in the front ranks of a New York peace procession that included sixty priests, nuns, rabbis, and ministers, walking from Jewish synagogue to Protestant church to St. Patrick's Cathedral, then on to the United Nations. Suddenly not only lay people like Tom and me but clergy and theologians were becoming opponents of the Vietnam War.

Hard Times

As 1967 began, my domestic life was in ruins. Jean had her own apartment and led her own independent life. Ben rotated between us. I was struggling with depression.

Then I met Linda Henry. We were both participants in a small group that met once a week for an informal Mass in the Harlem apartment of a mutual friend. David Kirk of Emmaus House was the usual celebrant. Both of us were survivors of failed marriages, in Linda's case to a noted jazz musician. She was smart, focused, attractive, good humored, artistically gifted, and as lonely as I was. We quickly fell in love and before long were living together in an apartment on East Ninth Street, half a block from Saint Mark's-on-the-Bowery.

While our union was blessed at a civil ceremony at the house of John Heidbrink, from the point of view of the Catholic Church, it was an unblessable relationship. In the eyes of the Church I was still married to Jean; and, until that marriage revived or was annulled, I was obliged to live a celibate life.

My irregular situation so distressed Dorothy Day that she demanded I withdraw from my work with the Catholic Peace Fellowship. "As you can well understand it is hard to write this," she wrote me in March 1967.

> *But I have been thinking about this for weeks and wondering what to do, and also what to say to you. . . . First, when God asks great things of us, great sacrifices, He intends to do great things with us, though they will seem small, they will be most important. Who knows the power of the spirit? God's grace is more powerful than all the nuclear weapons that could possibly be accumulated. Second, when we are asked to show our love for God, our desire for Him, . . . we have to give proof of it. . . . He is asking us to prefer him to all beauty and loveliness,*

to all other love. He is giving us a chance to prove our faith, our hope,
our charity. . . . I feel so deeply about this that I am afraid that I must
ask you to take my name from your stationery as one of the sponsors. I
hate saying this, but I do not think that while you are the head of the
CPF it can be considered a Catholic Peace Fellowship, if you continue
your relationship. I think the manly thing to do would be to resign, if
you cannot give up Linda. I would understand that. . . . With love to
you, and to Linda, and begging you to forgive me for the pain I may
have caused you.[1]

I wasn't surprised at Dorothy for her challenging me in this way and
in fact thought the demand she made was entirely reasonable. Her own
celibate life, her "long loneliness," bore witness to the sacrifice she had
made after her own attempt at marriage had failed. But before making
a decision I shared her letter with the rest of the advisory board, indicating my readiness to leave the staff if others agreed with Dorothy. To
my surprise none of them did. Merton wrote letters to both Dorothy
and me that, to my amazement, led Dorothy to withdraw her demand
that I leave CPF. She even remained on the CPF's board of advisors.

In a letter to me, Merton wrote:

I might say at once that I do not in any way judge your relationship
with Linda, and I think I take a much more flexible view of it than
Dorothy does. . . . I am much more prepared to concede that before God
you are perhaps doing no real moral wrong. But as I say, God alone
knows that, and there will still be many who will judge otherwise.

Dorothy is a person of great integrity and consistency and this hits
one between the eyes in the way she sums it up, hard as it may be. I can
see where she is in a sense quite right in demanding a like consistency
from others who act as "Catholics" formally and explicitly in the eyes of
the whole world. Perhaps it would be desirable for everyone to be as she
would desire, and as the traditional Church position would demand.
Yet we have to face the fact that this inflexible position is called into
question not just by mavericks and radicals: there are enormously seri-
ous unsolved questions being debated in the Church, especially in the
area of marriage, by the most reputable theologians, and the situation

---

1. The full text of Dorothy's letter is in *All the Way to Heaven: The Selected*
Letters of Dorothy Day, ed. Robert Ellsberg (Milwaukee, WI: Marquette University
Press, 2010), 332–33.

is such first that everyone outside the Church is quite aware of it, and second that it is no longer completely possible and fair to impose the old inflexible (though I think better and truer) position as a matter of strict obligation on everyone without further appeal. . . .

On the other hand, I do agree with her that quite apart from the question of sin, it would be better for the head of the Catholic Peace Fellowship to have made the kind of sacrifice she speaks of, and that a lot of us have to make in one way or another. Nevertheless, all that having been said, I do not think that it is quite fair of her to make it an either/or. Either you resign or her name drops from the list of sponsors—or you give up Linda.

In the new situation where many might be willing to concede that you were not in the wrong and when scandal is not given . . . in the way it once would have been, I don't think it is fully just to be so categorical. . . .

One thing I will say: now I am talking in terms of the traditional and accepted theology which Dorothy herself must accept. If there is some way you can continue living with Linda, in which, according to the judgment of a reputable authority—even one with whom Dorothy does not necessarily agree—you are not "in sin" (and here the boundaries may be far wider than Dorothy herself would impose), you preserve every right to maintain your position and she does not have any right to question it, except perhaps insofar as "appearances" may need to be "saved" and there I assume she is no more intolerant than any other normal person.

In other words the Church grants you the right to follow your conscience as formed with the approval of a reputable theological opinion or arbiter. This is not new, this is old. No one can question it. It is of course quite possible that the situation cannot be saved in this way. If not, I still think Dorothy should regard it more as your own personal business, be content to offer you charitable advice, and stop short of withdrawing her name from the list of sponsors. . . .

It might, ideally speaking, be better for you to resign: but in practice if this means the collapse of the CPF, which it well might, then you should not do so. I pray that you may see what God is asking of you, really and truly, and that he may give you the strength to do just that, as best you can. Pray for me too, Jim. I hate to see anyone in *such a bind. God love you. Happy Easter. My love to both you and Linda. . . .*[2]

With both Merton's support and finally Dorothy's, I stayed on as CPF cosecretary.

It was about that time I had a soul-changing dream that helped me overcome the bitter tide that was rising within me. At the time, antiwar demonstrations were turning in a hate-driven, self-righteous direction, with President Lyndon Johnson the focal point of growing rage. Protesters in front of the White House were often chanting such mantras as "Hey, hey, LBJ, how many kids did you kill today?" Crude caricatures of Johnson were being carried in parades. Writing about it in a letter to Merton, I added:

Nor do I want to sound self-righteous about the problem, for it afflicts me too. For a while I had a photo of the president at the center of the dartboard that hung on the kitchen wall and found it amusing to throw darts at the image. No more. The other night I had a dream about getting on a public bus and discovering L.B.J. was one of the passengers and that there was an empty seat next to him. I sat down and introduced myself and we got into a conversation about the war. We didn't agree—he said the same kinds of things that I had heard him say at press conferences—but it was a real if troubled human exchange. Then, at his suggestion, we got off the bus and went for a walk in the countryside, at this point saying nothing. Gazing downward, I watched our shoes as we kicked up the golden fall leaves that were thick on the ground. We were both silent, just the sound of our shoes plowing the leaves. At that point I woke up and the dream ended. I got out of bed, my mind momentarily blank, and stepped into the kitchen, where I saw the dartboard. The photo of Johnson looked like it had been sprayed with bullets. I just made it back to the bed, collapsed and wept. I felt like a murderer. So you see I'm not talking about problems others have but my own problem, my own sin.

That dream marked a turn. Whatever I might do about peacemaking in the years to come, it had better not be fueled by hatred and dartboard fantasies of homicide.

---

2. Merton, *The Hidden Ground of Love*, 301–3.

From Protest to Resistance

Meanwhile the death toll was steadily rising in Vietnam. By 1967 there were nearly half a million US soldiers on the ground and the number kept rising. Many who had backed the war were having second thoughts. For the first time in American history, a majority of Americans were in opposition to an American war in progress.

But now both Phil and Dan Berrigan began to question their ties to both the Catholic Peace Fellowship and the Fellowship of Reconciliation. On December 2, Phil wrote to Tom and me to announce his withdrawal. The activities of both organizations, he was convinced, fell far short of the prison-risking resistance that the times demanded.

I'm ready to admit . . . that people in both organizations are doing their utmost, and doing it conscientiously. That's their affair. But in face of what this war has become, with its contribution to probable nuclear war—they are out of it. Tom says that the movement must be orchestrated. Perhaps. But the term reminds me of white liberal jargon—jargon used by people who still will be building their broad base [of support in society] as the bombs come in. I will refuse to indict anyone's conscience, but I don't have to cheer their work, which seems to me . . . devoid of risk or suffering. . . . [Dan and I] have been led to different roads, ones which seem to us more at grips with this awful war and the insanity of our country.

To stop this war, I would give my life tomorrow, and I can't be blamed if I have little time for those who want to run ads in the New York Times. . . . Both Dan and I are seriously dealing with clergymen and laymen, professionals and family people, who have come to the point of civil disobedience and the prospect of jail, and are even foundering with convictions beyond that point. As [President] Johnson continues to have his war, and that means the probability of invading

North Vietnam, we will either witness from jail, or we will go ahead with social disruption, including nonviolent attacks against the machinery of this war. . . .

In a word, I believe in revolution, and I hope to continue a nonviolent contribution to it. In my view, we are not going to save this country and mankind without it. And I am centrally concerned with the Gospel view that the massive suffering of this war and American imperialism around the world will only be confronted by people who are willing to go with suffering as the first move to justice.

While not withdrawing from CPF, Dan also felt it was time to step onto thinner ice. As he put it in a letter to me dated December 3,

The question is whether we are helping people get radical, [whether we are] content to stay small and do things and encourage actions which will be evangelical and identifiable as such. Or are we trying to present an opposite "power" in the image of the opposite number, or at least something "presentable" to large numbers of Catholics, and therefore morally neutral—or liberal—but not radical at the roots.

For Tom and me the two letters occasioned pain, bewilderment, and defensiveness. As I reminded both Dan and Phil, in fact what the CPF was doing really mattered. Tom and I had been speaking at rallies, conferences, and teach-ins all over the country as well as in churches and seminaries. There were now half-a-dozen or so vigorous regional CPF groups. We were playing an effective role in encouraging thousands of potential soldiers not to fight. Before Vietnam, Catholic conscientious objectors had been a very rare breed; not so during the Vietnam War. A priest, Lyle Young of the Emmaus House community, had joined the CPF staff to assist us in counseling those who were seeking draft-board recognition as conscientious objectors—on average fifty people a week—and, thanks in large measure to CPF assistance, in most cases obtaining such recognition. The newly published CPF booklet I had written, *Catholics and Conscientious Objection*, was in intense demand.[1] Having obtained an imprimatur from the Archdiocese of New York, it passed through many doors that would otherwise have been double-

---

1. It is available online: http://jimandnancyforest.com/2015/08/catholics-and-conscientious-objection/.

locked. (In the course of the Vietnam War more than 300,000 copies of the booklet were sold or given away.)

But for Phil such activities fell short. That many refused to take part in war did not change the fact that, however reluctantly, most young men who received draft notices complied, put on uniforms, learned to kill, and did whatever they were ordered to do. The war moved forward on its merciless track.

By 1968, acts of antiwar protest were increasingly becoming acts of civil disobedience. Dan and Phil were central figures in one of the most dramatic and emblematic. It took place in a quiet suburb of Baltimore, Maryland, on May 17.

It was proving to be a warm and sunny day in Catonsville when three cars pulled into a parking lot behind the Knights of Columbus Hall, a Catholic organization that took pride in the religious identity of the Italian navigator who had "discovered" America. A casual passerby wouldn't have imagined a draft board was located on the upper floor of the clapboard structure. From this office, official letters—Phil Berrigan called them death certificates—were sent to local young men ordering them to report for physical inspection and, should they be found ablebodied, involuntary induction into the armed forces.

Nine passengers emerged from the cars, two women and seven men, one of whom, Phil, was wearing a Roman collar. There was nothing strange about them, though what would have struck an observer as odd were the two wire-mesh wastebaskets they carried with them.

While one of the group stayed below as lookout, the other eight entered the building, ascended the stairs, and walked into the draft board office, where three clerks were at work on their typewriters. Minutes later they returned, their wastebaskets now full—378 files, according to testimony given at the trial. Two bottles of homemade napalm, a flammable liquid widely used in Vietnam that sticks to the skin and causes death or severe burns, were poured on the files. A match was lit, and a roar of flame engulfed the paper. Several reporters, a photographer, and a TV cameraman watched it all. They had been tipped off that "a remarkable news event" would occur at Knights of Columbus Hall shortly after noon that day. Exactly what was to happen they had no idea. As the files burned, the nine recited the Our Father. "We hope," said Dan, "that our action will make it more difficult for men to kill one another." Reporters were given a press packet that included a statement whose key sentence was the declaration that "some property has no right to exist." While the files were still burning, the police arrived and took down names and other details. Then several FBI agents arrived and did the same.

Soon the nine, all handcuffed, were in a van bound for processing and arraignment.

Dan Berrigan had written a statement about the event. It quickly gained wide circulation as a manifesto of resistance to the Vietnam War, and became, after that war was long over, a modern classic of dissident literature:

> *Our apologies, good friends, for the fracture of good order, the burning of paper instead of children, the angering of the orderlies in the front parlor of the charnel house. We could not, so help us God, do otherwise. For we are sick at heart. Our hearts give us no rest for thinking of the Land of Burning Children. . . . All of us who act against the law turn to the poor of the world, to the Vietnamese, to the victims, to the soldiers who kill and die for the wrong reasons, or for no reason at all, because they were so ordered by the authorities of that public order which is in effect a massive institutionalized disorder. We say: Killing is disorder. Life and gentleness and community and unselfishness are the only order we recognize. For the sake of that order we risk our liberty, our good name. The time is past when good men may be silent, when obedience can segregate men from public risk, when the poor can die without defense. How many indeed must die before our voices are heard? How many must be tortured, dislocated, starved, maddened? How long must the world's resources be raped in the service of legalized murder? When at what point will you say no to this war? We have chosen to say, with the gift of our liberty, if necessary our lives: the violence stops here, the death stops here, the suppression of the truth stops here, this war stops here.*

Before long I was press secretary for the Catonsville Nine Defense Committee.

If few people were prepared to court lengthy prison sentences, many others were prepared to take significant risks. One of them was America's most famous and respected pediatrician, Dr. Benjamin Spock, whose books on child raising sold in the millions of copies. In 1967 he had decided it was time to make clear the depth of his opposition to the war by burning a draft card. As he was too old to have one himself, he asked if he might burn mine. I said yes, only to discover I no longer had one—it had been thrown away. I hurriedly requested a replacement from the Red Bank draft board. It came just in time for Dr. Spock to set it alight at a press conference in Manhattan. About the same time I was privileged to sit next to him as we placed our backs against the Whitehall Street Induction Center, the very place I'd taken the military oath nine years earlier. "Many parents," wrote Michael Stewart Foley in the *New York Times*, "seemed to appreciate Dr. Spock risking his reputation to protest against the war, for sticking his neck out on behalf of their now draft-age children."[2]

Of course efforts to promote peace need not involve drama or the risk of time behind bars. Books too can contribute to peacemaking. One such book came into being thanks to Betty Bartelme, a senior editor at Macmillan. Betty was one of the people who often attended Friday night meetings at the Catholic Worker. Earlier in her life, she had been part of the New York Catholic Worker community. One day in 1967 Tom, Betty, and I met for lunch and got talking about how many first-rate writers had been published in the *Catholic Worker* since the first issue appeared in May 1933. Betty suggested that it was time to put together an anthology of some of the better pieces. She was confident Macmillan would offer a contract if Tom and I were willing to edit such a compilation. Tom's wife, Monica, came up with the perfect title: *A Penny a Copy*. Dorothy welcomed the idea and helped us assemble a complete set of back issues, several hundred in all. As we were heavily loaded with CPF work, our reading of each and every copy took half a year, and the labor-intensive typing done by Marjorie Hughes of the most promising articles nearly as long, but a cloth-bound book was in print by 1968 with a classic Berenice Abbot photo on the cover. Taken in 1936, it was a view of a tenement-lined street on the Lower East Side, with a glimpse in the distance of a pier of the Williamsburg Bridge—the elbow-to-elbow, garlic-scented world into which the Catholic Worker was born. Wine flowed freely at a cheerful publication party hosted by the Paraclete, Manhattan's principal Catholic bookshop.

---

2. Dr. Spock and four others were later indicted for signing and circulating the "Call to Resist Illegitimate Authority" (a petition urging Americans to support draft resisters and others who would break the law to stop the Vietnam War) and for their involvement in draft card burnings and related protests. See Jessica Mitford's book, *The Trial of Dr. Spock* (New York: Knopf, 1969).

Thich Nhat Hanh

By the end of 1967 I was dividing my work time between the Catholic Peace Fellowship—I remained its cosecretary—and the Fellowship of Reconciliation, which had appointed me director of its Vietnam Program. I was given an office at Shadowcliff, a mansion that served as the FOR headquarters in Nyack, a town on the west bank of the Hudson River about an hour's drive north of Manhattan. For fifty dollars the FOR sold me a battered VW Beetle that had been rusting in the parking lot, used only for a daily run to the post office. Now it made possible my daily commute back and forth from East Harlem, where Linda and I had an apartment near the community we were part of, Emmaus House. The FOR also paid for me to take driving lessons as I hadn't a clue about how to drive a car. It was a skill I learned in the heavy traffic of the FDR Drive, the elevated highway that hugs Manhattan's East River.

Initially my FOR job meant taking a CPF project called "Meals of Reconciliation" and building it into an FOR program meant to reach, as in fact it did, churches and synagogues all over the United States.

The original stimulus for the project had come from a letter Merton had sent me:

> It seems to me that the basic problem is not political, it is apolitical and human. One of the most important things is to keep cutting deliberately through political lines and barriers and emphasizing the fact that these are largely fabrications and that there is another dimension, a genuine reality, totally opposed to the fictions of politics: the human dimension which politics pretends to arrogate entirely [to itself]. . . . This is the necessary first step along the long way . . . of purifying, humanizing and somehow illuminating politics themselves. Is this possible? . . . At least we must try. . . . Hence the desirability of manifestly non-political

177

witness, non-aligned, non-labeled, fighting for the reality of man and his rights and needs . . . against all alignments.[1]

Our hope was that Meals of Reconciliation would help those taking part move beyond a Cold War mentality, beyond ideology and politics, and enter the human dimension in which killing others becomes unthinkable. The meals served were also opportunities for participants to make donations to help civilian war victims in both North and South Vietnam.

These semi-eucharistic meals were very simple. Instead of bread and wine, participants gathered to share rice and tea, plus, when possible, examples of Vietnamese cookery. The project's overriding goal was to shrink the distance between America and Vietnam. Meals of Reconciliation introduced those taking part to elements of Vietnamese literature, poetry, and music. Vietnam was a culture, a way of life, that was being targeted, and the destruction was heartbreaking. "Blessed are they who mourn," Jesus declared. We hoped those taking part in one of them might leave in a state of mourning that could widen and deepen their antiwar commitment.

No two Meals of Reconciliation were identical, though rice and tea were always at the core. People who had been in Vietnam gave brief talks. A handbook I had edited included a selection of possible readings, mainly poetry. The poet whose work was invariably used at Meals of Reconciliation was Thich Nhat Hanh, a monk from Saigon whose name was then unknown beyond his homeland.

Thich Nhat Hanh had begun building a relationship with the Fellowship of Reconciliation after meeting FOR executive director Al Hassler when Hassler came to Saigon in 1965. A friendship took root between Hassler and Nhat Hanh that deeply influenced both men's lives and eventually played a major part in helping an unknown Buddhist monk become a world-renowned teacher of mindfulness.

One of the principal figures in Vietnam's peace movement, Nhat Hanh was a monk and Zen master who was also the leading figure in the development of "engaged Buddhism," a pathway that linked insights gained from meditation and the teachings of the Buddha to situations of suffering and injustice. He was founder of the School of Youth for Social Service, which brought young volunteers to serve in

---

1. Merton, *The Hidden Ground of Love*, letter dated December 8, 1962, 272.

hundreds of rural commu-
nities. One of the precepts
of a "rule of inter-being"
that Nhat Hanh had writ-
ten called on his students
"not to avoid suffering or
close your eyes before suffering. Do not lose awareness
of the existence of suffering
in the life of the world. Find
ways to be with those who
are suffering, including personal contact, visits, images,
and sounds. By such means,
awaken yourself and others
to the reality of suffering in
the world."

Al Hassler was so
impressed with Nhat Hanh
that he organized lecture
trips for him in America and
arranged a series of meetings
for him with religious leaders, senators, congressmen,
newspaper editors, and even

Thich Nhat Hanh with Thomas Merton at the Abbey of Gethsemane

Secretary of Defense Robert McNamara. Meetings were also arranged
with Martin Luther King Jr. and Thomas Merton, both of whom
nominated Nhat Hanh for the Nobel Peace Prize. Hassler found a
publisher for Nhat Hanh's first English-language book, *Vietnam: Lotus
in a Sea of Fire*.

In May 1966 Merton welcomed Nhat Hanh to the Abbey of Gethsemani. The two stayed up into the night, sharing the chant of their
respective traditions, discussing methods of prayer and meditation,
comparing Western and Eastern aspects of monastic life, and talking
about the war. "Thich Nhat Hanh is a perfectly formed monk," Merton said to his novices the day after their two-day conversation, telling them that his guest's arrival was really the answer to a prayer. In
meeting Nhat Hanh, Merton felt he had met Vietnam. "What is the
war like?" Merton had asked. "Everything is destroyed," Nhat Hanh

replied. These three words, Merton told his novices, were the answer of a true monk—not a long-winded analysis but just the essence: "Everything is destroyed."

They discussed monastic formation, which, whether Buddhist or Christian, has much to do with discovering the significance of "insignificant" activities: cutting vegetables, pulling weeds, sweeping floors, washing dishes, waiting in line, walking from here to there. Nhat Hanh summed up the essential attitude needed in one word: mindfulness. For example, it doesn't help to rush from a "less sacred" to a "more sacred" part of the monastery where, once you arrive, you change gears and move more reverently. "Before you can meditate," Nhat Hanh told Merton and Merton told his novices, "you must learn how to close the door." Aware of how often they ran to the church in order to be on time to chant the monastic offices, leaving behind them a trail of slammed doors, the novices laughed.

Thich Nhat Hanh, fluent in English and French, became a voice for all those Vietnamese who were victims of the opposing sides in the war but whose sufferings were mainly due to the Goliath-might of the US military.

I had met and briefly spoken with Thich Nhat Hanh at the FOR headquarters and immediately was enchanted not only by what he had to say about his homeland but by his entire manner. His voice was as gentle as a wind bell. He spoke slowly, carefully, sparingly. I was impressed by the silences he placed between words and phrases. His attentive, wide-open eyes were as unguarded as I imagined the eyes of Jesus or the Buddha might be. No pretense, no self-importance, no rhetoric. Afterward I said to Al Hassler, "I could listen to this guy for hours even if he were reading aloud from a telephone book." Al laughed. "Me too!"

Al was the person who normally accompanied Nhat Hanh wherever he went, but occasionally another staff member might have that privilege. One evening, when Al was not feeling well, I was pressed into the job. I was to

Thich Nhat Hanh with Martin Luther King Jr.

pick Nhat Hanh up at an apartment near Columbia University and take him by subway to a small gathering at a ritzy address on Park Avenue in midtown Manhattan.

The event we attended turned out to be a waste of time. The principal guest was an Indian guru whose ego could have filled every floor of the Empire State Building. He wore a pale saffron robe and pale saffron sandals, had a box of pale saffron tissues at his side, and every sentence he pronounced about the path to enlightenment seemed made of pale saffron words. I wouldn't have been surprised to see him driven off afterward in a pale saffron Rolls-Royce. I don't recall Nhat Hanh saying a single word while we were there, but his expression was one of discomfort.

Slipping away at the earliest possible moment, we returned to the street. I suggested perhaps a cup of tea wouldn't be a bad idea. Nhat Hanh agreed. We found a nearby neon-lit café. And there it was that I decided to ask a question that I thought only a Zen master could answer.

Not many weeks before, while at the University of Oklahoma to give a lecture on Vietnam, at the invitation of a member of the chemistry faculty I had tried the hallucinogenic drug LSD. It was an experiment way off my beaten track. I avoided both marijuana and hashish, but Aldous Huxley's book *The Doors of Perception* had stirred an interest in "mind-expanding" drugs. LSD, a not-yet-illegal drug, had been described by my chemist friend as triggering "a profound spiritual experience." For some, he said, it had been "a shortcut to enlightenment."

That night-long experience—in fact it seemed centuries long—had indeed "blown my mind." For perhaps ten hours I dived into my subconscious brain in which eternity was a reality rather than a concept. I was able to watch a fragment of sound drift slowly into my head and observe how my neurons received that sound and eventually made decisions about it, deciding it was, for example, a syllable of a word or a note of music, a sound to be welcomed or a danger-related noise that required my moving away. Just to hear and decode a simple sentence was a major event experienced in hyperslow motion. The traffic-directing, sorting-out, editing-room part of the brain was, I found, a bright, colorful metropolis methodically making sense of the avalanche of data constantly being provided by my senses, at the same time comparing this with that, taking a fresh look at relevant memories, making wild guesses, considering what if any response might be required to the events going on around me. Slowly emerging from the experience at dawn, I felt I had lived an infinity of lifetimes. I wondered if indeed this might be enlightenment.

Now I was face to face with one of the few people who would know, but to ask seemed risky. Might a Zen master be scandalized by such a question? How dare I imagine there were chemical shortcuts to enlightenment! What impertinence! But what the hell, I decided. I'll never have another chance to know. And so I asked.

Nhat Hanh's eyes widened in surprise. There was no trace of irritation, only curiosity. Looking back, I think he was astonished that there were people involved in antiwar protests who were interested in enlightenment. "Please tell me what you experienced," he said. I did my best to do so and have rarely been listened to so attentively. When I finished, Nhat Hanh said, "Perhaps it is not enlightenment—no drug can do that—but you are on the way." He told me he had once tried marijuana but would never do so again—he had not been able to sleep for days afterward.

There was a deep sense of connection, an almost audible click. Then he asked if in the future I would accompany him on his travels whenever Al Hassler was unavailable. "If you say yes, you have to be good at saying no," he added. "Every third day for me is a day of mindfulness. On those days under no circumstances will I give any talk or participate in any meeting, no matter how important it may seem. On those days I need someone who can be a stone wall. Can you do that? Others have said they could but in actual practice could not. For them the proposed event was too important. Also I want no more than two events per day on the days between."

I assured him I was good at saying no. I could say no to the president or to the pope. I liked the word no. After that evening we traveled together a great deal, East Coast to West. I had many opportunities to say no to interview requests and meetings with important people, opportunities that, on any other day, would have been worthwhile. My no was waterproof.

It was from Nhat Hanh that I first became aware of walking and attention to breathing as opportunities to repair the damaged connection between the physical and spiritual. In conversation Nhat Hanh had sometimes spoken of the importance of what he called "mindful breathing," a phrase that seemed quite odd to me at first. Yet I was aware that his walking was somehow different from mine and could imagine this might have something to do with his way of breathing. Even if we were late for an appointment, he always walked in an attentive, unhurried way.

It wasn't until we climbed the steps to my sixth-floor apartment in East Harlem that I began to understand. Though in my late twenties and quite fit, I was always out of breath by the time I reached my front door. Nhat Hanh, on the other hand, seemed rested. I asked him how he did that. "You have to learn how to breathe while you walk," he replied. "Let's go back to the bottom and walk up again. I will show you how to breathe while climbing stairs." On the way back up, he quietly described how he was breathing. It wasn't a difficult lesson. Linking slow, attentive breaths with taking the stairs made an astonishing difference. The climb took a little longer, but when I reached my door I found myself refreshed instead of depleted.

On the road, Nhat Hanh was always the first to wake. His nights were short. When he decided it was time to wake me, he would sit at the foot of whatever bed or couch I was using and quietly say, "Jim! Jim! [pronounced Zheem! Zheem!] The ginger tea is ready." Indeed there was a pot of tea in his hand, the perfume smell of fresh ginger in the air, a happy smile on his face, and a teasing look in his eyes.

Almost every night there was an invitation for us to have a meal with a family that had played a part in arranging whatever Nhat Hanh was doing locally but with rare exceptions the response I had to make was, "No thank you—Thich Nhat Hanh is too tired." We would be brought to wherever we were staying, say good night, and then look for a Chinese restaurant, the simpler and plainer the better.

By now Thich Nhat Hanh was becoming "Thây" (pronounced tie), the Vietnamese word for teacher. He was certainly a teacher for me, though occasionally the roles were reversed. Thây was extremely curious about Christianity, not only as a theory or theology but as a way of life. I often told stories about Christian saints whom I held in especially high regard—Francis of Assisi, for example. We also talked about the Buddha. Thây saw him as a man who had found out how to be completely awake. Thây speculated that Jesus was also someone who was fully awake.

"It is better to look into the eyes of a Zen master than to read all the books," Thây told me when I asked his suggestions for books to read about Buddhism.

Our meals were playful. Thây wanted me to become comfortable with chopsticks. He enjoyed making me practice lifting melting ice cubes out of glasses of water. Much laughter.

Thây noticed things that I hardly saw and took absolutely for granted, as happened one day at the University of Michigan. He had been invited to give a lecture on the war in Vietnam, to be followed by a poetry reading. Waiting for the elevator doors to open, I noticed Thây gazing at the electric clock above the elevator doors. Then he said, "You know, Jim, a few hundred years ago it would not have been a clock, it would have been a crucifix." So simple but so startling a comment. He was right. More than a tool of coordination, the clock had become a quasi-religious object in our world, a symbol of unity, a social conveyer belt, a symbol so powerful that it could depose the crucifix.

One day we were in walking in a seedy district of San Francisco, the Tenderloin, and we passed a sex store with wide windows. Photos of everything a passer-by might have wondered about concerning what human genitals could do was on display. Embarrassed, I pretended I didn't see the store, imagining Thây would do the same. But no. He stopped, calmly gazing at the pornography. Then he pointed to a sign in the window that read, "You must be 21 years old and able to prove it to enter this store." "Jim," asked Thây, "are you 21?" I noticed the twinkle in his eyes and realized the question was about the advantages of being a child. "No, I'm not 21." "Good," said Thây. "Neither am I. We don't have to go inside."

One of our trips was to Montana, where Thây was a speaker at a day-long university "teach-in" on Vietnam. The event went well, with about a thousand students and faculty taking part, including a US senator as well as a representative from the State Department. But afterward, because of the weather, there was a twenty-four-hour delay with the return flight. Thây liked my suggestion that we use our rented car and unexpected free time for a visit to nearby Yellowstone National Park. Neither of us had ever been there. We were lucky to get in—because of a blizzard, the roads had been blocked but snow plows had just cleared the main road. Ours was the first car of the day to arrive at the park's Montana entrance. Once in, a surprise awaited us, a sort of welcoming committee. A few miles into the park, I stopped the car so we could admire a mother bear playing in the deep snow with her two cubs. Then one of the cubs clambered onto the hood and began licking the window. The mother came closer—clearly she was guarding her child. Thây began laughing, then kissed the window just where the cub's pink tongue was engaged.

One evening, while Thây was speaking at a large Protestant church in St. Louis about what the war was doing to Vietnamese peasants, one man stood up and spoke with searing scorn of the "supposed compassion of this Mister Hanh." He asked, "If you care so much about your people, Mister Hanh, why are you here? If you care so much for the people who are wounded, why don't you spend your time with them?" At this point my recollection of his words is replaced by the memory of anger overwhelming me. The stranger's anger had become my anger, only directed back at him rather than Thây. When the man finished, I looked toward Nhat Hanh in bewilderment. What could he or anyone say? The spirit of war had suddenly filled the church. It was hard to breathe.

There was a prolonged silence. Then Nhat Hanh began to speak—quietly, with astonishing calm, even with a sense of personal caring for the man who had just strafed him. Thây's words seemed like rain falling on fire. "If you want a tree to grow," he said, "it does not help to water the leaves. You have to water the roots. Many of the roots of the war are here, in your country. To help the people who are to be bombed, to try to protect them from this suffering, it is necessary to come here."

The atmosphere in the room was transformed. In the man's fury we had experienced our own fury. We had seen the world as through a bomb bay. In Nhat Hanh's response we had experienced an alternate possibility: the possibility—brought to Christians by a Buddhist and to Americans by an "enemy"—of overcoming hatred with love, of breaking the seemingly endless counterreactive chain of violence.

But after his response, Nhat Hanh whispered something to the chairman and walked abruptly from the room. Sensing something was wrong, I left the book table I had been stationed at and followed Thây outside. It was a cool, clear night. Thây stood on the sidewalk at the edge of the church parking lot. He was struggling for air like someone who had been deeply underwater and who had barely managed to swim to the surface before drowning. I had never seen him like this. It was several minutes before I dared ask him how he was or what had happened.

Thây explained that the man's comments had been deeply upsetting. He had wanted to respond to him with anger. So he had made himself breathe deeply and very slowly in order to find a way to respond with calm and understanding. But the breathing had been too slow and too deep.

"But why not be angry with him?" I asked. "Even pacifists have a right to be angry."

"If it were just myself, yes," said Thây. "But I am here to represent the Vietnamese peasants. I have to show those who came here tonight what we can be at our best."

It isn't easy to describe the influence Thây had on me. Partly it was simply helpful guidance about what I would call prayer and Thây would call mindfulness. In contrast with Dan and Phil Berrigan, Thây exerted no pressure to do more than I was doing to end the war in Vietnam. But because of living with Thây, Vietnam was no longer a distant country. It was as close as Thây's voice. When I was invited to be part of a community that would carry out a Catonsville-like burning of draft records, part of the reason I said yes was my love of Thich Nhat Hanh.

The Milwaukee Fourteen

It was the summer of 1968. Dan Berrigan had just been released on bail and Jim Douglass, a cofounder of the Catholic Peace Fellowship, was in town. Jim and I decided to visit Dan at a parish in the Bronx where he was briefly staying before returning to his chaplaincy work at Cornell. Sitting on wooden chairs in the weedy backyard of the rectory, we discovered that Dan, usually remarkably upbeat, was depressed. The reason quickly became apparent. Several months had passed since the nine had put Catonsville on the map, and, so far as Dan knew, no one was preparing a similar action. Both Jim and I were dumbfounded—we had both seen the draft-record burning in Maryland as a one-of-a-kind happening, not a prototype. We were speechless. On the subway back to Manhattan, we discussed the reasons we couldn't do anything that was likely to cost years in prison. At the top of the list was the fact that we both were parents of young children. Yet I was troubled by my hesitations. Shouldn't peacemaking be as costly as war making? Should so much be asked of soldiers and so much less of opponents of war?

Soon afterward I was in Washington to attend the annual meeting of the National Liturgical Conference, a group dedicated to the renewal of worship in the Catholic Church. Dorothy Day was the principal speaker. After being greeted by a standing ovation, she confessed she was "more at home washing a batch of dishes than standing before such an august audience." She spoke about the connection that had long existed between the Catholic Worker and Benedictine monks working for liturgical renewal. "It was the liturgy," Dorothy said, "which led us to pray the psalms with the church, leading us to a joyful understanding in prayer. It was the liturgy which brought us close to Scripture." Coming to know many of the psalms by heart, she said, had helped sustain vigils for peace and justice as well as times in jail.

Dorothy referred to the "hard sayings" in the Gospels—love of ene-mies, forgiving seventy times seven, refusing to respond to violence with violence, turning the other cheek, going the second mile. She named various people in the Catholic Worker movement who were in prison that very day because of their attempts to shape their lives around the "hard sayings" of Jesus—Tom Cornell, David Miller, Bob Gilliam, Jimmy Wilson, and others.

She drew particular attention to Phil and Dan Berrigan and the wit-ness of the Catonsville Nine and their "revolutionary act of destroying draft records." Their motivation, she stressed, was "love of brother and compassion for men conscripted and dying in Vietnam and other countries of the world to which we have sold arms and planes." She was aware that some had judged the destruction of draft records as an act of violence, but Dorothy disagreed. "It was a nonviolent act," she argued, "in that it was directed only against the symbols of man's present-day enslavement and not against man, and at the same time it was the vio-lence of the Lord Himself when he overturned the tables of commerce in the Temple."[1]

I was deeply moved by what Dorothy had said. Afterward, walk-ing the streets of Washington with George Mische, one of the nine, he told me that a second Catonsville-like action was taking shape and asked if I was interested in joining it. Without hesitation and to my astonishment, the word "yes" flew out of my mouth. "Great!" George replied. When and where the event was to take place, he said, was as yet unknown. Several people, including two priests, had expressed readiness. He was adding my name to the list.

---

1. In the weeks that followed, Dorothy had second thoughts about the tactic of property destruction as a means of protest. "We ought not do to others what we would not have them do to us," she said. She also worried that less dramatic efforts to end the war would be judged less valuable than actions that were likely to result in long prison sentences. Early in 1969, she reminded *Catholic Worker* readers that peacemaking most often took quite ordinary forms. "The thing is to recognize that not all are called, not all have the vocation, to demonstrate in this way . . . to endure the pain and the long, drawn-out, nerve-wracking suffering of prison life. We do what we can, and the whole field of the works of mercy is open to us. . . . All work, whether building, increasing food production, running credit unions, working in factories that produce for human needs, working in the handicrafts—all these things can come under the heading of the works of mercy, which are the opposite of the works of war." For more about Dorothy's change of mind, see the collection of her letters, *All the Way to Heaven*, ed. Ellsberg, 365–67.

My next stop happened to be Milwaukee, where Dan Berrigan and I had both agreed to speak at a conference of Franciscan teaching nuns. For the several days we were there, we stayed at Casa Maria, the local Catholic Worker house of hospitality. Our hosts were Michael and Nettie Cullen. Michael was an enthusiastic Irishman, with a brogue thick as potato soup, while Nettie, with her midwestern accent and practical manner, was as American as pumpkin pie.

On our second night at Casa Maria, Dan and I found ourselves drinking beer in a crowded kitchen in which several of those present, Michael among them, made clear they were eager to follow the Catonsville example. We learned that all Milwaukee's nine draft boards were conveniently located in adjacent offices on the second floor of a downtown office building, in front of which was a small park dedicated to America's war dead. The situation was, Michael pointed out, "the ideal spot for burning draft files."

George Mische's list of potential volunteers quickly enlarged. The next step was a weekend gathering of the twenty or so people from August 23 to August 25 at St. Paul's Abbey, a monastery in northwest New Jersey. Paul Mayer, coordinator of the Catonsville Nine Defense Committee, made the arrangements. The gathering resembled a retreat, with Mass each morning and a period of Bible study later in the day. In addition there were sessions at which we got to know one another, discuss our motives and backgrounds, and make decisions about who would take part in the action, who would form a support team, and which of several cities being considered should be chosen.

By the time the retreat ended it had been agreed that Milwaukee was the best option, in part because four of the participants lived there. Fourteen people committed themselves to take part: Don Cotton, Michael Cullen, Father Robert Cunnane, Jerry Gardner, Bob Graf, Father Jim Harney, Jon Higgenbotham, Father Al Janicke, Doug Marvy, Father Anthony Mullaney, Fred Ojile, Brother Basil O'Leary, Father Larry Rosebaugh, and myself.[2] Twelve were Catholics, five of them priests. The oldest member of the group was a professor of economics. Another was a Benedictine monk. A date was set, September 24, just four weeks away. We decided to gather in Milwaukee two days beforehand.

---

2. Information about each of the fourteen can be found at www.nonviolent worm.org/Milwaukee14Today.

I agreed to draft a group declaration. Here are extracts from the final document:

> *We who burn these records of our society's war machine are participants in a movement of resistance to slavery, a struggle that remains as unresolved in America as in most of the world. Man remains an object to be rewarded insofar as he is obedient and useful, to be punished when he dares declare his liberation. Our action concentrates on the Selective Service System because its relation to murder is immediate. Men are drafted—or "volunteer" for fear of being drafted—as killers for the state. Their victims litter the planet. In Vietnam alone, where nearly 30,000 Americans have died, no one can count the Vietnamese dead, crippled, the mentally maimed.*
>
> *Today we destroy Selective Service System files because we need to be reminded that property is not sacred. Property belongs to the human scene only if man does. . . . Property is repeatedly made enemy of life: gas ovens in Germany, concentration camps in Russia, occupation tanks in Czechoslovakia, pieces of paper in draft offices, slum holdings, factories of death machines, germs and nerve gas. . . .*
>
> *In destroying these links in the military chain of command, we forge*

anew the good sense of the Second Vatican Council: "Human dig-nity demands that each person act according to a free conscience that is personally motivated from within, not under mere external pressure or blind internal impulse."

Others worked on an action plan. Doug Marvy took on the task of finding a way to open the doors to the nine boards half an hour after the staff left for the day. Others mapped the boards, locating the cabinets containing the files of people in the 1-A category—those who had passed their physicals and would soon receive orders to report for military service.

Amazingly the action came off as planned. The fourteen of us walked in pairs from a variety of starting points, converging at the office building that housed the draft boards. My knees shook every inch of the way. The nine doors were opened, the many burlap sacks we had brought with us were filled to bursting with 1-A files—10,000 of them, it was estimated during the trial—and dragged out to the park across the street. Napalm, made ourselves according to a recipe found in the US Army Special Forces Handbook, was poured on the files and a match struck. The fourteen of us lined up on one side of the bonfire and prayed the Our Father and sang "We Shall Overcome."

The police and fire departments were slow to arrive. Had we wished, we could have quietly walked back to Casa Maria, but the trial to fol-low was as important to us as the destruction of the files. I doubt the police had ever arrested a more cheerful or cooperative, in fact elated, set of prisoners. We had set out to declare nonviolent war on military conscription and to do our bit to impede the war in Vietnam, and had achieved all we had dreamed of.

I recall these events with gratitude, pride, embarrassment, and amazement, but at the same time I'm disturbed that it never occurred to me to back out. I still have mixed feelings about having been one of the Milwaukee Fourteen. The hardest part of preparing for the action was arranging Ben's care during the prolonged absence I anticipated. Thanks mainly to my mother, it all worked out remarkably well—Ben has happy memories of living with her in that period of his life and takes pride in what I did. Still it troubles me that I put work for social change ahead of my responsibilities for him, much as my father had done to me during my own childhood. Dad had often remarked that I was "a chip off the old block." Perhaps I should have been less so.

Trial

One doesn't have to have undergone arrest to know what happened next. The ritual has been endlessly and accurately reenacted in countless crime dramas: handcuffs, transport by police car or van to the nearest police station, the emptying of pockets and removal of pens and wrist watches followed by finger printing and the taking of mug shots. The same had happened to me six years earlier when I had been among those blocking the entrance to the Atomic Energy Commission in New York. I felt as if I were playing a familiar role in a film.

As night was falling, we were delivered to the Milwaukee County Jail where we were briefly deposited in a "drunk tank" and then moved to a dormitory with seven bunk beds—a perfect fit for the fourteen of us. The county jail was our home for a month.

In court for arraignment the next day, we found ourselves charged with three felonies: burglary for breaking into the nine draft boards, theft for removing draft files, and arson for burning the files.

The judge who arraigned us had a remarkable name: Christ Seraphim. He was a notorious foe of Milwaukee's civil rights movement and a past president of the Eagles Club, a whites-only fraternity. He set bail that would have been more appropriate for kidnappers, rapists, or armed robbers: $430,000 in toto—approximately $3,000,000 in today's money. It took a month, but finally the amount was reduced by a different judge. Thanks to generous loans from supporters (one couple mortgaged their house), we were set free pending trial. We had half a year to prepare our defense as well as to organize public meetings and events, from discussion forums to poetry readings to helping people who were organizing new draft board actions.[1]

---

1. By the time the war in Vietnam ended, nearly three hundred draft board raids had occurred. In addition, the headquarters of the Dow Chemical Corporation,

There was a major surprise at the end of our second night behind bars. Hearing a chorus of cheers outside, we looked out our third-story window to discover that a crowd, led by the comedian and civil rights leader Dick Gregory, had gathered on the streets below. Earlier in the evening Gregory had given a talk at Marquette University and then led his audience to the jail to say thank you to the fourteen. "You'll receive better treatment from the government if you cheat on your income tax than if you burn your draft card," Gregory told his audience. At his side was Father James Groppi, an often-arrested leader in the local battle against racism and ghetto housing. Soon afterward, Groppi became cochairman of our defense committee.

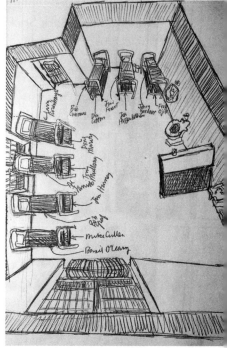

The time in jail proved to be a great blessing—a month in which we really got to know one another. Each day there were seminars led by one or another member of the group. Doug Marvy told us what it had been like, while in the Navy, to live in the Antarctic and to closely follow the lives of penguins. Basil O'Leary taught us the basics of economics, in the course of which he commented, "Everything, every institution, is to be weighed in terms of its effect on people." Bob Graf, who had been a Jesuit for seven years, introduced us to the life of St. Ignatius Loyola. Tony Mullaney did sessions on the Holy Rule of St. Benedict. Larry Rosebaugh focused on the parables of Jesus. Mike Cullen talked about Irish history and culture. I led a discussion on the history of the Catholic Worker movement. We all shared life stories— events in our lives that had finally led us to the nine draft boards of Milwaukee. Discussion of the forthcoming trial was, necessarily, a major topic. Local priests managed to visit and celebrate Mass with us.

---

the infamous manufacturer of napalm, was targeted. The documentary film *Hit & Stay: A History of Faith and Resistance,* by Joe Tropea and Skizz Cyzyk, provides an excellent overview. The DVD, produced by BRINKvision, can be ordered online.

Several lawyers volunteered their services—Percy Julian, William Kuntsler, and Mark Stickgold—and did a great deal to help us prepare our defense, but in the end we made a decision to represent ourselves rather than have lawyers speaking on our behalf. This gave us greater leeway to express our views. Mark Stickgold, a professor of law at Wayne State University in Michigan, stayed on as legal adviser.

The Abbey of Gethsemani in Kentucky was one of my main stops during the half year of being free on bail before the trial. Thomas Merton had died a few months before, on December 10, 1968. I felt orphaned by his absence. While I knew he hadn't fully approved of the sort of action I had participated in, I also knew he would have been supportive of me personally and would have helped in any way he could. His many letters had played such an important role in my life for nearly seven years. I thought one useful thing I might attempt doing while in prison was to edit his letters to me with the goal of making available, in a booklet, extracts potentially helpful to others. "Thomas Merton's Advice to Peacemakers" was the title I had in mind.[2]

The trial began in the Milwaukee County District Court on May 5, 1969, with Judge Charles Larson presiding. Larson, a man in his sixties, was Republican, the Wisconsin Commander of the American Legion, father of a Vietnam veteran, and a devout Roman Catholic. Having five Catholic priests and one Christian Brother in the dock for protesting war was not an experience he could ever have imagined or wished for. Surprisingly, he was a kind and relatively patient man who allowed testimony (albeit rarely with the jury present) many other judges would have muzzled.

Two lawyers from the district attorney's office conducted the prosecution, both of whom, we discovered, sympathized with our antiwar views if not our methods. One was white, Deputy District Attorney Allen Samson, the other black, Assistant District Attorney Harold Jackson Jr. Both were twenty-nine. "The immorality of this war bothers me more than its unconstitutionality," Samson said in an interview. "We're using Vietnam the way Russia used Hungary and Czechoslovakia. If I were boss I'd have our boys home by tomorrow noon. I'm more antiwar than anyone in the courtroom, but I don't burn draft records. It's bad for

---

2. It didn't happen at the time, but what I envisioned in 1969 as a booklet finally evolved into a book, *The Root of War Is Fear: Thomas Merton's Advice to Peacemakers*, published by Orbis Books in 2016.

the peace movement." Jackson agreed. "I'm as antiwar as anyone in the courtroom," he said. "Our draft laws are obscene. But these draft-file burners are the worst thing that could happen to us liberals. They've polarized the community so much I thought I would have to resign."

We sat on the left side of the courtroom at a long table heavily laden with law volumes and other books.[3] We looked like "a graduate seminar at a respectable university," Francine du Plessix Gray wrote in a lengthy essay about the trial published in the *New York Review of Books*.[4] A sheriff told her that we were "the classiest bunch of defendants ever."

The first day was taken up with jury selection. We took turns interviewing the candidates. After I had asked one potential juror too abstract a question, Judge Larson advised me, "Not everybody is a philosopher like you, Mr. Forest. You have a doctor of philosophy degree, is that correct?" I confessed I had no degrees at all—"I am a high school dropout, your honor." But it was good advice. Afterward I stuck to simpler questions.

Following jury selection—eight men, four women, eleven of them white, eight of them Catholics, none of them critical of the Vietnam War—the prosecution proceeded to make its case. Evidence entered during the first five days of the trial included a box of charred draft records, nine screwdrivers, two gasoline cans, and photos of draft files in flames. Witness testimony was given by policemen, two cleaning women, a photographer, journalists, passersby, and Selective Service employees.

On our side, we readily admitted we had done what we were charged with doing but contended that our actions were intended to prevent greater crimes and thus were legally justifiable. We were attempting to impede a war that was, as expert witnesses would testify, illegal, unconstitutional, and immoral. Our purpose, we stated repeatedly, was to save lives. We sought permission of the court to argue the protection of "defensive privilege"—statute 939.48 in the Wisconsin legal code—which declares that actions normally punishable under the criminal code may be considered "privileged," that is noncriminal, if the action is taken with the "reasonable belief" that it may prevent bodily harm

---

3. By the time the trial began we were down to twelve—Mike Cullen and Jerry Gardner had opted for separate trials with representation by their own attorneys.

4. Francine du Plessix Gray, "The Ultra-Resistance: On the Trial of the Milwaukee 14," http://jimandnancyforest.com/2006/11/m14trial/.

to another party. A classic example: a driver running a red light to get a gravely injured person to the hospital. We were prepared to show that we had earlier tried a wide range of legal methods of stopping the war and that our act of civil disobedience was a last resort.

To prove that it was reasonable to believe that our actions were justifiable, we sought the court's consent to present scholarly judgments contained in books, documents, and legal journals testifying to the illegality of the Vietnam War. We also hoped to demonstrate that our action was in accordance with Christian doctrine. The exhibits we offered—all rejected by Judge Larson—ranged from the *Congressional Record*'s list of the war dead and Pope John's encyclical *Pacem in Terris*, to Gordon Zahn's book on the Catholic Church in Hitler's Germany, and the New Testament. (Remarkably the prosecution was willing to admit the New Testament as an exhibit, but Judge Larson ruled that "to admit [the New Testament] into evidence may create substantial danger of undue prejudice or of misleading the jury.")

It was not always easy to connect Judge Larson's rulings with the life-and-death issues being raised by our trial, but at least Larson wrestled with the implications of our "justification" defense.

"Mr. Forest," Larson asked me in one exchange, "I want to ask you a question. Was John Wilkes Booth justified when, believing he was acting for the welfare of the Confederacy, he shot and killed Abraham Lincoln?" "I would simply point out," I replied, "that the only charges against us are damage to property, not to persons, and that, in fact, we were trying to *prevent* people from getting killed. So, the direction is the opposite. I'm not saying that the jury should find us innocent. I'm simply hoping that the court will allow us to try to demonstrate to you and to the jury the reasonableness of our belief and to decide for themselves whether, in fact, it was reasonable. The jury must determine whether the threat was apparent . . . whether we could reasonably believe as we did. Therefore all the evidence relevant to establishing either one of these points we believe must be admitted into evidence so that the jury can decide these points. . . . In *Weston versus State,* 28 Wisconsin 2nd, 136 of 1964, the court agrees with this analysis. The court in this instance allowed evidence to be introduced under 939.48, the justification defense, and then gave an instruction to the jury explaining that theory." ("Well, Jim comes from a family of lawyers," one of my co-defendants audibly remarked.)

"Let the record show," said Larson, "that while these defendants are in court without counsel, time and time again they have cited law which is very pertinent and relevant, law which requires a learned legal mind to ferret out. . . . The Court therefore wants the record to show that although it does not appear so in the courtroom, clearly they are receiving legal assistance."[5]

I didn't deny it. "We would like the opportunity to let the jurors decide," I continued, "with all the facts before them, and not just the fact that doors were opened, papers removed, and files burned. . . . It seems to me that when people are dying every hour, American boys, Vietnamese soldiers and civilians, women, children, the old, the young, that it's certainly imminent peril that we're speaking of. . . . We would like the jury to decide whether the peril is imminent or not. . . . By analogy, consider the situation of a Jew in Nazi Germany. He didn't have to be walking into the ovens to be in imminent danger. He was in danger if he was a Jew and could be found."

"Mr. Forest," Larson responded, "why have you assumed the heavy burden of making such determinations?"

"I think I stand on fairly solid ground in American tradition," I answered, "although I admit there are many who would question whether I'm right. It may well be that the jury will decide I'm wrong. I am prepared for that. But it seems that many times in the history of this nation small minorities have had to act. . . . It was only a small minority that first sought to establish these United States. It was, at first, only a small minority that believed that slavery was wrong."

"You call this civil disobedience, Mr. Forest?"

"Yes, your honor, in the same sense that it was civil disobedience, in the 1850s, to help prevent an escaped slave from being forcibly returned to slavery."

Not all the exchanges in court had to do with issues of historical importance. A nice moment occurred after I saw clear indications that District Attorney Sampson was suffering from an overfull bladder. He had asked Larson for "a very brief recess" but been told to be patient. However, when I seconded Sampson's request, Larson grasped the

---

5. He was correct. Law professor Mark Stickgold helped prepare us for the trial, taught us how to find and cite relevant case law, instructed us in courtroom etiquette, and attended the trial, meeting with us afterward to join in evaluating what had happened that day and to help us prepare for the next day.

urgency and gave us a ten-minute break. Sampson gave me a grateful smile and a thumbs-up as he hurried out of the courtroom.

We brought three expert witnesses to Milwaukee who were qualified to testify on the reasonableness of our views on the war and the place of civil disobedience in American history: Howard Zinn, professor of government at Boston University and author of *A People's History of the United States*, war crimes expert John Fried, and Marvin Gettleman, author of *Vietnam: History, Documents, and Opinions*.

Zinn came first. "The tradition of civil disobedience in this country goes as far back as the colonial period," Zinn testified, "reaching a height during the American Revolution. It has been enunciated by the Fathers of our country, written into the Declaration of Independence, carried on in the movement to end slavery, and carried on in the movement to win decent conditions for laboring people. The tradition of civil disobedience goes back as far as Thomas Jefferson and it comes right up to today. . . . People distinguished in the field of law and philosophy recognize that there's a vast difference between a person who commits an ordinary crime and a person who commits an act which technically is a crime, but which in essence is a social act."

Zinn was beginning to answer a question about acts of civil disobedience committed against the fugitive slave laws in the 1850s when Judge Larson stopped him. "We are not here to consider the fugitive slave laws. Such testimony is inflammatory and immaterial."

The only substantial comment that Zinn was allowed to make was in response to a question concerning the relationship of civil disobedience to democratic process. "Whatever progress has been made in the United States in eliminating social evils," he responded before being cut off, "has been due in part to the courage of some people in committing acts of civil disobedience. If these acts were considered ordinary crimes, this country would be far worse off than we are today." After a hailstorm of attempted questions and forbidden responses, and after a warning of arrest from Larson, Zinn left the witness box.

John Fried came next. Following World War II, he had been chief consultant to the American judges at the Nuremberg war crime trials of leading Nazis as well as a United Nations adviser on international law and also an adviser on international law at the Pentagon. We hoped he would be allowed to testify on "a hierarchy of law in the international world order."

The prosecution and Judge Larson objected that testimony drawn from such documents as the UN Charter and the Nuremberg Principles concerning the US violations of international law would be irrelevant to charges of burglary, arson, and theft. Amazingly, after heated argument, Fried was allowed to answer a number of questions, though in the absence of the jury. "I say with a very, very grave heart and after very, very careful study that the US military intervention in Vietnam," Fried said, "does violate essential and basic provisions of the United Nations Charter, and this is not an isolated opinion of myself."

"What recourse does a citizen have," Basil O'Leary asked Fried, "when his country pursues war in violation of international treaties which the citizen holds have been violated?"

Expecting an objection, Larson looked toward the prosecution table. "No objection," said Jackson. "If he can answer that, God bless him."

Fried replied, "The International Tribunal at Nuremberg, at which the United States was represented, stated that it is the moral choice of the individual if he feels that for him obedience to the higher order— to the world order—is more important . . . then he has to take the moral choice and do the things which he considers morally proper. That is the great ethical and moral method of Nuremberg."

He added: "The United Nations Charter does not give the rules for conduct during wartime. There are other treaties, like the Hague Treaties of 1907 long preceding the Charters of the Geneva Conventions of 1929 and 1949. In the hierarchy of law, international world order as stipulated in treaties . . . is the highest. If, then, a dichotomy develops between international law and domestic law, the dilemma for the government and for the individual is great."

"No more questions," said Basil.

Our last witness, Marvin Gettleman, was an expert on the history of the Vietnam War. His testimony would have shown that the war in Vietnam was crippling the nation's war on poverty. Larson ruled such testimony was irrelevant. Unpredictably, prosecutor Samson asked Larson to be patient because "everyone knows that the war is taking money away from urban planning." Gettleman was dismissed.

After days of passionate endeavor on our part, Larson ruled that we had failed to prove that military conscription constituted an "imminent" threat to anyone's life and thus we could not argue that, in destroying draft records, we were protecting lives, and that the "justification" defense was "not applicable in this case." He added, "I shall not permit any testimony about the fairness of the draft or the fact that it discriminates against some, and as far as the Vietnam War is moral or anything else, it is not relevant here."

Prohibited from presenting evidence on the illegality and immorality of the war in Vietnam, our only way of communicating to the jury what lay behind our action was through our own testimony. In the course of several days we took turns cross-examining each other.

One of the high points of the trial was the afternoon in which Tony Mullaney, a Benedictine monk, explained what had brought him to interfere with the work of the Selective Service System. He proceeded to identify several aspects of his state of mind.

"The motto of the Benedictine order has always been *Pax*—Latin for peace. A monk's vows can be summed up as a single vow to set up the conditions whereby man can be fully human. The monk is supposed to be a sign of hope, he is supposed to be a sign that history can be moved in the direction laid down in the Gospels, and therefore a sign that we are responsible for history and the direction that history takes."

Tony described the justifiable anger "that stems from a correct assessment of a present moment in history. My anger on September 24th was based on first-hand evidence that I had that the draft was doing violence to the consciences of young men, doing real psychological damage to young men." No less important were the experiences he had in Roxbury, an area of Boston "where poverty is perhaps at its worst. In Roxbury, your defenses are shattered the day you arrive."

Another element was "fear of a very deep and very pervasive polarization that is going on in the United States. . . . We are a nation that's very seriously divided . . . black–white, rich–poor, young–old . . . the growing gap between the powerful and the powerless. My participating in the burning of draft records was my attempt to say something about the polarization, which, if it is not checked, is going to lead to great disaster in this nation."

Finally, Tony read aloud the 1,500-word statement that the Milwaukee Fourteen had handed to reporters at the time of our action. Despite objections that Tony was giving "an oration on social matters," he was allowed to read through this entire document.

"Tony, Reverend Doctor," Fred Ojile asked in his cross-examination, "when does the question of who determines destruction of property become pertinent in the decision-making process?" "The decision to destroy property," Tony replied, "has to be confronted whenever the person has reasonably concluded that there is no longer any relationship between that property and the enhancement of those values to which he is committed, through his membership in various communities such as the American community, the family of nations, and so forth. In other words, when property no longer enhances the dignity of the person. Property is an instrument. It does not have substantial value; it has instrumental value."

Bob Graf spoke with emotion about what was at the center of his thoughts on September 24: "I'm inside the draft board, and I'm taking files which I believe to be those of my brothers and neighbors. . . . The only sensation I can remember that day was that of my arm being extremely tired as I was trying to do as much as possible to get as many people freed as I could. And in this act of liberation my arm was just getting tired, and I guess it's like the stories you hear when someone is drowning and someone runs out to save him; his arm, his body, his whole body gets tired in the act of saving the drowning person."

When it was my turn to describe my intentions, I stressed that breaking a law need not imply contempt for the law: "One aspect of our action was the idea that our action would not add to an atmosphere of lawlessness in this country, but, on the contrary, help restore law and order in our society. You have heard it said, and it was my belief at the time as it is today, that our public officials are failing to take proper cognizance of the Constitution of this country and the law of the land. Our leaders are paying a great deal of attention to small laws, but overlooking the very big laws which are the most important ones to this country and its future."

I also emphasized our commitment to nonviolence: "One of my main concerns was to reopen the possibility of protest being nonviolent in our society. Many people have said when Martin Luther King died, nonviolence died with him. We don't believe that. We wanted to keep open the possibility of people undertaking their protests in the context of nonviolence, with respect for life, and to keep people from becoming so frustrated that protest would simply become destructive."

On May 26, the eleventh and last day of the trial, Larson gave the jury its charge: "The law does not recognize political, religious, or moral convictions, or some higher law, as justification for the commission of a crime, no matter how good the motive may be. . . . People who believe that the Vietnam War is illegal or unconstitutional or morally wrong have the right to protest in various ways but not to

Courtroom scene minutes after we were found guilty

break the law." The jury deliberated for only seventy minutes before returning its verdict. All of us were guilty as charged.

Dozens of spectators rose and sang "We Shall Overcome." Judge Larson ordered marshals to clear the courtroom. Quite a number, mostly of student age, had to be dragged out. "I pity the nation that fears its young," said Tony to Judge Larson.

As the end of the trial, Assistant District Attorney Jackson confessed to a journalist how shaken he was by the events in the courtroom. "I'm more torn by this case than I was at the beginning. I see nothing but honesty and intelligence here, depth of perception and integrity, an atmosphere that I can only describe as very loving." After the trial was over, Jackson resigned from his job in order to devote himself to black civil rights cases. "Negroes in this country are being sent to jail like Jews to Auschwitz," he said in his office on his last day. "There's not enough legal talent around to help them." He explained that the trial of the Milwaukee Fourteen had been a turning point. "That trial tore me up," he said. "I'm still not sure what they accomplished politically. But whatever religion is, they're where it's at. . . . I suppose the essence of religiousness is to break rules at the proper time. . . . What the hell do you expect when a great priest like [Tony] Mullaney leaves his monastery after nineteen years to see what life is like in Roxbury, Massachusetts?"

Sabbatical

A fter the trial, I spent just over a year under lock and key in Wisconsin, more than half of that time at Waupun, a prison that closely resembled the penitentiaries re-created by Hollywood in classic black-and-white crime movies starring such iconic gangsters as James Cagney and George Raft: castle-like walls, barred cells four tiers high with metal catwalks, metal staircases, metal bunk beds, metal toilets, and the metallic slams as steel gates and cell doors were opened and closed.

Waupun, opened in 1851, was Wisconsin's oldest and most guarded lockup—a maximum-security prison. Maximum it was. The population of convicts housed there was a thousand or so, mainly those convicted of the most serious crimes: murder, manslaughter, armed robbery, rape, and child molesting. It was an odd environment for a young writer who had a principled objection to war and other forms of violence, but in many ways I gradually came to find being there a blessing. My monastic side came to the rescue, but also the good luck of being locked up in Wisconsin. In the seventies, Wisconsin was regarded as having the best state prison system in the United States. If I was nowhere near paradise, in most other states it would have been significantly worse.

Linda was the first who came to visit, an event she described in a letter to a mutual friend, Francine du Plessix Gray: "Jim looked very well. He looked about nineteen years old with his head clean-shaven, and without his mustache. He says the food is good, cafeteria-style. . . . For the first few days he's not been allowed any books except his Bible and his breviary. He's been saying his hours. We sat and talked about our marriage and about how we would grow through this, how it might be the best thing for our marriage. When I hugged Jim he smelled so good, a smell of clean plain soap and of fresh clean linen, he smelled like a nun, or like a child when you put him to bed."[1]

My first seven days were spent in twenty-four-hour-a-day isolation—similar to solitary but not as grim—while a decision was made about what work I would be assigned to. I felt like a caged squirrel. My main human contact was with an elderly prisoner-trustee delivering a tray of food three times a day. This was the hardest week for me, a week of fear. Fear was not unreasonable. I drew on years of reading stories about prison brutality, drugs, gangs, racial rivalries, riots, and rape. I was full of dread. But when I was finally assigned to a cell block and released into the general prison population my anxieties quickly receded. Waiting in line in the cafeteria the first day after isolation, I felt a tap on my shoulder. A huge man with scarred features was standing behind me. I expected him to say, "Who the hell gave you permission to stand in front of me?" Instead he quietly asked, "Would you like a caramel?" He pushed a cellophane-wrapped candy into my hand and told me his name was George.

Initially I was assigned to the laundry. Six days a week, truckloads of sheets, pillowcases, and clothing from various state institutions, including mental hospitals, orphanages, and other prisons, were sorted, washed, ironed, and folded. It was work with an outhouse smell as the sheets were often smeared with feces. Flies by the thousands were drawn into the delivery area.

Eventually I was moved into the section where ironing was done with industrial steam presses. Here my first prison friendship took root while I was working side by side with a man in his mid-sixties—I'll call him Thomas Jones. He was then in his eleventh year of serving a life sentence for murder. Though as kind and caring a man as I've ever met, Thomas had the handicap of being black and near the bottom of the economic ladder—not helpful when it comes to police, lawyers, and judges. I asked what led to his conviction. The story he told was simple and tragic. "I'd rented a back room of a neighborhood bar," Thomas told me, "a place to celebrate with family and friends our twenty-fifth

---

1. Linda's letter was included in a two-part essay by Francine du Plessix Gray, "The Ultra-Resistance," published in the *New York Review of Books*, September 25, and October 2, 1969. The text of the Gray article is online at http://jimandnancyforest.com/2006/11/m14trial/. Linda's letter was also used by Leonard Bernstein in his oratorio *The Mass*.

wedding anniversary. But two drunken boys crashed the party and spoke in an insulting way to my wife. By that time I wasn't sober myself. I went out to my car, took my handgun out of the glove compartment, and returned to the party. I swear to God I didn't mean to hurt no one. All I wanted was to scare those boys. I was just waving the gun around. But somehow I pulled the trigger. If I had any target in mind, it was the ceiling, but that one bullet hit one of those boys in the head and it killed him. Biggest mistake of my life." Thomas was not convicted of accidental manslaughter, as a white man with a good lawyer might have been. He was doing time for premeditated first-degree murder.

I was to meet quite a few men who were inside the walls for their inability to hire a good lawyer. In my view, many were convicted of crimes they didn't commit—race often playing a significant part. Drugs were another common factor leading to years in the penal zoo.

I was so much luckier than most inmates. For starters I had many caring friends on the outside providing a network of support. One of them, Francine du Plessix Gray, gave me a typewriter—a handsome red and orange, Italian-made Olivetti portable. Making use of the trial

transcript I had borrowed from the court, over many weeks I typed up a 250-page abridgement of the huge text.[2] I also used my Olivetti for correspondence, writing projects, and for helping illiterate prisoners who needed assistance with letters home or in their efforts to obtain a retrial or parole.

Correspondence was a lifeline. One of those who kept in touch was Thich Nhat Hanh. In the first of his letters he wrote: "Do you remember the tangerine we ate when we were together?

My Christmas letter to Ben

---

2. The pages are online at http://jimandnancyforest.com/wp-content/uploads/2014/10/Milwaukee-14-abridged-trial-transcript-sm.pdf.

Ben's drawing of his happy father in jail

Eat it and be one with it. Tomorrow it will be no more." He helped me embrace imprisonment day by day.

The letters I sent to Ben, now seven, were more graphic than verbal—watercolor drawings with text typed around the illustrations. Each page was a kind of children's story. (Obtaining permission to have a drawing pen—a Rapidograph—and a set of watercolors in my cell had not been easy.)

With my mother's help, Ben responded in kind. Of all the communications I received while locked up, the most cherished is a crayon drawing Ben made for his Sunday school class at Mother's church. The topic that week, Mother explained, was St. Paul. The teacher leading the group mentioned that St. Paul had been imprisoned for his faith. "So is my dad," Ben announced with pride. "He's in jail right now!" The drawing he made that day showed me behind prison bars with a big smile and victoriously raised arms. Framed, it now hangs in our house.

The most surprising gift that made its way to my cell during my thirteen months in prison was a photo of Earth taken by an astronaut on the Apollo 11 moon voyage in July 1969.

Millions of people at the time watched the moon landing on television. In my case, I listened in a cell fourteen bars wide via a pair of aging, low-tech earphones. Having seen so many science fiction films, and having read so much science fiction, I had plenty of props to assist my imagination. It wasn't hard picturing the crew of three crossing the airless sea of space, then two of them actually landing and standing on the moon's gray, dusty surface.

A major surprise was yet to come: the delivery of a carefully wrapped packet from NASA containing an 8½ x 11-inch color photo of the Earth made from the actual negative. I doubt the photo could have reached the White House much sooner than it reached me. The same image was soon to appear on various magazine covers, but none had the richness of color and fineness of detail of the original photo.

The prison administration made it difficult for me to receive the gift as it hadn't been sent by an "authorized correspondent." I was given a form to sign that had two options: authorization to destroy the unopened packet or to return it to the sender. After an appeal to the warden, the packet was at last delivered to my cell and for the rest of my time in prison rested on top of my book-laden table. It has been a treasured icon for me ever since. I often bring a laminated print with me when I give lectures—it has been held by thousands of people. Recently I've made badges of it to give to friends.

The Whole Earth, as seen from Apollo 11, July 16, 1969

The photo celebrates the astronauts' most astonishing discovery—not the colorless, airless, arid moon, now embellished with boot prints and a US flag, but our own planet, seen whole, small, and vulnerable, a colorful island of cloud-shrouded life in the vast black night of space.

The packet contained no letter. Who with NASA had sent it? I have no way of knowing, but my guess is that it came from one of the Apollo 11 astronauts. If so, the donor was a career officer in the US Air Force saying thank you to an antiwar protester locked in a small cell in middle America. My guess is he had seen a press report of the trial and that something I was quoted as saying had touched him.

One possible sender was Apollo 11 crew member Michael Collins, who wrote the following in *Carrying the Fire: An Astronaut's Journeys*:

I really believe that if the political leaders of the world could see their planet from a distance of 100,000 miles their outlook could be fundamentally changed. That all-important [national] border would be invisible. . . . The tiny globe would continue to turn, serenely ignoring its subdivisions, presenting a unified facade that would cry out for unified understanding, for homogeneous treatment. The Earth must become as it appears: blue and white, not capitalist or Communist; blue and white, not rich or poor; blue and white, not envious or envied.[3]

People who have gazed at the Earth from space seem to experience a similar life-changing astonishment. "You spend even a little time contemplating the Earth from orbit and the most deeply ingrained nationalisms begin to erode," astrophysicist Carl Sagan once commented. Political squabbles on Earth, he added, "seem the squabbles of mites on a plum." This experience is sometimes called "the Overview Effect."

That effect caught Alan Shepard by surprise: "If somebody'd said before the flight, 'Are you going to get carried away looking at the Earth from the moon?' I would have said, 'No, no way.' But yet when I first looked back at the Earth, standing on the moon, I cried."

The Russian cosmonaut Yuri Artyushkin said, "It isn't important in which sea or lake you observe a slick of pollution or in the forests of which country a fire breaks out, or on which continent a hurricane arises. You are standing guard over the whole of our Earth."[4]

Apollo 14 astronaut Edgar Mitchell, the sixth human being to walk on the moon, said, after his return, that looking at the Earth from the moon "you develop an instant global consciousness, a people orientation, an intense dissatisfaction with the state of the world, and a compulsion to do something about it. From out there on the moon, international politics look so petty. You want to grab a politician by the scruff of the neck and drag him a quarter of a million miles out and say, 'Look at that, you son of a bitch.'"

Many hours of my time in prison were spent contemplating that photo, and it still stops me in my tracks.

My sojourn in prison was also a time of reading. Remarkably, the

---

3. Michael Collins, *Carrying the Fire: An Astronaut's Journeys* (New York: Farrar, 1974).

4. "Fifty Years Ago We Landed on the Moon. Why Should We Care Now?," *New York Times*, June 14, 2019, www.nytimes.com/2019/06/14/books/review/moon-landing-anniversary.html.

prison library was an integral part of the state university library system. I could obtain any book I requested. I've ever since referred to those thirteen months as my sabbatical year. Dorothy Day had often urged me, indeed nearly ordered me, to read Dostoevsky's greatest work, *The Brothers Karamazov*. At last I did so and found that there is no better place to give such a book the unhurried attention it deserves than prison. I went on to read his *Crime and Punishment*. Next came Tolstoy's *War and Peace*. Curious to know more about Tolstoy, I read a brilliant memoir about a visit with him written by Maxim Gorky, which in turn led me to Gorky's enthralling autobiographies: *My Childhood, In the World,* and *My Universities*. In them I met Gorky's saintly grandmother, whose vividly described prayer life left a lasting impression. One Russian author led to another—Alexander Pushkin, Nikolai Gogol, Nikolai Leskov, and, from the Soviet era, Aleksandr Solzhenitsyn, another fellow prisoner. What providence! I had no idea at the time that my reading was laying a solid foundation for work I would later undertake in Russia.

There were other books and authors that left a mark on me, not least J. R. R. Tolkien's *Lord of the Rings*—a parable of modest hobbits ready to give away their lives in order to destroy a ring that enslaves. Frodo and Sam's ring-destroying action had something in common with our destruction of draft records.

Poetry was important: Robert Bly, Denise Levertov, Gary Snyder, and Galway Kinnell sent book after book. The small table in my cell was hard pressed to hold them all.

Most important was the New Testament. Starting with Matthew, I read a chapter a day and then, when I reached the end, began over.

Complementing the Gospels, there was the rosary. After years of regarding the rosary as something mainly for pious ladies of modest education, I found myself praying "Hail Marys" as I was marched from building to building at Waupun or as I gazed through remote windows at glimpses of the sky. I discovered I needed no string of actual beads—the ten fingers I was born with served the purpose.

God and my guardian angel must have been laughing. Thanks to an act of civil disobedience, I had stumbled off the conveyer belt that carries peace activists along at the same speed and ambition as corporate executives and movie stars. I had once aspired to the contemplative life and, in a funny sort of way, found it for a year in the company of convicts.

My time at Waupun came in two slices that together added up to just over seven months. There was an in-between period at Camp Gordon, a minimum-security compound in northwest Wisconsin whose inmates did maintenance work at state parks and, when needed, fought forest fires. The forestry work inspired such poems as this:

Prisoner Forest
on hands and knees
thick grass, blooming clover.
He is supposed to be looking for
a needle valve fallen off the lawn mower
but actually he's watching a bee
moving with Bolshevik determination
from blossom to blossom.
Not very much like Prisoner Forest.

And this:

In a woods of poplar, jack pine, birch,
knee-high ferns dripping with last night's rain,
sixteen of us in orange and yellow helmets,
the bull gang.
Axe blows sound like rocks falling into a stream.
"Just let me at these trees with a flame-thrower,"
says a blond, gray-eyed kid with instant-oatmeal skin.
Paisan asks: "You ever seen a flame-thrower, kid?"
Paisan comes from New York—
East 111th Street and 2nd Avenue, Little Italy.
He has World War II scars on his legs.
"150 feet of flame, kid? You make one mistake
with one them cocksuckers and your ass'll be burned
from here to kingdom come, you goddam right."
"You ever eat Vietcong flesh?" he asks.
Wind in the poplar leaves rustles like clothes
being taken off, like kisses.
Ferns sparkling with rain drops,
the sky soft enough to be sucked,
but eyes have been so long blistered
that all the tongue can taste
is burned brother's flesh.

If the words were sometimes grim, the work was mainly pleasant, but the several redneck guards who had charge of the camp took sadistic glee in withholding my mail, even such journals as *Natural History* and *National Geographic*. Finally, after threatening to stop working, I was sent back to Waupun. During my second stint there I worked in a factory that made metal furniture for state institutions.

My last four months were spent at Fox Lake, a medium-security facility in central Wisconsin that was, as prisons go, a remarkably decent place—modern buildings, each prisoner with his own small room, and guards and staff who treated us kindly. After a short period working in a factory that made wooden furniture, I became assistant to the Catholic chaplain, Jim Koneazny, a priest who was outspoken in his support of the Milwaukee Fourteen. We became good friends and stayed in touch until his death from cancer a few years ago.

Were there no horror stories? In my case no. Two or three guys wondered if I might like to get to know them sexually—they accepted my negative response without protest or threats. At Camp Gordon I was once struck in the face by a Native American prisoner who assumed anyone with white skin was his enemy. He apologized the same day and we became friends. I never felt in danger at Waupun, but this may be due in part to a black inmate who came from East Harlem, my neighborhood too, and appointed himself my bodyguard. He was a contract killer by trade who had been caught in Milwaukee with a dead body on the pavement and a smoking gun in his hand. "Bad timing, man," he explained.

When I was freed on parole in early August, a social worker who had become a friend gave me a going-away present: a green dwarf parrot named Gandalf.

Linda was waiting at the prison gate ready to drive back to New York in her VW Beetle. Seeing her was both a joy and a sorrow. Despite brave hopes to the contrary, several months before she had written to say that our marriage was over—her life was taking new turns. In fact, doing time behind walls rarely benefits committed relationships, a perennial fact that was even truer in the centrifugal sixties. It was a period of experiments, many of which seemed promising but often proved doomed. That our marriage was one of the casualties was not surprising, only painful.

On the Road to Emmaus

Ireturned to New York from prison with two high-priority resolutions: to learn how to make coffee that tasted as good as the smell of freshly ground coffee beans and to get a bike.

Coffee was at the top of the list, and I knew just where to go. I had often walked past a coffee roasting shop in Greenwich Village. Mr. McNulty, the owner, welcomed me and my questions. "The main thing you need," he told me, "is a good coffee bean." "And how," I asked, "do you tell one bean from another?" "It's simple. Taste the  bean. Just take two or three beans, put them in your mouth, chew them slowly, and taste reveals the rest. Brewed coffee will never taste better than the bean." He put sample after sample in my hand. "You see what I mean? Start with whole beans, taste before you buy, grind the beans yourself, and the rest is easy." After half an hour with Mr. McNulty, I walked out of his small shop with a Melita ceramic coffee pot, two packs of filter paper, two bags of coffee beans, and an inexpensive electric coffee grinder. Ever since that day I've connected being freed from prison with the smell and taste of a good cup of coffee.

That same week I bought a bike—English, green, three-speed, and second hand. Bikes were a rarely used means of getting around Manhattan in those days. Dodging buses, trucks, taxis, and autos was at times like navigating a stampede of wild bulls. I mainly used paths in Central Park to make my way downtown to *Commonweal* magazine, where I worked as an assistant editor during the first months after being released. Biking, especially in the park, was yet another celebration of freedom.

Ben, now eight, was still living in New Jersey with my mother and doing well both as part of her household and at school. It didn't seem a good idea to uproot him. For the time being, I was a weekend parent.

My home was Emmaus House in East Harlem, a neighborhood in upper Manhattan that had been solidly Italian but was now shifting ethnic boundaries as its Puerto Rican population expanded. Our block was on the borderline. We had a four-story brownstone building at 241 East 116th Street. The main floor had tall windows, high ceilings, and, behind the living room, a spacious kitchen. There was a garden behind the house whose several grape vines bore witness to the wine that was once made in the basement, now serving as the Emmaus office.

The community took its name from the Gospel story about two traumatized disciples fleeing Jerusalem after the execution of Jesus. A stranger joined the

David Kirk, founder of Emmaus House

despairing pair along the way. When the three stopped for a meal in the village of Emmaus, the outsider was recognized as Jesus risen from the dead. "And they knew him in the breaking of bread," wrote Luke. It is perhaps the most compelling of all the resurrection stories.

Half a block to the east was the Republican Club, regarded in the neighborhood as the local headquarters of the Mafia. "Mafia, definitely," said a nearby Italian baker, "but not altogether bad for the neighborhood. Their being here is the reason there's so little crime on East 116th Street. No purse snatching, no burglaries. The mafioso, they don't welcome small-time crooks."

I had been close to the Emmaus community before burning draft records and a friend of its founder even before Emmaus got started. In 1961, when I was part of the Catholic Worker staff, one of the people I had met was Emmaus founder David Kirk. In those days he was a graduate student at Columbia University. He spoke of his hopes of someday starting something along Catholic Worker lines.

It wasn't until 1967, with the purchase of the building in East Harlem, that Emmaus crossed the border from vision to reality, with four people living in the house and half a dozen others in nearby apartments. Emmaus became a house of hospitality as well as a center for peace and social justice activities, a school, and a base for helping people recently released from prison.

David liked to say the community didn't come to East Harlem to help the poor; we came because we ouselves were poor. We tried to be good neighbors, most notably by starting the Emmaus tutoring program, directed by Kathryn Mahon, a local elementary school teacher. Kathy had moved in years before the rest of us, believing the only way she could reach her students was to experience the challenges they faced in daily life.

Speaking with a velvety, unhurried, southern accent, David reminded me of Huckleberry Finn. In Mark Twain's novel about an escape on the Mississippi River, Huckleberry Finn floats away on a raft with a runaway slave. In the same tradition, in 1947, when David was twelve, he befriended a black man, recently employed by his father, who was accused of murdering his wife. Certain that the man was innocent and equally sure that no black man could count on a fair trial in the Deep South, David brought food every day to the man's hiding place, then helped him escape over the state line to Louisiana.

In 1956, David was part of a small group of students who risked their lives helping protect Autherine Lucy, the first black student to enroll at the University of Alabama. David was beaten by white racists for his protective action but counted himself lucky not to have been killed.

Friendship with a civil rights–oriented priest led David to faith and baptism. Lebanese-born Father Joseph Raya was a Melkite, an Orthodox church of the Eastern Rite in communion with Rome. "Father Joseph taught me a new way of looking at God, humanity, and the church," David explained. "It was different because—in contrast with most of Western Christianity—it drew from the radical wells of early Christian sources. It put the stress on awareness of the God of love unfolding himself in time and history, its spirituality of the heart, its confidence in the basic goodness of people, in the potential deification of the human person."

Inevitably David heard of Dorothy Day and began corresponding with her. His decision to do postgraduate study at Columbia University was linked to his wanting to live near the Catholic Worker and help in its work. Dorothy became a mentor. "Everything I have, anything I have achieved, I owe to Dorothy," David would say. "She formed me."

The way opened for David to study at the Beda College in Rome from 1959 to 1963 during the Second Vatican Council. He made contact with the leader of the Melkite Church, Patriarch Maximos IV of Antioch, a prominent figure at the council. Maximos took a special interest in this young radical Christian and ordained him a priest. "In the ordination formula where it says, 'You are ordained for the Church of God,'" David told me, "Maximos added the words, 'for the poor, and for the unity of Christians.'" With Maximos's blessing, David returned to America, first to Birmingham, Alabama, for a year of pastoral internship with Father Joseph Raya, and then to New York, where Emmaus House was born. Thanks to David's talent for raising money, he bought the brownstone that became Emmaus's first home.

Emmaus House came to be regarded as a center of the "underground church," especially for its experimental worship. While occasionally a somewhat streamlined version of the ultratraditional Eastern-Rite liturgy was celebrated, more often it was an informal version of the Western Catholic Mass with prayers revised to reflect awareness of such societal issues as war, racism, sexism, and addiction. "We were inclined to be experimental," David recalled in later years. There was even occasional revision of canonical texts, a process that brought those involved to regard the original versions with enhanced respect. "The moral is, it is indeed," wrote Hilaire Belloc, "you must not monkey with the Creed."

And there were classes. Under the auspices of the New York Theological Seminary, I taught a course on Jewish and Christian prophets. At the College of New Rochelle I was responsible for a one-semester class on "urban theology." The "urban" element involved reading such topical books as Harvey Cox's then-bestseller *The Secular City*, but also included such anti-urban works as Henry David Thoreau's *Walden*. Discovering that my students were at best skeptical about the existence of God, discussion shifted away from both urban and rural theology to more basic questions: What is meant by the word "God"? How can a creator exist who allows events like Hiroshima and Auschwitz to happen? Or for children to be born with incurable diseases? Are ecstatic moments in life actually mystical experiences? For that topic, I wrote on the blackboard a sentence from Léon Bloy: "Joy is the most infallible sign of the presence of God."

The Emmaus community published an occasional journal, *The Bread Is Rising*, designed with baroque abandon by Richard Mann, a young priest from Australia. "As the journal is free," Richard noted in one issue, "no one should complain about how rarely it is published."

In a project led by Father Lyle Young, an Emmaus cofounder, we became deeply involved in prison ministry. This included not only working with people currently in captivity but helping to find housing and jobs for them after they were freed. Lyle also worked part-time at the Catholic Peace Fellowship counseling young men who were apply-ing for recognition as conscientious objectors.

Compared to the Catholic Worker house downtown, the hospitality side of our work was on a small scale and, while I was there, mainly had to do with teenage runaways. A typical example was a seventeen-year-old named Eric, a boy from Pennsylvania who had shoulder-length golden hair plus pacifist views about the war in Vietnam. His outraged antipacifist father ordered Eric to get a haircut or leave the house. Refusing, Eric had somehow found his way to the Port Author-ity Bus Terminal and from there to us. He had been our guest for several days before an accident occurred—as he was leaning over the kitchen stove on which water was being boiled, his long hair caught fire. It was quickly extinguished but there was a nasty burn across his shoulders. We summoned an ambulance. Once he was in the hospital, I called his parents to let them know what had happened. There was a tearful father-and-son reconciliation at the hospital in the days that followed. Months later, Eric wrote with the news that he was back at home and still had long hair. His father was supporting his decision to seek recognition as a conscientious objector.

Some of our guests put us to the test. A man named Marc, with us for three months, had resolved under no circumstances to have any money, not as much as a penny, though he was quite willing to make use of money in other people's pockets so long as he didn't have to touch it. He would sometimes announce that he had to take the sub-way in order to meet with a friend downtown or in Brooklyn and therefore needed someone to accompany him to the subway station to buy him a token. Sooner or later one of us would give in, as otherwise, standing statue-like in the middle of the office, Marc was a nuisance. Our attempts to argue him out of his obsession had no impact. He cheerfully reminded us of Jesus's instruction that his disciples "should take nothing for their journey, save a staff only; no scrip, no bread, no money in their purse." Our suggestion that he should therefore walk to Brooklyn led him to remind us, "What you have done to me you have done to Christ."

We were campaigners as well. We joined protest marches to appeal for more affordable housing and demonstrated for draft-card burners when they were being sent away to prison. Supporting the United Farm Workers Union and its boycott of California grapes, we were often present for picket lines in front of supermarkets in upper Manhattan.

It was the Nixon period. Nixon plus J. Edgar Hoover were quite a combination. Before his resignation in 1974, every effort was made by Nixon to project an image of presidential indifference to protests, small and large, but the truth was quite the opposite. The Senate Watergate hearings and the release and publication of the Nixon tapes revealed a president obsessed with spying on his critics and punishing them harshly. What he called his "enemies list" was long indeed.

When Dan Berrigan, after several months of playing hide-and-seek with the FBI, was at last captured in August 1970, I phoned folksinger Pete Seeger, told him of Dan's arrest, and asked if he would sing at a demonstration the next day near the federal courthouse on Foley Square in Manhattan. "With the greatest pleasure," Seeger replied. We made a handout featuring a day-old photo of radiant Dan in handcuffs.

Welcoming Dan Berrigan upon his release from Danbury Prison

Beneath it was the headline DAN BERRIGAN IS FREE. "Would that more of us," the text declared, "were as free as Daniel Berrigan." Not long afterward I had the privilege of introducing Seeger at a benefit concert for Emmaus that he did at the College of New Rochelle.

During the summer and fall of 1971, the FBI became a major presence in our lives due to our close relationship with two nuns, Sisters

Dan celebrates his first post-prison Mass at the Catholic Worker

of Charity Judy Peluso and Karen Lydon, who lived a block away at St. Paul's Convent. Due to arthritis, Judy walked with a cane, her pain often visible in her eyes, while fresh-faced Karen could have been typecast as an angelic nun in a fifties Hollywood movie. Judy and Karen had taken part in a draft board action, and both were suspected of being involved in a break-in of an FBI office that led to the release of secret memos about the FBI's illegal activities against antiwar campaigners. The latter event was especially irritating to FBI director J. Edgar Hoover. The convent was put under overt twenty-four-hour-a-day FBI surveillance—a car with engine running and two agents on board was placed directly in front of the convent entrance and an apartment rented across the street with convent-aimed telephoto lenses visible in its front windows. Whenever Judy or Karen left the building, they were followed. One day Judy, focal point of so many FBI cameras, had the effrontery to come out of the convent to take a snapshot of the FBI car parked by the front door. The agent at the wheel drove the car onto the pavement and pinned Judy to the wall.

One of the nuns, Florence Speth, went to the local precinct proposing that the police arrest "the suspicious men, possibly peddlers or potential rapists," who were loitering around the convent. The precinct captain knew, of course, that the loiterers were FBI agents and convinced her not to file an official report—"The feds could take over the precinct and we don't want that to happen." The community found other ways to bewilder the agents: "Since our phone was being tapped, we made up wild stories for our audience of eavesdroppers." She added, "The whole thing would have been a nightmare had it not been so ridiculous."

On one occasion a friend visiting the convent brought out a sponge and pail of soapy water and the car, agents within, was given a good scrubbing.

Carol Vericker, another nun at St. Paul's Convent, had both an uncle and a cousin who were with the FBI. Though not herself engaged in protests, she had refused—like all the other nuns at St. Paul's—to answer questions about Judy and Karen. To the FBI, the uncle-cousin factor made Carol seem the nun most likely to tell all. She was ordered to appear before a grand jury in Brooklyn where she would be obliged to answer questions or go to jail for contempt. After much soul searching, Carol decided jail was the more Christian choice. To provide moral support, I accompanied her to the courthouse and waited outside. She brought with her a small suitcase containing a toothbrush, a change of clothes, and other things she might need in prison. Though she answered no questions about her sisters and thus was charged with contempt, amazingly Carol was not immediately jailed, nor were any other community members summoned to appear. With the help of lawyers from the Center for Constitutional Rights, the contempt conviction was later overturned by the US Court of Appeals.

There was surveillance of Emmaus House as well. I was often followed. I sometimes attempted to converse with the agents—"Aren't you troubled by the war in Vietnam?" was a question I repeatedly asked—but only got irritated glares in response. On one occasion I managed to make a game of it—getting into a subway car with the agent doing the same, then getting off, the agent doing the same, then getting back on again, as if we were playing musical chairs.

A Sojourn in Paris

It was 1971. I had been at Emmaus House a year when an invitation came for me to take part in an international antiwar meeting being hosted by the Quaker International Center in Paris. The Emmaus community encouraged me to say yes, and a friend paid for the air ticket. I traveled on a no-frills charter airline. If there was a single frill on that flight, I failed to spot it.

Part of the reason for being eager to go was my hope of seeing Thich Nhat Hanh and even staying with him; he was now based in Paris as head of the Vietnamese Buddhist Peace Delegation.

Arriving soon after sunrise, my first thought was to get something to eat. The only problem was that I had very little money, no credit card, and knew hardly a word of French beyond *oui* and *non,* while the airport café menu was entirely in French. I ended up requesting *fromage* because this mysterious word sounded invitingly edible and the price was less than a *sandwich*, a word that required no translation. Coming at the very end of the menu, I had guessed *fromage* might mean ice cream. Instead I had discovered how to order cheese.

By the time of departure, I hadn't received a response from Nhat Hanh, the only person I knew in Paris. Once there I discovered I had left his phone number and address in New York. All I had was the address for the Quaker center on Rue de Vaugirard.

I bought a map of Paris and found that, if I took the airport bus to its terminus in the Latin Quarter, I was near the east end of Rue de Vaugirard. This meant that I could get where I was going on foot, saving my freshly purchased francs for more essential needs. What I had failed to notice on my map was how lengthy is Rue de Vaugirard. Before long I began to feel as if I was on pilgrimage to China. I wore holes through the soles of my shoes and my socks as well. I must have walked for two hours before reaching the Quaker center. Once there, with the help of an English-speaking Quaker, I got the address and phone number of the Vietnamese Buddhist Peace Delegation. I called, was told to come right over, and given instructions for getting there by Metro.

The Vietnamese Buddhist Peace Delegation: with such an impressive name, I imagined their offices might be in the diplomatic quarter, something simple of course, in keeping with their Buddhist affirmation, but nothing resembling what I found. The office was in a neighborhood not unlike East Harlem except here the streets were older, narrower, and twisted. The address was 11 rue de la Goutte d'Or—the Street of the Drop of Gold. The delegation's office was on the top floor, a room with several desks and a view across the rooftops of St. Bernard's Church with its flying buttresses and charcoal black steeple.

Two people were there. One was a young blond woman who looked familiar. She smiled and said, "Don't you remember me? I'm Laura Hassler, Al Hassler's daughter." We laughed. While a high school student, she had been one of Ben's babysitters. That had been five years earlier, when I was directing the Fellowship of Reconciliation's Vietnam program and was married to Linda Henry. Laura had since graduated from Swarthmore and afterward worked with a group in Philadelphia raising medical help for the war's civilian casualties.

The other person was Cao Ngoc Phuong. I recognized her name. While a professor of biology at the universities of Hue and Saigon, she had been a leader of peace actions that led to her imprisonment by Saigon authorities. Protest from academic figures in several countries had resulted in her release. When friends in the government let her know that she was about to be arrested again, she was smuggled out of Vietnam. Now she was Nhat Hanh's principal collaborator. She wore traditional Vietnamese clothing—black silk trousers with a slim brown dress, open along the sides to the waist for ease of movement in chairless, couchless houses.

An hour later, at sunset, Laura and Phuong took me to the community's home, driving in washing-machine traffic around the edge of Paris in a Citroën *deux chevaux* that seemed made of tin foil. Phuong drove like a tiger. We survived, finally arriving at Maisons-Alfort, a town of brick houses, a few modern apartment buildings, and many trees. We were in the southeast of Paris, near the juncture of the Seine with the Marne.

The apartment itself might as well have been in Vietnam—a large room with rice mats on the floor, a small corner table covered with books and papers, other books in rows at the floor's edge, an altar, and a neatly blanketed mattress on the floor beneath the windows. No tables or chairs. Off to one side was a compact kitchen. A small room in one corner contained several more thin mattresses. In a closet-sized space there was a toilet, and across from that a bathroom that had been taken over by a mimeograph machine.

Thich Nhat Hanh—or Thây, as everyone called him—was waiting for us. It was now four years since we had traveled together in America, but our conversations resumed as if we had been apart only a few weeks. I was again struck by his deep calm and gentle voice.

Of the many photos I have taken of Thich Nhat Hanh, this is my favorite

After supper we had a long conversation about being a monk, a vocation he had embraced when he was sixteen. "I was initiated into the monastic life by a master," Thây said. "My elder didn't give me things to learn—he just put me into community life. We didn't begin by doctrine. We began by living the community monastic life. The very morning I came, they asked me to carry water and work in the garden. He recommended that I look carefully at the others, to see the way they do things. By that time I already had received some education of a Western nature, so I thought the kind of education in the monastery was not very advanced, because they gave me something to learn by heart—not theory but practice.

"For instance, when you wash your hands, you have to raise in your mind a thought that goes along with washing your hands. You would think to yourself, 'While I wash my hands, I wish that everybody would have clean hands capable of handling the truth.' So whatever you do, you have to become concentrated on it with a thought, and this is how we are trained for meditation. You get stronger concentration of mind. They had me learn things by heart. I thought it wasn't very advanced, but I finally found it very important. The most important thing is that they don't want to initiate you with philosophy, theory, doctrine; they want to push you right away into life, into that kind of monastic life. You learn better that way."

After the first four years in the monastery near Hue, Thây was sent to a Buddhist institute where he continued monastic life through to profession and later became founder of a new monastic community. In the early 1960s, he studied and lectured at Princeton and Columbia.

In 1964, when he returned to Vietnam, the war had reduced much of Vietnamese monasticism to rubble. Where the monasteries had physically survived, the monks had either fled or been forcibly evicted by the Saigon government, then under the leadership of an intolerant Catholic, Ngo Dinh Diem. The monks could have rebanded into less visible monastic communities, continuing life as before, and some did, but many others didn't. Increasingly, they became opponents of the war and active in helping the victims—activities that their critics judged as unmonastic.

Nhat Hanh explained, "But there is really not much division between the two kinds of life. The monastery is like a laboratory. A scientist, if he wants to do his scientific work, has to be in his lab; he has to refrain from such things as smoking, listening to the radio, chewing gum—things like that. It is not because these things are evil. But if you want to work for something, you have to stop doing those things which interrupt your work. So monastic life is a lab in which you work hard to obtain something. It is not an end in itself—it is a means."

Nhat Hanh's voice was quiet, with frequent pauses. His words seemed to float on a river of silence.

"Now," he continued, "the essence of Buddhism is compassion and wisdom. But if that compassion and wisdom are not translated into life, it would not be compassion and wisdom! So it is not a problem of speculation. If you have compassion and wisdom and find yourself in a situation of suffering, you will do what your conscience dictates. The only thing we believe is that action should be rooted in a nonaction base, which is the spiritual source of wisdom and compassion. For without wisdom and compassion, action would only further trouble the world.

"That is why conserving monastic life is very, very important. But monastic life is also for life. There is really not much separation between monastic and nonmonastic life. The hard thing is trying to find the needed work while preserving your spiritual strength."

Out of his Buddhist "nonaction" base, Thây had founded Van Hanh University in Saigon, named for a monk of the eleventh century whose followers initiated a nonviolent movement that resulted in discouraging the Chinese from invading Vietnam, a chapter in the history of nonviolent movements unknown in the West. The university, along with La Boi Publishing House, also founded by Thây, became an intellectual and spiritual base for "engaged Buddhism."

To supplement the academic format of the university, Thây went on to found the School of Youth for Social Service as a faculty of the university. The school became one of the principal channels for relief and direct action through which increasing numbers of young people found a way to assist refugees, to help in village reconstruction, to set up emergency medical centers, to teach better methods of agriculture and sanitation, and to begin small schools.

When I had first gotten to know Thây in 1968, I had been impressed by his hopefulness. My first impression of him in Paris was that much of that hope had wilted. I sensed a deep sadness in him, as if he were a rabbi at Auschwitz. There was a clue to this sadness in the room in which we were sitting. Against one wall was a low, black table that served as an altar. On it was a candle, some flowers, the stems of burned rods of incense, and a photograph of Thich Tanh Van, who had been director, since Thây's departure, of the School of Youth for Social Service. Laura gave me a mimeographed sheet announcing Tanh Van's death. On June 2, fewer than forty days prior to my arrival in Paris, Tanh Van was returning from relief work when his small car was hit by a US army truck. Tanh Van was refused admittance to an army hospital. Two days later he died. Thousands came to the funeral.

Thich Tanh Van had been Thây's most beloved student and closest friend. Both Thây and Phuong had been devastated by this loss. "He cannot be replaced," Thây told me later while showing me photos of Tanh Van.

The next day several Vietnamese visitors arrived. Their conversation explored the question of Tanh Van's next incarnation. It was implicit that Tanh Van had reached that rare degree of wholeness in which it would be possible for him to freely choose. Some thought Tanh Van would now leave the world of suffering forever and enter the "pure land" of complete peace and final liberation, others that he would return to the Vietnam of the present where once again he would share in the suffering.

There was another source of Thây's depression. Four years before, there had been much interest in the United States in the Buddhists' nonviolent struggle. Many Americans seemed to find a new source of energy for peace work in response to their awareness of what the Buddhists were doing in Vietnam. But now, many peace activists seemed indifferent to the Buddhists' struggle, though it was continuing as intensely as ever. There was criticism of the Buddhists for putting their primary emphasis on obtaining a cease-fire rather than on the nature and composition of a future government. One peace periodical went so far as to connect the Buddhist movement in Vietnam to the CIA. Representatives of the Vietnamese Buddhist Peace Delegation had not been invited to several recent international peace gatherings, including the one that had brought me to Paris. Nhat Hanh was, he was told, "politically unacceptable."

So, while many Buddhist monks, nuns, and lay people were in prison cells and "tiger cages" (holes in the ground with bamboo bars over the top) for their peace struggle, and thousands were refusing to fight, their struggle was old news in the world peace movement. While a leader of relief and peace work lay dead in Vietnam because there was no room for him in a hospital, the peace movement had quietly closed its eyes to the existence of the movement Thich Tanh Van had shared in making.

During the weeks we were together, the sorrow that I had sensed in Thây and Phuong began to lift. Not that there hadn't been moments of peace and even happiness, as when I arrived, but a new current gradually returned. I began noticing it during our meals.

Over supper one day Laura mentioned a puzzling Vietnamese saying, "Only the rice loves you." We talked about the broken-grain rice we were eating. It hadn't come from the food market but from a pet store. Broken grains of rice cost less than half the usual price—a big saving in a household where nearly everyone had five or six bowls of rice a day. But the man at the pet store was puzzled by these huge purchases. "How do the birds you feed eat so much?" the shop owner asked Phuong. She told us her reply: "Well, they are very big birds." We laughed. Then Thây offered me another bowl of rice. I shook my head no. He opened his eyes extra wide and said, "Don't you want the rice to love you?" What could I say? He took my bowl, filled it, and handed it back, saying, "Special delivery!"

One evening a discussion was going on the living room, but I had been given the task that evening of doing the washing up. The pots, pans, and dishes seemed to reach halfway to the ceiling of that narrow kitchen. I felt annoyed—I was stuck with an infinity of dirty dishes while a lively conversation was happening just out of earshot in the living room. Suddenly Nhat Hanh, sensing my irritation, was standing next to me. "Jim," he asked, "what is the best way to wash the dishes?" I knew I was suddenly facing one of those very tricky Zen questions. I tried to think what would be a good Zen answer, but all I could come up with was, "You should wash the dishes to get them clean." "No," said Nhat Hanh. "You should wash the dishes to wash the dishes." Noticing the blank look in my eyes, he then added, "You should wash each dish as if it were the baby Jesus." A light went on. I have been drawing on that advice ever since.

That night Thây brought a book to me and opened it to a reproduction of an old Zen master's painting: a dead, twisted branch coming in from one side, and growing out of it a new and fragile limb, very thin and covered with blossoms. There was no need to know the meaning of the Chinese words, or any words. A Christian might say it was a way of showing the resurrection: life rising out of death. A simple painting of hope, hope as experience, as evident in the gospel of trees as it is in the gospels of words.

I was reminded of some words of Thây's in the introduction to his play, *The Path of Return Continues the Journey*, about the death of four of his school's volunteer workers in 1967:

> *Love enables us to see things which those who are without love cannot see. Who will be gone and who will stay? Where do we come from and where shall we go? Are the other shore and this shore one or two? Is there a river that separates the two sides, a river which no boat can cross? Is such an absurdly complete separation possible? Please come over to my boat. I will show you that there is a river, but there is no separation. Do not hesitate: I will row the boat myself. You can join me in rowing, too, but let us row slowly, and very, very quietly.*

While I was gazing at the Zen painting of the branches, Thây turned the page. No word had been spoken. This time there was a painting of a monkey with large eyes and a face that seemed, in its few brush strokes, full of expectation. There was an oval shape in the water, just beyond the monkey's reach. Thây translated the adjacent Chinese ideographs:

> *The monkey is reaching for the*
> *   moon in the water.*
> *Until death overtakes him, he'll*
> *   never give up.*
> *If he'd let go the branch and*
> *   disappear in the deep pool,*
> *the whole world would shine with*
> *   dazzling pureness.*

I said to Thây that it seemed to me that I had let go of the branch several times, and several times entered into dazzling pureness. That day, I think, Thây had let go of the branch once again. Some new corner in his rebirth process had been turned. The seed had fallen into the ground, died, and now there was a bit of green breaking open the ground's surface.

The next day Thây asked if I would draw a picture in my journal for a new poem he had written. He gave me the English words:

> *Excitedly the sky gives birth to a new dusk.*
> *The blue-eyed bird hops among crystal leaves.*
> *Awakened from forgetfulness*
> *my soul gives birth to a new dawn.*
> *The lake of mind silently reflects a peaceful moon.*

The new sense of hope, of possibility, didn't dilute, however, the painful words that arrived each day in envelopes from Vietnam. In particular there were detailed reports from a senior nun trying to help refugees coming to Buddhist centers near Hue, fleeing US obliteration bombing in Quang Tri province. B-52 raids were reducing towns and villages to ashes and splinters. Those who were escaping did not dare go to Saigon government refugee camps because these were often the target of attacks by the Vietcong, who didn't want the people to believe

Saigon could offer them security even as refugees. But the Buddhist centers—schools, pagodas, and monasteries—while being relatively safe from bomb and mortar attacks, had nothing to offer materially other than what could be begged door to door in the city. One Sunday morning, another letter from the nun arrived. There were now fifteen thousand people, she said, three thousand more than reported in the previous week's letter. Still there was no rice or tins of condensed milk for the infants.

In the same mail came another letter. It bore the return address of a large religious relief organization. The letter's author, though expressing regret for the refugees' difficulties, suggested that the problem be referred to another staff member. "Could you write so-and-so?" he suggested. In fact, Phuong had written so-and-so weeks earlier. It had been his suggestion to address the present correspondent.

"I am really angry," Thây said. His voice was quiet, but the words shook. He held the agency's letter in his hand. Scattered on the floor were photos that had come with the nun's letter. There was a picture of the tents in which the refugees were staying; others were of a mass funeral. A photo that I still remember was of an old woman wandering aimlessly, one trouser leg rolled up. Though the woman had lived her many decades in a very modest culture, she had forgotten her shirt. Much of her hair was gone. Before losing her sanity, she had stood for days in an underground shelter up to her chest in water as the earth shook continuously with the explosion of bombs. All her relatives had been killed, the nun had written on the back. Now, though being cared for in a refugee center, she was wandering with vacant eyes calling the names of her dead children.

Shortly before I left, another harsh blow was struck: the Saigon regime had ordered that Buddhist monks between the ages of eighteen and forty-three be drafted into the army. In several areas pagodas and other Buddhist centers had been surrounded by police, and monks were being taken away at gunpoint. It was a new step in the "Vietnamization" of the war, a favorite term of US presidents and generals.

So it went. The conference that had been my reason for coming to Paris was long over and, in any event, had been peripheral. For me, each day was shaped by Thây and Phuong reading aloud the most recent letters. Events were no longer simply black type on newsprint or gray images on a television screen. They came to us in handwritten letters.

> ...«Is there a river that separates the two
> sides, a river which no boat can cross?
> Is such an absurdly complete
> separation possible?
> Please come over to my boat.
> I will show you that there is a
> river, but there is no separation.
> Do not hesitate:
> I will row the boat myself.
> You can join me in rowing too,
> but let us row slowly,
> and very, very quietly. »
>
> nhat hanh
>
> love enables us to see things which those without love cannot see

Even though the depression of the first two weeks lifted and we were able to laugh with each other over meals and eat more bowls of "special delivery" rice, there were still nights when I watched tears slipping down the side of Phuong's face as she lay under the window on the blankets, staring through the ceiling, Laura reaching out sometimes to touch her foot or hand.

"Please stay longer," Thây said to me when I spoke of returning to the United States. "There are many ways you can help." In the end I stayed for a month, but it was finally Thây who convinced me to leave—not because of anything he said but by his example of putting children first. Vietnamese refugee families living in or near Paris often came to visit. What impressed me most during these encounters was how quickly and easily Thây bonded with the children. No guest was more important. Watching him connect so unreservedly to our youngest visitors, it dawned on me that Ben needed me and I needed Ben and that I was on the wrong side of the ocean. It was a painful realization, all the more so as during those four weeks, Laura and I had fallen in love and decided to marry. We wanted to be together rather than apart. The last thing I wanted was to leave. But the rest of our courtship would have to be by letter rather than face to face.

I flew back to America.

Apprentice Father

Back at Emmaus House, I packed up my books and clothing and moved into what years earlier had been my room in my mother's house in Red Bank, New Jersey. I found it a major challenge to leave the city—I had become a city boy. But my being in Red Bank—for how long wasn't clear—would mean continuity rather than disruption for Ben: his living in the same house, attending the same school, having the same friends, with his grandmother still part of his daily life. The only major change was having his father close at hand rather than (at best) a weekend parent. Ben, now nine, was ecstatic. For me the move was a giant step into adulthood. Thanks to Nhat Hanh's example, I was beginning to become the kind of father that I wished my own father had been for me.

Also it was a good moment to change bases. David Kirk had fallen seriously ill and was in a state of slow recovery. The work of Emmaus House was in recess awaiting his revival. With several others from Emmaus plus Dan Berrigan, I helped establish the Thomas Merton Life Center, a project to make Merton's writings, especially regarding social issues, better known and better practiced. An office was donated to us by Bishop Paul Moore, longtime friend of the Catholic Worker, in the basement of the Episcopal Cathedral of St. John the Divine on the edge of the Columbia University campus. Corpus Christi parish, where Merton had been baptized, was nearby. We were in one of Merton's old neighborhoods.

Along with many other Red Bankers, I began commuting daily to New York. On the occasions when nighttime events made overnight stays necessary, I was given use of a guest room in Bishop Moore's residence on the cathedral grounds.

The Merton Center set up seminars and lectures and took an active role in demonstrations. One of our focal points was helping build support in the New York area for the United Farm Workers Union and its "salad bowl" boycott. It was the largest farm worker strike in American history. The strikers finally won higher wages for the men and women, mainly migrants, who worked for grape and lettuce growers.

In 1973, at Bishop Moore's invitation, Cesar Chavez, leader of the union, came to speak at the cathedral, an event that packed the huge church. Both Dorothy Day and Cardinal Terence Cooke were present. I was standing at her side when Dorothy asked Cooke to donate some unused archdiocesan property that could become a house of hospitality for women. Cooke, clearly taken with the idea and somewhat in awe of Dorothy, promised to investigate and see if some suitable church-owned building might be available. (Eventually, with financial support from a Trappist monastery in upstate New York, a former music school on East Third Street was purchased and converted into the Catholic Worker's Maryhouse. It became Dorothy's last home. She died there in 1980.)

Dan Berrigan with the Thomas Merton Community in New York

Our Merton Center attracted not only people who wanted to know more about Merton but also occasional visitors who had been friends of Merton's, among them the Nicaraguan poet Ernesto Cardenal, once one of Merton's novices. We spent an afternoon in conversation about the monk who had done so much to shape both our lives. A few lines in one of Ernesto's poems recorded our meeting:

> *Jim Forest (a pacifist) with a big mustache*
> *younger than I thought. He wrote me once.*
> *He told me that Merton gave him a crucifix that I made in Gethsemani.*
> *He's in from Washington, from a protest march*
> *from the Watergate building to the Justice Department.*[1]

But of all the activities that I helped with and actions I took part in, my core project in that period of my life was becoming a practicing parent. It was a learning process for both Ben and me. One element of the process was weaning Ben from a TV-centered life into one engaged in outside-the-house activity. I remember Ben resolutely turning off the television after dinner soon after I moved to Red Bank and going out to the backyard where he repeatedly threw a ball into the air and caught it, a solo game needing a second pair of hands. While washing dishes, I watched from the kitchen until, my chore finished, I went out to join him. Playing catch was a connecting step for both of us.

With financial help from Dan Berrigan and the skills of a local carpenter, the attic of my mother's house was converted into an independent apartment. At the time it seemed not only a major achievement but even spacious. With marriage to Laura planned for later in the year, it seemed to me a temporary paradise. I wasn't sure what came next, but felt excited as the path ahead revealed itself.

"Next" proved to be the return to Nyack, New York. I was hired by the Fellowship of Reconciliation to edit their monthly journal, *Fellowship*. I couldn't have been more pleased—I had charge of the principal peace publication in North America. The printer's ink in my veins rejoiced.

The move to Nyack coincided with marriage to Laura, an event that took place at Shadowcliff, the FOR headquarters. We rented a nearby house on the edge of the Hudson. The shift from Red Bank to Nyack was painless for Ben. He enjoyed living a minute's walk from a small boat yard. Laura opened an office at Shadowcliff to raise support for Buddhist relief work in Vietnam.

Our first child, Daniel, was born in October.

---

1. Ernesto Cardenal, *Pluriverse: New and Selected Poems* (New York: New Directions, 2009), 157.

Al Hassler

Among the blessings of being back at the Fellowship of Reconciliation was the close relationship that developed with Al Hassler.

Al had been part of the FOR staff since 1942, when he was hired to edit *Fellowship* magazine. During World War II, he spent two years in prison as a conscientious objector, a story he afterward related with good humor in his first book, *Diary of a Self-Made Convict*. After his release from prison in 1946, he resumed his work as editor of *Fellowship*. In 1958 he was appointed the FOR's executive secretary.

Al was a man who had the rare gift of seeing beyond the day's headlines, crises, and controversies and taking a longer, deeper view. It was an inspired idea of Al's that led, in 1957, to the production of a graphic novel, published in four-color, comic-book format, about the Montgomery Bus Boycott. It was a struggle that had ended victoriously with a Supreme Court ruling against racial segregation in public transportation. It was thanks to the boycott, in which FOR staff played a major role, that Martin Luther King first gained national recognition. It struck Al that here was a story that should be told in the most accessible way possible, something that could attract the interest of kids as well as adults. In consultation with King, Al drafted the text and did a rough layout, then convinced comic-book artist Al Capp and his staff to contribute the artwork. More than a

Al Hassler with grandson Dan

portrait of the first civil rights campaign led by Dr. King, the publication served as a compact introduction to nonviolent methods of social struggle. In the five years that followed, while the civil rights movement steadily expanded, a quarter-million copies were printed and, in later decades, hundreds of thousands more. It remains in print in a variety of languages.

One of Al's later achievements was bringing Thich Nhat Hanh to the world's attention. The two had met in Saigon in 1965. They quickly took to each other. No one else Al had encountered was able to communicate so vividly what the war was like from the standpoint of ordinary Vietnamese people. Yet his was not only an antiwar voice. Nhat Hanh opened a window on the riches of Vietnamese culture, its poetry and music, its food and literature, its wisdom and its form of "engaged Buddhism." A friendship took root that remained important in both their lives.

Al was also among the first to connect work for the protection of the environment with efforts to prevent war, founding Dai Dong in 1969 as a project of the International Fellowship of Reconciliation (IFOR). Dai Dong was Vietnamese for "a world of togetherness," a name chosen in a non-Western language to signal global inclusivity. Dai Dong's first mission was the organization of a meeting in Switzerland of prominent environmental scientists who drafted the Menton Statement, ultimately signed by four thousand of their colleagues in more than forty countries. The text connected environmental issues with the problems of poverty, injustice, militarization, and war. Dai Dong's next step was organizing an independent conference side by side with the first UN Conference on the Environment, held in Stockholm, Sweden, in June 1972. Al was the prime mover.

"If your enemy hungers"—FOR campaign urging food aid to famine victims

Al told me about the Fellowship's China campaign in 1954 and '55.

"There's a story we haven't told very often because it was told to us in great confidence, but that was nearly twenty years ago. There was a famine in China, extremely grave. We urged people to send President Eisenhower small sacks of grain or breakfast cereal. The empty sacks were provided by the FOR with an attached message, 'If your enemy is hungry, feed him. Send surplus food to China.' The campaign got a lot of press attention at the time, but the surplus food was never sent. On the surface our project was an utter failure. But then quite by accident we learned from someone who had been on Eisenhower's press staff that our campaign had been discussed at three separate cabinet meetings. Also discussed at these meetings was a recommendation from the Joint Chiefs of Staff that the United States bomb mainland China in response to the Quemoy-Matsu crisis. [Quemoy and Matsu were islands off the coast of China.] At the third meeting the president turned to a cabinet member responsible for the Food for Peace program and asked, 'How many of those grain bags have come in?' The answer was 45,000, plus tens of thousands of letters. Eisenhower's response was that if that many Americans were trying to find a conciliatory solution with China, it wasn't the time to bomb China. The Pentagon proposal was vetoed. But we learned all this by pure chance! That's the point. You do something and seem to fail—but in the process of failure you sometimes accomplish something else quite unexpected, something of greater importance. As A. J. Muste used to say, 'All the really great things in history came as a surprise. Nobody predicted them.'"

I once asked Al about a somewhat battered, sentimentalized word, "love." "For a long time," Al responded, "we tried to point out that there were different kinds of love—*agape* and *eros*—but that really doesn't come across to most people. When you talk about love, people think of a very intimate sort of relationship, but that's manifestly impossible with each of the billions of people alive today—or even more the one person who is doing something extraordinarily destructive.

"The three elements that are essential to an understanding of love are compassion, humility, and understanding—compassion in the sense of awareness, sensitivity, and understanding of other persons and their weaknesses, even the ones you think are very strong—their mortality, their limitations, the fact that they suffer in ways we don't know about or understand—and humility in understanding just how narrow is the gap between people we regard as morally good—ourselves!—and the people whom we regard as morally bad—*them*—the ones who oppose us.

"You can't get anywhere with it unless you realize that love means understanding and compassion—then it opens up. Compassion, not in the sense of lessening your opposition to Hitler, for example, and what he is doing, but compassion for a man who clearly had suffered terribly, who was terribly distorted, who had so little real happiness and joy.

"[The writer] Milton Mayer has written about a Quaker meeting for worship at which A. J. Muste stood up and said, 'If I can't love Hitler, I can't love at all.' The equivalent for us would be to say, 'If I can't love Richard Nixon, I cannot love at all.' In the case of someone like Nixon you only have to look at any of the hundreds of recent pictures of Nixon to see the suffering that he's going through, a suffering that he probably doesn't yet understand—a man who doesn't understand himself, his personality, or the reaction of people to him—a man who really feels that he is being persecuted. You can only feel sorry for him. You can only feel compassion even as you resist the destruction he is causing.

With several co-workers (including Nancy Flier, at the right) at FOR headquarters in Nyack

"That's the essence of pacifism for me. The realization that we are, as it's put in the New Testament, 'all sinners who have fallen short of the glory of God.' We have no right to be self-righteous, but only to be pitying, compassionate, helpful. But of course we fail at this all the time. Pacifism is an aspiration, not an achievement."

An Island Surrounded
by Footlights

Perhaps the best part of being *Fellowship*'s editor was that my work brought me into frontline contact with peacemakers willing to put their own lives at risk in order to protect others. In the summer of 1976, I spent a month in Europe, in part to report on a conflict that was costing many lives in Northern Ireland.

Arriving in Belfast, I soon realized green was a perilous color. In the Protestant parts of Belfast, I would have been better off not wearing a green jacket, while in the Catholic neighborhoods my orange backpack was not a prudent color choice. In fractured societies, colors are often charged with political meaning.

Armored British military vehicles resembling giant black beetles patrolled the streets. Skull-like ruined buildings gave the city a cemetery appearance. Remnants of walls were spray painted with paramilitary images and slogans. There was more fear in the air than oxygen. A bored soldier took aim at me with his rifle, then grinned and gave me a friendly wave. No one entered Belfast that summer complacent about leaving alive.

Belfast was on the knife-edge of civil war. In one isolated Catholic area that I visited, a peninsula of houses was surrounded on three sides by Protestants. In recent days Catholic families had been heaping heavy furniture against the doors before going to bed to make it harder for armed intruders to break in.

I was twice arrested by British military forces, once near the cramped little house of a Catholic priest and peace worker, Desmond Wilson, with whom I was staying, and once in the barricaded city center after taking a photo of a soldier guarding at a heavily fortified checkpoint.

"We're all on stage," Desmond Wilson told me. "Ireland is the only country in the world entirely surrounded by footlights. The only problem is that not all the players leave the stage alive."

On the first night of my visit Father Desmond's living room was packed with twenty or so local Catholics along with a Protestant politician, Bob Cooper, a large, calm man who had recently resigned the leadership of the Alliance Party in order to direct a British-funded agency whose task was to end discrimination in employment. Breathing air that was dense with cigarette smoke, he absorbed polite ridicule. He was accused of being "British window dressing camouflaging the Troubles" and an obstruction to work on "real problems." He never hurried to reply and made no effort to glamorize his work or minimize what he was up against. Inevitably, he agreed, when fears and animosities can be swept under religious labels, discrimination based on religious prejudice is easy to come by. So far as jobs are concerned, Catholics were at the back of the line, and Protestant Cooper didn't hesitate to say so.

In the hypernervous world of Northern Ireland, one was either Protestant or Catholic. "If you're an atheist," Desmond explained, "then you're either a Protestant atheist or a Catholic atheist." But was it in fact a religious war? I heard it argued both ways, dogmatically and passionately, by Protestant and Catholic alike. There were Protestants, like the notorious Reverend Ian Paisley, who saw it largely in religious terms. What about loving your enemy? Paisley argued there was no biblical mandate to love the anti-Christ, that the pope is just that, and his followers were burdened with the same curse and fate. He had his Catholic counterparts, raised in a rigid catechism that preaches no salvation outside the Roman Catholic Church—*Extra ecclesiam nulla salus*—and to hell, literally, with all the others.

But such parochially justified mercilessness wasn't the norm. "When they shoot at us," as one bitter man put it to me, "they're not shooting at us because we're Catholics. It just happens that we're all Catholics." It just happens. The labels had to do with different pasts, different ancestors, different sets of sufferings and injustices—all complicated by the poverty of Northern Ireland and the resultant job competition. The extreme—and quite ecumenical—unemployment was linked with festering memories of a brutal history. The Catholics, even those who hadn't been in church since their childhood except for weddings and funerals, tenaciously remembered the earlier centuries when the death sentence was passed for mere possession of a crucifix or rosary or any hint of "Romanism." And the Protestants recalled the steep price paid in blood and suffering by their ancestors for trying to build a reformed church and a state that respected their consciences. It wasn't a religious war, but there were no convenient labels to turn to in describing the war's borders other than Protestant and Catholic. Religious labels marked tribal borders.

The nighttime noise of bombs exploding made sleep elusive. Bomb blasts were common events. I talked with a mother whose young son had recently been severely injured by a bomb planted next to a toilet on a Dublin-bound train.

I spent several days in the care of Will Warren, a retired seventy-year-old English Quaker who had spent the past five years searching for ways to end the violence. Financial support for his work came from the Fellowship of Reconciliation of Northern Ireland. Will was a plainspoken man who had no university degrees. He had worked in print shops, read galley proofs, known unemployment. He became a pacifist during World War I when his father, a Baptist deacon, "got in trouble for thinking Jesus wasn't in favor of killing." At the time his father thought that he was the only pacifist in the world. During the next war, Will recalls his mother's refusal to sign a petition that circulated in their neighborhood after German bombs destroyed several local homes, including that of the Warren family. The petition called on the government to take retaliatory action on German cities—the British counterblitz hadn't yet begun. For not signing, no local shopkeeper would wait on her. Will had to do all the family shopping afterward.

"I came here with the intention of talking to the men of violence, to try to talk them into renouncing violence or at least using less of it," Will explained. In fact, while it had taken years to build up a degree of trust, he had made headway. He served, on occasion, as an intermediary between opposing paramilitary groups. "There are people alive today who wouldn't be if I hadn't been here," he said, with no vanity in the statement. He felt guilty that on at least one occasion he had saved the life of a man accused of being a British spy by suggesting he be "knee-capped" instead. "I saved his life but wasn't able to save his legs!"

Will and I visited a home in Derry (or Londonderry, as Protestants preferred) where there was a Catholic crucifix on one wall and under it the complete works of Stalin. The one volume I opened creaked loudly—it had never been opened. "Those books," our hostess told me, "were a gift from another visitor, someone from Russia, I think. But I have no time to read." There were no other books in the house. Her husband was in prison, his wife struggling to raise the children and keep her small council house tidy. While pouring a cup of tea for us, she described how a prison guard had grabbed one of her sons by his hair and lifted him off the floor when he attempted to hug his father, a forbidden intimacy. "In such small cruelties seeds of future violence are planted," Will later commented.

Through Will I met Duncim Murphy, whose job was to find ways to bring kids from the two communities together in hopes that bonds would begin to develop. The previous night he had been in a local pub when a bomb exploded. "What do you do," I asked, "when a bomb explodes?" "You feel your arms. They're okay. You feel your legs. They're okay. You feel your eyes and ears. They're okay. If they're okay, you order another beer." He laughed. "One thing both sides have in common is a taste for Guinness! And both sides like to target pubs."

I asked if he was hopeful that one day there will be peace in Northern Ireland. How would it come about?

He gave a bitter response. "What will it take? Drop the atom bomb on Belfast. Start over again with Adam and Eve. Then it'll be four or five thousand years before there's another civil war here."

The only hope Duncim could find for ending the conflict was a mobilization of the mothers. "They're the only ones who can solve it. If you had twenty thousand mothers out, who's going to shoot them? Mothers without weapons—they could maintain the peace." (His words were prophetic. Weeks later Mairead Corrigan and Betty Williams led a mothers' march for peace that brought thirty-five thousand people, mainly women, to the streets of Belfast, an event that many regard as having prevented civil war. The following year Corrigan and Williams were awarded the Nobel Prize for Peace.)

As Duncim put it in Belfast, "We have to keep building bridges. When you take a life, you can't give it back. There are no nine lives, not for cats and not for people. One's all you get. It's priceless."

No One Should Die

"If you're looking for peace," I've often joked, "avoid the peace movement." One of the ironies of working for peace is that it puts the would-be peacemaker in a social context in which conflict can be intense and nasty. At times I've speculated that the peace movement's main contribution to world peace may be that it absorbs some of the planet's most hot-tempered people and keeps them a safe distance from lethal weapons. Movements of dissent attract people who are in a relationship of dissent not only with various aspects of mainstream society but often with one another.

Among the more painful conflicts I've been part of grew out of my conviction that unborn children, however small, dependent, and unfinished, are human beings and deserve protection before delivery no less than afterward—thus every effort should be made to find alternatives to abortion without criminalizing those who, in desperation, have abortions.

"The means are the end in the process of becoming" is a truism that happens to be true. Violent methods, such as abortion, have destructive consequences. It is because of the radical conviction that killing is not the route to the creation of a better world that peace groups like the Fellowship of Reconciliation have opposed not only war but capital punishment. And yet the FOR is far from the only peace group that has taken no stand for or against abortion. Over the years there has been close to nothing in FOR publications about abortion as a topic that deserves attention, discussion, and response among all those who think all human life ought to be safeguarded.

Every now and then editors get the opportunity to risk their jobs. Probably the bravest thing I did during the several years I edited *Fellowship* (mid-1973 to December 1976) was to publish an article by Dan

Berrigan on this ultracontroversial topic. The occasion was a special issue of *Fellowship* following the capture of Saigon by Hanoi-backed forces on April 30, 1975. That day the Vietnam War ended abruptly. It was an event involving the hurried withdrawal of American civilian and military personnel in Saigon, along with many South Vietnamese civilians who were linked with the defeated regime, in the largest helicopter evacuation in history. The war had cost more than a million Vietnamese lives, tens of thousands of them children, plus nearly sixty thousand American lives. Millions more had been wounded both in body and soul. Vast areas of Vietnam's countryside had been drenched in blood and polluted with toxic chemicals.

After more than a decade of war in Indochina, it was a no-brainer that I needed to put together a special issue of *Fellowship* on this long-awaited event. Dan Berrigan was one of seventeen prominent antiwar activists to whom I sent this brief invitation: "The war's end offers a moment for meditation on the lessons to be learned, the amnesia to be avoided, and the ways in which we can better become a peacemaking community."

Dan's unexpected response was an appeal to peace activists, as a next step, to focus our energies on saving unborn lives from death by abortion. I knew I was putting not only Dan but myself on the firing line in publishing it. Here's what Dan wrote:

"I am struck recently by the harrowing fact that the chief assault [in war] is against children. A sentence of Dietrich Bonhoeffer keeps invading me: 'How are the unborn to live?' When I go to my theological class here in Detroit, my classroom window faces a sign: 'Abortions'—and a phone number. As though one were offering groceries, tax advice, or used cars. It strikes me that Bonhoeffer's sentence takes on a new horrific resonance. How are the unborn to live? . . . In the past five years . . . some two million nearly-born people in our midst have been so disposed of. Perhaps someday soon people who did get born may invade such centers, where doctors relieve women of the unwelcome burden named You or I. . . .

"Maybe we have a few new questions about old matters. Is our morality in any sense superior to that of those ancient peoples who commonly exposed the newborn to death? Can we help everyone walk into the full spectrum and rainbow of life, from womb to old age, so that no one is expendable? Especially in the religious pacifist community, we who believe no political idolatry can excuse the taking of life, can we help remind and symbolize the splendid range of nonviolence: from before birth to the aged?

"How do we remind people, our people, of the virulence of short-term solutions, 'definitive solutions'? . . . Was not our first political act just getting born? . . .

"What I'm asking is whether pacifists might risk, as we have already risked so much on other unpalatable questions, rethinking the acceptance of abortion? . . . We have had to raise hard questions in the past about the readiness of so much of the 'peace' movement to see death occur, so long as the perpetrator is a 'liberator.' May we not also helpfully question other current dogmas of our western, war-ridden, itchy, competing and mechanistic selves?

"Maybe in mutual nurture of unwanted life, male and female rage can join their lost longing, in an old Christian, Jewish, Buddhist teaching . . . and say, 'No one should die!' Maybe the most hopeful statement [we can make] is a nonviolent statement, 'Everyone should live.'"[1]

Portrait of Dan Berrigan by Robert McGovern

Predictably, publishing Dan's article got me into a great deal of hot water with many friends and colleagues and put me at risk of unemployment, as I told Dan by phone a week after the issue's publication. "Sorry to hear it, but not at all surprised," said Dan. "I've been getting some heat too. I expected it. Beware of irate pacifists! Being pro-abortion has become the litmus test for being pro-woman." Dan noted how words, phrases, and slogans have been enlisted to dehumanize the human beings in the womb. "It's an unborn child only if it's wanted—if unwanted it's demoted to embryo or fetus. To dare recognizing that it's an unborn child, and thus deserves protection, is to be against choice, and choice is what the American way of life—and way of death—is all about."

---

1. Complete text is in Jim Forest, *At Play in the Lions' Den: A Biography and Memoir of Daniel Berrigan* (Maryknoll, NY: Orbis Books, 2017), 206–8.

Nearly half a century has passed, but the abortion debate remains as divisive as ever. One aspect of the problem is the fact that so many people who militantly oppose abortion are passionately pro-death in other contexts. How rare are those who are consistently pro-life, that is, trying in every arena and every stage of life to prevent killing, thus opposing the death penalty, war, euthanasia, abortion, death caused by social neglect, and attacks on the environment. Dan was one of the few peace advocates to be as concerned for inhabitants of the womb as for Vietnamese peasants under attack. His inclusive concern for any threatened life in every context made him a minority even within minorities—and me as well.

With Ben, Dan Berrigan, and Ed Kehoe, in Nyack, 1976

To See, or Not to See . . .

One of the most bizarre experiences I had during my years working with various peace organizations was the opposition I encountered from a number of fellow antiwar activists when I began circulating reports Thich Nhat Hanh had shared with me concerning human rights violations in postwar, reunified, Marxist Vietnam.

One of the documents Nhat Hanh sent me was a letter from twelve nuns who, on November 2, 1975, immolated themselves as a protest against the Hanoi regime's antireligious, repressive measures. Nhat Hanh's monastic sources reported that hundreds of thousands of people were being detained—not only men and women associated with the defeated Saigon government, as one might expect, but Buddhist monks and lay people who had previously been jailed by the defeated Saigon regime. Additional corroborative evidence of heavy-handed repression came from reports by such respected French journalists as Jean Lacouture and Patrice De Beer, both of whom had spent considerable time in Vietnam during the war and who became the first Western journalists allowed into the country by the Hanoi government.

The information led me to write an article for *Fellowship*, "Reunification without Reconciliation," and soon after, in the late summer of 1976, to draft a letter addressed to Hanoi's prime minister urging the government to open its cosmetically labeled "re-education camps" for inspection by staff of Amnesty International and the International Red Cross. Here are the key paragraphs:

> *Beginning soon after the victory of North Vietnam and the Provisional Revolutionary Government in the Spring of 1975, and sharply increasing in recent months, reports have reached us indicating grievous and systematic violations of human rights by your government. The evidence is too specific and persuasive for us to ignore.*

Especially with regard to those imprisoned or otherwise detained, in May a Vietnamese official stated that 200,000 were being held in re-education camps while some respected foreign journalists in Vietnam have estimated 300,000 detainees. The actions of your government constitute a great disappointment to all those who expected . . . an example of reconciliation built on tolerance. We realize that those held include individuals responsible for aspects of the war and the repressive mechanisms of the former Saigon government. But, having believed your fervent past expressions of commitment to human rights, we are deeply saddened to hear of the arrest and detention of a wide range of persons, including religious, cultural and political figures who opposed the Saigon government despite considerable personal risks . . . [various names were cited].

Differences among us on what could be hoped for in the revolution's victory did not in the past hamper our solidarity in opposing America's intervention. Our agreement, then and now, transcends differences in ideology and analysis, being firmly grounded in our concern for the lives of the Vietnamese people. We have recognized that the credibility of our witness is related to the candor with which we demonstrate our concerns and our commitment to certain ethical precepts regardless of politics. . . .

We therefore call upon you to honor the concern for human rights which you have expressed both in formal agreements and in countless conversations with peace activists. We call for a complete public accounting of those detained or imprisoned indicating, as well, the charges for which they are held. We call on the government of Vietnam to facilitate on-the-spot inspection by the United Nations, Amnesty International, the International Red Cross or other independent international agencies in order to assure that those in the government's charge are treated in accord with international covenants regarding human rights. We call on you to release any individuals who are held purely because of their religious or political convictions. We call for government recognition of the right to open and free communication.

The letter was cosigned by ninety prominent war resisters, including Joan Baez, Robert Bly, Tom Cornell, Dorothy Day, Richard Deats, James and Shelley Douglass, Bishop Carroll Dozier, Daniel Ellsberg, Robert Ellsberg, Howard Fast, Allen Ginsberg, Bishop Thomas Gumbleton, Al Hassler, Ken Kesey, Alice and Staughton Lynd, W. S. Merwin, Paul O'Dwyer, Ira Sandperl, Rabbi Steven Schwarzschild, Gary

Snyder, Allan Solomonow, Mobi Warren, Rabbi Arnold Jacob Wolf, and Howard Zinn.

I had no premonition of the firestorm the letter would ignite, with myself at ground zero. Though I was only one of the drafters, the document became known as "the Forest Appeal."

Several noted antiwar activists accused me of being a CIA agent. I ought to be sent to a re-education camp myself, one of them declared. "Should you pursue the matter," a member of the national staff of the American Friends Service Committee in Philadelphia warned me, "it will cost you your career in the peace movement." Until that moment I had no idea I had a "career"—I thought of what I was doing as a vocation. Even Dan and Phil Berrigan, who had been among the first to sign the appeal, decided to unsign it. (Dan later apologized and wrote his own appeal to the Hanoi authorities.)

Dave Dellinger, with whom I had worked closely during my year with *Liberation* magazine, accused me of "circulating every remotely credible rumor . . . that would discredit the new Vietnamese government." Louis Schneider, executive secretary of the American Friends Service Committee, wrote a letter to all signers of the appeal saying that the evidence offered in the letter "is either open to serious question or is insufficiently substantiated in order to be able to make particular allegations concerning certain individuals who may have suffered a loss of human rights. Indeed, in certain instances, including the alleged immolation, there is contradictory information. Until such questions are dispelled or more authentic documentation is adduced, our colleagues demur to subscribe either to generalizations or to representations on behalf of particular individuals who may have been cited."

Happily, there was a good deal of support as well. Joan Baez called me one morning to describe the intense pressure she was under to withdraw her signature and wanted to assure me that she had no intention of doing so. Then, to cheer me up, she sang a newly written song over the phone. To a distinguished friend who warned her of my possible CIA employment, Joan had responded, "Jim Forest is much too nice—and much too disorganized—to work for the CIA."

In fact how does one prove he isn't working for the CIA? I quickly realized that denial only adds fuel to the fires of suspicion. The only thing one can do is joke about it.

In an open letter explaining why he and his wife Alice were not withdrawing their signatures, historian Staughton Lynd wrote, "Any revolutionary government finds itself much less threatened by the ordinary adherents of the overthrown regime, who often enough have opportunistic motives for throwing their support to the new men of power, than by persons who opposed the old regime for principled reasons other than the reasons of the victors. It is this kind of person who fares worst the day after the revolution. In Russia, the Social Revolutionaries, the Workers Opposition, the Kronstadt rebels were persons of this kind."

The appeal and list of signers was hand delivered by Robert Ellsberg and myself to the office of the Vietnamese ambassador to the UN on November 16. On December 29, a press conference to make the appeal public was held by the International League for Human Rights not far from the UN headquarters in New York. The issues addressed by the appeal, said Roger Baldwin, president of the league, "cover suppression of language held to be critical of the [Hanoi] government or its policies, thus contravening Article 19 of the Universal Declaration of Human Rights. In similar fashion, other articles of the Declaration appear to be violated in the detention of political prisoners solely for activities not involving violence or organized opposition."

During the acrimonious months in which debate raged, it became increasingly clear how divisive the issue of human rights can be, even shattering friendships. People who had marched hand in hand in anti-war demonstrations, and even shared the same cell for acts of resistance, found themselves furiously at odds when confronted with reports of systematic human rights violations in postwar Vietnam. To see, or not to see. . . .

For me, the affair, though exhausting, was an education. While I had occasionally been labeled a Communist by those on the right, I had never before been accused of being a CIA agent. For many political radicals, outrage at human rights violations was limited mainly, even solely, to America and its allies. In most cases, the more left-leaning one was, the more determined to see the Hanoi regime through rose-colored glasses. The violation of human rights in "socialist" countries tended to be ignored, denied, or even justified.

Did my initiative cost me my "career" in the peace movement? Not at all, although I've never been career minded. Two days after the press conference I was in the air on a Holland-bound flight where for the coming twelve years I would lead the staff of the International Fellowship of Reconciliation.

European Migrant

Since its founding in 1919, the headquarters of the International Fellowship of Reconciliation had moved time and time again, most often to get out of the way of war. Over the decades its bases had included Vienna, London, Berlin, Paris, Copenhagen, and most recently Belgium's capital city. Now IFOR was poised for another move. The immediate reason was that the staff had never felt welcome in Brussels. "We've been here three years," one of them told me, "and not once been invited to anyone's house for a meal! We might as well be in a space station."

Besides meeting with peacemakers in Northern Ireland, one of my responsibilities during my European trip in the summer of 1976 had been to visit several IFOR branches—in Italy, France, Germany, Britain, and Holland—in search of a better place from which the secretariat could carry on its work of representing, connecting, and strengthening the IFOR-associated groups that circled the globe. In each country I found a warm welcome, but in terms of legal structures (getting visas and work permits for a multinational staff, arranging housing, and solving other practical problems) it didn't take long to realize that Holland offered the most supportive environment. Since the late nineteenth century, Holland had been a place of welcome for initiatives seeking the peaceful settlement of international disputes. The first Hague Peace Conference had been held there in 1899. The International Court of Justice had been established in The Hague in 1945. Just after the First World War, Holland had also been IFOR's birthplace.

But where in Holland? Amsterdam had seemed the obvious place, but visiting friends in nearby Alkmaar made that smaller city a promising alternative. The Hof van Sonoy, a landmark in the city center that had once been the Monastery of St. Mary Magdalene, was undergoing restoration. Its trustees were looking for tenants doing nonprofit work. One wing of the three-sided structure was offered to us—more space than we had in Brussels, an attractive environment, low rent, and within walking distance of the train station and post office. The location, the enthusiasm of our two Dutch branches, and the readiness of local friends to lend a helping hand made Alkmaar an easy choice.

At the same time, IFOR was seeking a new person to head the staff. I applied and, in the autumn of 1976, was appointed. The only major problem was that IFOR was close to penniless. The treasurer, Peter Eterman, warned me that he could only guarantee my salary for six months. "Are you and Laura sure," he asked, "that you want to make so big a move with so small a safety net beneath you? You'll be diving into a pool with almost no water in it." Without hesitation we decided to make the plunge. Among other things it would put Laura on the same side of the Atlantic as her retired parents, now part of a retirement community in Spain. We would also be close to Nhat Hanh. For my part, it was a long-held wish to live in Europe. In my thirty-five years of life I had often changed addresses, but never had I been more excited about making a move.

On the first day of January 1977, our family—now with two small children, Daniel and Wendy, plus Ben, in his teens—boarded a night flight to Amsterdam. Shortly after dawn the next morning, our friends in Alkmaar, Kirsten and Thomas Roep, met the flight and drove us to the two-floor apartment on the city's west edge that had been rented on our behalf. It had been a last-minute find—the only furnishings in place were several foam mattresses, a few chairs, a small table, dishes, glasses, pots and pans, and an old refrigerator containing such basics as bread, milk, butter and cheese. A bare light bulb dangled from the ceiling of each room. It was an austere start.

Grateful for the mattresses, we decided to take a nap, but I found myself too excited to sleep. Europe had suddenly

Reading a story to Wendy and Dan

become my home address, though I had no idea at the time that I would still be here in my old age.

While the rest of the family slept, I set off for a walk into the heart of the city. As I walked, the buildings—all of them of brick—gradually got older, smaller, and more tightly packed. Smaller canals flowed into larger ones. A major canal circled the old town; once there had been a substantial defensive wall there, but now it was a park. I passed an eighteenth-century windmill, its blades turning. A little farther on was Alkmaar's oldest major structure, the former cathedral of St. Laurence, completed in 1518. After the Reformation, the patron saint had been disowned, the altar removed, and statues smashed. The huge Gothic structure became simply the *Grote Kerk*, the Great Church, used for Calvinist worship. A hundred meters farther on was the *stadhuis*, the town hall, nearly as old as the church. The canal-wrapped, island-like core of the city was crowded with shops. At a shop that sold bikes, I bought a three-speed model and rode it back to our apartment. At last I was tired enough to sleep.

Connections occurred quickly. In less than a week Ben and Dan were placed in local schools and soon began speaking Dutch—words, phrases, whole sentences. (I found most younger Dutch people spoke English, often fluently. They had learned it not only in classrooms but from television. Many programs and films originated in the United States or Britain and were broadcast with Dutch subtitles.)

We soon found used furniture at a nonprofit cooperative, where household items, small and large, were received from donors and arranged by the all-volunteer staff in a former warehouse and sold at very low prices to immigrants, students, and others pinching their guilders. The income received was donated to projects in developing countries. Our purchases included an old open-top washing machine with built-in wringer costing only twenty guilders. By the end of the month we had furnished the apartment.

The IFOR wing of Hof van Sonoy in Alkmaar

As days turned into weeks and months, Dutch culture slowly disclosed itself. What impressed me most was the social solidarity. Social structures revealed a sense that everyone is better off when no one is abandoned. No one was excluded from health care. Everyone had a family doctor. No one was sleeping on the streets at night. Beggars were close to non-existent. Public transportation was excellent—frequent buses and trains to every region and town, plus tram networks in the largest cities.

Besides public transportation, there were bike paths everywhere, a web of thousands of kilometers, and such a thing as rush-hour traffic on major biking routes. For more than a third of the population, bikes were, and still are, the principal mode of transport. Many people have more than one—a sturdy model for everyday use, a bike that folds up and can be brought on board trains, a racing bike, a bike designed to carry several children, etc. In today's population of seventeen million, there are an estimated twenty-two million working bikes.

I found that the Dutch were blunt but not rude, self-critical, and more inclined to problem solving than dreaming of utopia. There was a startling lack of privacy—I could walk down a street in the evening and, due to the uncurtained front windows, follow a TV program from living room to living room. "It's all because of Dutch Calvinism," joked our friend Kirsten Roep, a Dane by birth. "They need to show they're not sinning." Another friend said Calvinism had nothing to do with it: "The Dutch have a passion for windows and light, as the paintings of Johannes Vermeer and many other Golden Age artists bear witness. Given a choice between light and privacy, Dutch people tend to choose light."

One of Holland's surprises was that its abortion rate was so low—less than half that of the United States. A major factor is that sex education and birth control are something Dutch kids learn a lot about in school. Another factor is that social support for young mothers and single mothers is strong and solid. No one is abandoned. Health services leave no one out. It's not a sink-or-swim culture. The Dutch tend to be pragmatic. In regard to abortion, the question here is, What can we do to make abortion less common? The slogan of the main pro-life organization, VBOK, is, "There is help for *both* mother and child."

The Dutch are generally thought of as mainly Protestant, but in fact, the Catholic Church is the largest religious body in the Netherlands. But the joke is that every Dutch person is at base a Calvinist, even the atheists. "Scratch a Dutchman, find a Calvinist," a Dutch journalist told me. "One Calvinist trait is that we're embarrassed by outward signs of wealth. We're not impressed by status—even the queen and prime minister ride bikes. We favor moderation. Look at our beer glasses—they're much smaller than beer glasses in Germany or Belgium." (Four decades later the beer glasses are somewhat bigger.)

In 1977, "pillarization" was still in evidence. Pillarization was the practice of organizing life along sectarian lines to minimize social friction. A town might have a Catholic baker, a Protestant baker, and a secular baker; a Catholic school, a Protestant school, and a secular school. There were Catholic, Protestant, and secular TV and radio stations and a similar division of newspapers. By chance the first bike I purchased came from a Protestant bike shop. The two men working in the shop's repair section were singing "A Mighty Fortress is our God" while changing bike tires. (Traces of pillarization still exist, but the invisible walls that once stood so firmly are now full of holes.)

Town and city borders ended abruptly. Biking out of Alkmaar, one saw houses stop as if on a razor line—one was suddenly on narrow roads winding through farm fields. In this densely populated country, there was little sense of anything being where it is by accident. I half expected to find a microscopic registration number imprinted on each blade of grass.

Though I found the Dutch to be quite proud of their national identity, *patriotisme* was a word I rarely heard. In contrast with America, the Dutch flag was very little in evidence, even in classrooms, except on national holidays. Ben was surprised that his school day began without anyone saluting the flag or reciting a pledge of allegiance.

The Dutch are famous for toleration. Our friend Thomas Roep, professor of geology at the University of Amsterdam, credited Dutch collaborative social structures and tolerance of minorities to geography and water: "Dutch tolerance isn't sentimental or liberal—'I'm this and you're that but in the end, it really doesn't matter.' No, it's more, 'I'm going to heaven and you're going to hell, but in this world it's common sense that I cooperate with you because otherwise the dikes will break and we will all drown together.' Nearly a third of the country is below sea level, and nearly two-thirds of the land is engaged in a daily argument with the North Sea and the major rivers. From the start Holland's survival has required everyone's cooperation. Dutch water boards [independent bodies responsible for managing dikes, waterways, water levels, water quality, and sewage treatment in their particular regions] are among the oldest democratic structures in Europe."

In my corner of the IFOR office

The Dutch experience is that tolerance is a better solution than intolerance. Red-light districts have long been a fixture in every city and the larger towns, as it has seemed a more real-world solution than attempted suppression of prostitution. Similarly, for generations marijuana has been available at "coffee shops" in any sizable community, the alternative being a black market in weed, underworld involvement, and lots of young people in jail.

I had never experienced so democratic a society. It was not, as in the United States, a winner-take-all political system in which third parties are irrelevant and losers lose big. The Dutch government is always a fusion of several parties. There are more than a dozen parties, some to the right, some to the left, some in the wobbly center, some secular, and others with religious roots, each party with its own base and topics of concentration. Even very small parties are of consequence. If a party receives 0.67 percent of the vote, it means it has one person in Parliament. The ballot caster can vote for a party that he or she actually identifies with. So many of my votes in the United States had been for the person I thought was the least dangerous candidate, not for someone I actually supported.

Holland—a country smaller than Pennsylvania—never ceases to surprise me. When I arrived here, my crystal ball wasn't in sharp focus. I had imagined being here for three years, perhaps five. As I write these words, I've lived in this land of windmills, tulips, canals, and wooden shoes for forty-two years. It's long since become home. In 1995 Nancy and I became Dutch citizens.

Few of life's major events are premeditated. As we say in our family, "Life is what happens after you plan it."

Caring for Marigolds

With help from our two Dutch branches and local volunteers, the IFOR secretariat was quickly up and running. Our furnishings and files had been trucked from Brussels to Alkmaar in late December. A working office with a four-person staff became functional by the second week of January.

It was a sink-or-swim period, as there were serious divisions among the branches regarding IFOR's direction and identity. If IFOR was to survive, we needed to renew our mission as well as strengthen the bonds linking our twenty-seven branches and five affiliated groups in Europe, Asia, Africa, and North and South America. We had a rich history to look back on—our membership had included many heroes of nonviolent action, six of them recipients of the Nobel Prize for Peace. But in recent years many branches had been reducing their support, with some unsure that IFOR's work merited future funding. IFOR was close to broke. Renewal was urgently needed.

The major immediate task for our small staff was to prepare a five-day IFOR Council meeting that would convene in April at a conference center belonging to Dutch Mennonites and located northwest of Alkmaar in the dunes of Schoorl.

A core issue that needed sorting out at the council had to do with religious identity. IFOR had been founded by deeply committed Christians whose efforts at peacemaking were a form of discipleship. Nearly all of its branches remained Christian. The Fellowship of Reconciliation in the United States, the largest branch, was the most significant exception—since the late sixties its membership included Jews, Unitarians, Humanists, and Buddhists. IFOR had adopted a more secular self-definition and been nudging its resistant Christian branches to widen their membership borders. In place of a religious emphasis, for nearly a decade IFOR had stressed a commitment to nonviolence as providing us with sufficient common ground, but it wasn't working. Promoting nonviolence is not equivalent to a faith whose center point is Jesus. The result had been frustrating meetings at which the Christians felt it necessary to adopt a secular vocabulary that wasn't their own, while the non-Christians tried to modify their input so as not to offend Christians. Few felt they were in a hospitable space.

Aware of the tensions, Thich Nhat Hanh suggested we start the council meeting with a procession in which each participant carried a green, flowering plant. "Plants are sensitive to the emotions of nearby people, as has been demonstrated by scientists," he said. "They do not thrive in rooms where people hurl reproachful words at each other or glare at each other. Let each person be responsible for one plant." While a member from Switzerland played a violin, we each took a flowering marigold in our hands, felt its soil, placed it in a pot, and took responsibility for the growth of our own and each other's plants in the days ahead.

We were fifty delegates, young and old, of every skin color, representing eighteen countries and seventeen national branches plus our Latin American affiliate, Servicio Paz y Justicia.

Much that was said was memorable. The representative of the FOR in India, K. V. Mathew, commented on how striking it was that so many peace activists in the "developed" world showed signs of exhaustion and quiet despair, while those from poorer countries seemed empowered with hope. Cao Ngoc Phuong, representing the Unified Buddhist Church of Vietnam, described the sufferings that had been endured by young peace workers in her home country, who were sometimes targets of the US-allied Saigon regime and sometimes of the Vietcong yet "without hesitation put themselves in places of great danger and died for it." Argentinean Emilio Castro, president of the World Council of Churches, urged closer collaboration between IFOR and the WCC in developing nonviolent approaches to such social crises as apartheid in South Africa. Will and Nelly Warren, from the FOR in Northern Ireland, spoke about "the slow but necessary business of building links between paramilitaries, whether Catholic or Protestant, not simply writing them off as 'terrorists' but seeing in them their humanness and capacity for constructive work."

Listening to such voices, no one needed reminding that structures like IFOR were urgently needed. Our immediate task was a fresh declaration of IFOR's purpose and program. The basic text we finally agreed on was reassuring both to those groups whose membership was entirely Christian as well as to those with wider borders:

"The International Fellowship of Reconciliation is a transnational religious community committed to nonviolence as a principle of life for a world community of peace and liberation. Our vision is rooted in the various traditions of faith from which we are drawn. We who are Christians have found our way to this community through the teaching and example of Jesus, the power of self-giving love made visible on the cross and in the new life of the resurrection. We who are Jews have found our way through the interventions of God in our history, in our journeys out of captivity to the God who offers liberation. We who are Buddhists have found our way through the path of compassion and service. We who are Gandhians have found our way in such experiments with truth as were begun by Gandhi in South Africa and India. Whatever our convictions, whether traditional or nontraditional, we know we have in common membership in one creation, one family, one deep longing for a world of sharing and community. . . ."

Several program priorities were agreed on: disarmament work, promotion of human rights, and promotion of alternatives to nuclear energy. Work groups for Africa, India, Latin America, and Northern Ireland were established. A "Peace Press Project" was envisioned to more effectively bring news of nonviolent actions and campaigns to public attention.

The drafting of statements and setting of program priorities was necessary work, but more important was the sense that a fresh wind was blowing into IFOR's sails. The council participants left smiling and excited. National branches pledged increased financial support. And what about the plants? They thrived during those five days. I had rarely been so refreshed by a peace movement gathering. The council concluded with a Quaker-style silent meeting for worship followed by the planting of our yellow and orange marigolds in the grounds around the conference center. The experiment had worked. By holding ourselves accountable for the well-being of the marigolds, we had been more attentive and caring to each other. IFOR itself was replanted.

A Ceremony in Oslo,
a Meeting in Rome

O ne of the people missing from the IFOR Council in Schoorl was our co-worker Adolfo Perez Esquivel. From his office in Buenos Aires, Argentina, Adolfo led Servicio Paz y Justicia (Service for Justice and Peace), a continental network whose beginnings had much to do with the work of Hildegard and Jean Goss-Mayr, IFOR's longtime traveling secretaries.

On April 5, 1977, we received a frantic call from his wife, Amanda, reporting that Adolfo had been arrested. In that period, when Argentina was being ruled by a military dictatorship, this meant that within a matter of days Adolfo was likely to be dead, one of the disappeared—a *desaparecido*—like thousands of others murdered by the junta.

What could we do that might prevent Adolfo's death? The idea we came up with was to arrange Adolfo's nomination for the Nobel Peace Prize by former recipients of the prize and get reports of his nomination into the world press. From my recent trips to Belfast, I knew two of them, Mairead Corrigan and Betty Williams, founders of the Peace People movement. They had met Adolfo and were deeply impressed with the work of Servicio. I phoned them and we worked together on a nomination letter and then on press releases. Within a day, news of Adolfo's nomination was making its way into print in hundreds of newspapers. We had no illusions about Adolfo receiving the award— he was little known outside Latin America—but hoped the Argentinian generals would be made more cautious about Adolfo's life. And they were. Though he was repeatedly beaten and tortured, he wasn't executed. It took fourteen months of campaigning and appeals from several governments and such nongovernmental groups as Amnesty International, but finally Adolfo was freed.

258

IFOR staff had prepared a dossier for the Nobel committee about Adolfo's life and work, but we regarded it as a pro forma exercise. Following his release from prison, we gave little further thought to his nomination. Adolfo had survived and had resumed his work—this is all we had hoped for. Adolfo himself was our prize. But then in the late summer of 1978 the phone rang—a call from Oslo with the news that the committee had chosen Adolfo.

On December 10, along with Hildegard and Jean Goss-Mayr, I was in Oslo with Adolfo and his family, housed in what must have been the city's most prestigious hotel.

Describing himself as "a small voice for those who have no voice," in his acceptance speech Adolfo said: "I am convinced that the gospel power of nonviolence presents a choice that opens up for us a challenge of new and radical perspectives. It is an option which gives priority to the essential Christian value: the dignity of the human being, the sacred, transcendent, and irrevocable dignity that belongs to the human being by reason of being a child of God and a brother or sister in Christ, and therefore, our own brother and sister." I was impressed by Adolfo's emphasis on the contemplative foundation that is needed for peace work to be constructive. "For me it is essential to have the inner peace and serenity of prayer in order to listen to the silence of God, which speaks to us in our personal life and the history of our times, of the power of love."

Weeks before the trip to Oslo, Adolfo had phoned from Buenos Aires to ask me to arrange a meeting with Pope John Paul II following the Nobel ceremony. I called the papal nuncio in The Hague and explained Adolfo's hope for such a meeting, also warning him that the Argentinian hierarchy, so compromised in its association with the military junta, was likely to do all in its power to block such a meeting. The nuncio assured me there would be no problem. "The Holy Father decides on such matters himself," he said, "and my request will go directly to his desk." A few days later the nuncio called with the news that we could meet John Paul for a private audience on December 17.

Before the private audience there was the pope's weekly public audience in the Aula Paolo VI, a large hall close to St. Peter's Basilica. We were given places in the press gallery, which meant having an opportunity to watch from above as the pope walked down the aula's central aisle, repeatedly stopping and listening to people desperate to say something to him or receive a blessing. It took half an hour for him to make his way to the front of the hall. As a journalist, I had often watched famous people encountering crowds, but had never before seen anyone respond with such attentive care to so many people. It was astonishing. Pope John Paul impressed me as a man of inexhaustible energy.

After the general audience there were brief meetings with individual pilgrim groups, beginning with a crowd of people who were mainly in wheelchairs. These encounters were still going on when the Vatican staff person responsible for us escorted us to the papal throne room elsewhere in the same building.

When John Paul at last entered the room, we immediately got down to business. For Adolfo this was not simply an opportunity to greet the pope and receive a blessing. He had a definite agenda: first to thank John Paul for his efforts to prevent war between Argentina and Chile, an event that was far from unlikely at the time, and to present a letter signed by many young Argentinians and Chileans promising him that, in the event his efforts failed, they would refuse to fight. John Paul looked carefully at the letter and the many pages of signatures, and—speaking in Spanish—expressed gratitude for the courage of those who had made such a commitment.

Next Adolfo gave the pope a large album of photos, with explanatory text, of people who had been kidnapped in Argentina and never seen alive again—the *desaparecidos*. John Paul looked through the album page by page while the conversation with Adolfo continued. Adolfo described his experience of being kidnapped and tortured, and expressed his grief that the Argentinian hierarchy had been silent about the crimes committed by the junta.

A third item on the agenda concerned the church in El Salvador. Earlier in the year Archbishop—now Saint—Oscar Romero had been assassinated while celebrating Mass. Adolfo urged the pope to appoint the acting archbishop, Arturo Rivera Damas, to become Romero's successor. This was a controversial proposal. There were many in El Salvador's power structure who wanted a bishop who would bless their activities, not condemn them, as Romero had done. John Paul promised that what Adolfo asked for would be done. (Rivera Damas was later appointed archbishop of San Salvador.)

The pope had gifts for us. We each received a silver rosary. Adolfo had a gift for him as well, a copy of my biography of Thomas Merton, which had recently been published. Merton's writings, Adolfo told John Paul, had been a major influence in shaping his faith and vocation. This was the one moment in the audience when I had a brief exchange with the pope. Adolfo introduced me as the book's author. John Paul, switching from Spanish to English, asked me if I had known Merton. "Yes," I responded, "he was my spiritual father during the last seven years of his life." John Paul said he was an admirer of Merton's writing. A close friend, he said, was both the

Our meeting with Pope John Paul II

publisher of his own books in Poland and also of Polish translations of many Merton books. He had read them all and still had them in his library. He looked through my book, pausing over various photos.

At this point a bishop who had been standing behind the pope throughout the audience reminded him that our audience had taken considerably longer than had been scheduled. The pope apologized, gave us a final blessing, and left for his next appointment.

There is one other detail on the Rome visit worth recalling.

In the weeks before the trip to Rome I had tried but failed to arrange a meeting with the cardinal who headed the Pontifical Commission for Justice and Peace. The morning following our papal audience, Adolfo decided that, even without an appointment, we should go and seek a dialogue on the spot. After all, pictures of our meeting with John Paul were on the front page of all the Italian newspapers. If the pope would meet us, surely a cardinal would open his door.

We had a good friend on the cardinal's staff. Once we arrived at the commission offices, we asked the receptionist to contact him. A few minutes later he appeared, obviously in panic. "Please leave immediately," he begged. "The cardinal refuses to see you and does not want you in the building. If you don't leave, I will be fired and never have a job again in the Vatican civil service." He said he would meet us in fifteen minutes at a certain nearby café. Once there he explained that the Argentinian hierarchy had more influence in his department than the pope. It was a disturbing lesson in Vatican realities. Even the pope's example sometimes has little influence on his own curia.

Beggar-in-Chief

The title I had at the start of my tenure on the IFOR staff, coordinator, several years later was changed to general secretary. It might more accurately have been beggar-in-chief, as so much of my work involved inspiring donations from our associated branches plus foundations and supportive individuals, a work requiring much letter writing and face-to-face visits.

A significant part of the money I raised came in the form of lecture fees. I developed a lecture-plus-slide show to give audiences not only a verbal but a visual impression of what IFOR groups and members had done and were doing in Africa, Latin America, Eastern and Western Europe, South Asia, and the United States.

Looking through old issues of the IFOR journal, *Reconciliation International*, I'm reminded of the many projects we took part in—work to end apartheid in Rhodesia (now Zimbabwe) and South Africa, support for jailed peace activists and conscientious objectors in many countries, and engagement with disarmament programs of the United Nations and the World Council of Churches. We were also a partner with the church-backed campaign to get nuclear-armed missiles out of Holland.

Our work for the release of imprisoned Buddhist leaders in Vietnam was acknowledged in a touching July 1978 letter from Thich Nhat Hanh, who quoted one of the recently arrested monks, Thich Tri Minh: "No ideological or political doctrine should be considered more important than life and the love of our fellow human beings. Without ideological or political doctrines, we can still live in peace, but without respect for life, the world will be destroyed." Nhat Hanh commented: "I fear not many 'peace' organizations will notice [such arrests in Vietnam]. . . . If such a one were imprisoned in the United States, what a furor there would be from the very people who will pay no attention to this tragedy in Vietnam. It is very sad for us . . . so many we thought cared about the suffering in our country now seem blind and deaf. Without IFOR's continuing compassion, I would feel there was no longer a peace movement in the world. Your efforts are keeping us hopeful."

Enclosed with his letter was a small packet of peppercorns. Nhat Hanh explained: "Here are some black peppers grown by the staff of the School of Youth for Social Service after the liberation. This was the last crop before the government forced the school to disband. Smell them! They are tiny and wrinkled but strong. They do not kill yet they are very powerful."

Our work involved a lot of travel. Often I was away to participate in meetings of our branches and other organizations—in Switzerland to take part in World Council of Churches' events and assemblies, in Germany for Church and Peace conferences, in Belgium for consultations arranged by Pax Christi International.

One of the journeys I found most stimulating was arranged by the FOR in India. On February 8, 1978, I arrived in New Delhi for a three-week, ten-thousand-kilometer pilgrimage by train and bus that brought me from Delhi to Madras, from Kerala to Bombay (as Mumbai was then called). Each day had its surprises. I felt like one of the blind men in the fable—each of them able to touch only a small part of an elephant, each convinced that reports from the others were lies because his own experience of the elephant was so different. The part of the elephant I got to touch was mainly composed of people whose lives had, in various ways, been shaped by Gandhi.

Within an hour of arrival, FOR national secretary K. V. Mathew brought me to meet with India's prime minister, Moraji Desai. We had met once before, Desai recalled, in America in 1970, soon after I had been released from prison and not long before his own eighteen-month imprisonment by former Prime Minister Indira Gandhi. (Despite her name, Indira Gandhi was not a Gandhian; she had acquired her family name by marrying one of Gandhi's sons.) Knowing my interest in Mahatma Gandhi, he spoke of his participation in Gandhi-led acts of civil disobedience and his years in jail during the national freedom struggle, but it was his latest imprisonment, he said, that had been the most important, "a gift from God, not Mrs. Gandhi." Among Desai's criticisms of Mrs. Gandhi was her authorizing the development of nuclear weapons for India. "It was," he told me, "a historic mistake."

He hoped to help India step away from making or possessing such armaments, but it is a reversal that, as I write these words, has yet to happen.

It surprised me that Desai knew of IFOR and had been willing to meet me. "It was from Gandhi I first heard of IFOR," he explained. "Your organization—especially your former leader Muriel Lester— was an important ally. Gandhi was her guest when he came to London for the Round Table Conference in 1931. The Fellowship shows how much can be achieved by very few people," Desai commented. He picked up a rose from a vase on his table. "This rose," he said, "gives a fresh smell to the entire room, but it is only one rose. What gives it this power comes from a drop of essence smaller than a pinprick. What you are doing is like that."

Among the Gandhians I met in the days that followed was Cherian Thomas, who had been living with Gandhi at the Birla House in New Delhi during the last months of Gandhi's life and was with Gandhi the day he was shot. Taking me to Birla House, we found film director David Attenborough in the midst of reenacting Gandhi's murder for the film he was making about Gandhi's life.

During a break in the filming, we followed a path marked by concrete footprints. "Gandhi was a few minutes late for the daily prayer meeting," Cherian recalled. "When he came to this spot he saw a man and stopped to bless him. The man shot him point blank. Gandhi said only 'Hey Ram'—oh God—and he was dead. Gandhi had always refused guards. So many times he did dangerous things and lived. He always said no man could make his life one minute longer than God intended."

My travels in India brought me to ashrams, temples, mosques, and churches, to such castles as the Red Fort in Agra and the nearby Taj Mahal, to monsoon-soaked communities of improvised houses packed tightly together, to flood-isolated islands in tropical Kerala, to convents and hospitals founded by Mother Teresa, to places of pilgrimage such as the cathedral in Madras where relics of the apostle St. Thomas are kept. At one spot in the deep south, I spoke about the nonviolent Jesus to a crowd of a hundred thousand Christians gathered in a dry riverbed. I had never spoken to so many people at once.

While there was always someone to meet me at the end of each train or bus ride, I often made my way from place to place unaccompanied. There is much to be said for traveling alone in unknown places: no buffers, no translators, no explainers. The vulnerable pilgrim is pressed into a state of complete dependence on strangers. The most memorable passage of my first India trip occurred the first night—a train journey from Delhi to Calcutta (now Kolkata). I was the only non-Indian in the crowded carriage with its four-person-wide, wooden benches. As the sky darkened, narrow sleeping platforms were lowered from dividers that stood between compartments creating columns of beds four-planks high. The other passengers had known they needed to bring their own bedding—I had not. Using the contents of my small suitcase, I had to improvise what I could for padding. I made a sort of pillow by stuffing a shirt with underwear. There was little if any actual sleep that night. When morning came, families around me unpacked picnic meals and carried on with ordinary life as they might have at home. The smell was a thick mixture of oil, sweat, spices, all sorts of food and all things human.

Soon after dawn the train stopped at a major station, temporarily draining the cars of nearly all passengers as they rushed to food stands and bought cups of tea and newspapers on the station platform. I slowly made sense of what was going on. While gazing at all the activity through a partly opened window, the open hand of a beggar boy, palm up, reached urgently toward me. I found a coin in my pocket and put it between his outstretched fingers. Hand withdrawn, the boy  stared at the gift—one rupee—in happy amazement, then rushed off to proudly exhibit the coin to other boys. I learned how much a single coin could mean to those at the bottom of the economic ladder. The small change in my pocket was, for many, a life-saving treasure.

At the side of the train in the same station I watched families who lived on splinters of land between tracks beginning their daily ablutions. Using a twig, a boy stood next to a faucet earnestly brushing his teeth. Close to the faucet was a mat that, at night, served as his bed. His home was without roof or walls.

In Holland I was at the low end of the economic scale—in India, a rich man.

Lost and Found

Representing IFOR, its work and values, was an aspect of my job that I enjoyed and was good at, but a drawback was that I was on the road at least three months of the year and often out of touch with office and home. In those pre-digital-communication days, phone calls were costly and e-mail nonexistent. It wasn't easy for my co-workers and still harder for Laura. All my time away may have been a contributing factor to the collapse of our marriage in 1979. By that time we were the parents of three—Thomas had been born in December 1978. To write about it in detail would be of service to no one. It's enough to say that, for whatever reasons, Laura found herself in love with a Dutch friend and out of love with me. In 1980 we officially divorced.

Ben had returned to the United States before the breakup. Due to his dyslexia, Dutch schooling had been a steep climb for him—he knew he would do better in his native language. Perhaps he also sensed the unraveling of my marriage and guessed the ground would be more stable were he living with his grandmother in Red Bank. I had made a similar decision when I was sixteen.

Thich Nhat Hanh helped keep me from being sucked into a dangerously deep depression. I went to see him in France and found him nearly as sad as I was about my marital woes. Not optimistic about the breakup being reversible, he reminded me of spiritual exercises that help one let go.

Another helper was Henri Nouwen, a Dutch Catholic priest and writer who was then teaching at Yale University. Henri had become a friend soon after I left prison and had brought me to Yale two or three times to give lectures about Merton. The first months that I was living alone, Henri called on a more or less weekly basis to see how I was doing. As spring approached, he arranged for me to spend Easter with him in New Haven. After I had spent several days in his apartment, he sent me for a week-long retreat at a Trappist monastery in upstate New

York. The abbot, Dom John Eudes Bamberger, a psychiatrist as well as a monk, went for a long walk with me each day and, among other things, helped me see how intertwined anger and depression are. "Depression," he said, "is anger inside out." I left the abbey with a renewed capacity for laughter.

What else kept me going? The kids, first of all. Laura was quite willing that we collaborate in their care. The three of them often spent weekends with me. One night, while I was lying in bed silently praying for the children, who were sleeping on the floor beside me, three-year-old Wendy interrupted my prayers to tell me, "Daddy, there's an angel lying next to me." I looked, saw nothing, and asked, "What does it look like?" "Just like an angel—shining." I felt enormously comforted.

Henri Nouwen

Music was part of my therapy. For the first time in my literate life, I was barely able to read unless the reading was work connected, but found I could sit in front of a record player and listen to classical music, especially Mozart, and slip free of dark moods. Week by week I added another disk or two to my collection. For months, unless traveling, I doubt I spent a single evening alone without a time of quiet, wordless listening. I felt like a half-dead tree welcoming rain.

Last but not least, my work helped me. It demanded a great deal, forcing me to focus my thoughts and energy on persons and things other than my private disaster.

For at least a year I was convinced that any future marriage was impossible, nor did I long for one. My record of marital failure was proof that I wasn't suited for such a relationship. Celibacy was the only option, though it wasn't a route that attracted me for any positive reason.

Holidays played a healing role. The first summer that I was on my own I took a vacation in Ireland with Dan and Wendy plus Ben, who flew over from the United States. Inspired by a photo I'd seen in a tourist booklet, for two weeks we traveled in a horse-drawn, barrel-shaped gypsy wagon around the Dingle Peninsula on Ireland's southwest coast. From Tralee to Dunmore Head, Europe's westernmost point, we were pulled by a genial horse named Sergeant and followed by an affectionate dog we christened Spaghetti. Luck was on our side with the weather—

Dan and Wendy in Ireland

I don't recall a single rainy day. Ireland's narrow, winding, stone-bordered roads had little traffic in those days. The main sound was the clopping of Sergeant's hooves as we made our slow way from village to village. Each night we found a field that was open to campers, unhitched Sergeant to graze, and made our way to the nearest pub, which in Ireland (unlike England) is a gathering place for whole families as well as singers and musicians. A fireplace often sheltered a lively blaze. The kids loved the adventure. I could feel the mending going on within me.

The following summer, with Dan and Wendy, I went on a Van Gogh pilgrimage, visiting Arles, Saint-Rémy-de-Provence, the asylum of Saint-Paul-de-Mausole, where Van Gogh had been a patient, and Auvers-sur-Oise, where he died and is buried. The journey had its roots in many hours spent at the Van Gogh Museum in Amsterdam.

Along the way I found myself thinking of Nancy Flier, my former FOR co-worker and still a special friend—also mother of my god-daughter Caitlan, then age four. When I was living in Nyack, editing *Fellowship* magazine, Nancy and I often had lunch together, usually with co-workers, occasionally just the two of us, playing chess and discussing books. We had many common interests, including Merton's writings, which had played a part in Nancy's finding her way into the Catholic Church. Even after my move to Holland, we had an ongoing correspondence. When she left the FOR staff to work for a typograph-ical company, I sent her one of my bibliophile treasures, a handsome book on the history of book and type design from Gutenberg onward. I always made it a point, when in the United States, to visit Nancy and Cait.

While in the south of France, I bought a postcard of a flowering field in Provence and wrote on the back:

Dear Nancy, I'm in Arles, where Van Gogh once lived, and am camping near St.-Rémy, not far from where he died. The air is thick with the smell of herbs and the sunlight intense. I'm sitting in the shade above an ancient cloister, a quiet place, still soaked in the taste of Cotes de Rhone wine that I drank with a Japanese stranger I met. Love, Jim.

It's a postcard Nancy still has and keeps in a cookie tin she calls her treasure chest. At the time I wasn't knowingly writing a love letter—I just wanted to share a happy moment with a particularly dear friend—but looking back, I realize quite a lot was unconsciously written between the lines.

On a US speaking trip three months later that brought me to Nyack, we talked after the lecture, neither of us saying a word about love but both of us aware love was becoming an invisible bridge between us. Not long afterward, love letters began flying back and forth across the Atlantic.

In late December, I was back in America for a two-week visit, not only to see Ben and the rest of the family in Red Bank, but, the day after Christmas, to introduce Nancy to them. Driving to Red Bank from Nyack, Nancy brought a freshly baked pecan pie which Mother enjoyed remembering and praising for years afterward.

In April 1982, Nancy and Cait flew to Amsterdam. Wendy was thrilled to acquire a sister nearly her own age. A year later, on May 30, 1983, our daughter Anne was born. All told, between us we have six children. These last few decades we have been counting grandchildren—ten so far.

Let It Begin Here

"My fellow Americans," Ronald Reagan said in Florida in August 1984, "I'm pleased to tell you today that I've signed legislation that will outlaw Russia forever. We begin bombing in five minutes." He thought the microphone had been turned off and meant it as a joke, but a joke told by the president of the United States about starting a war with America's mortal enemy didn't fill the world with laughter. Cataclysmic war was only a button-push away. Day and night the United States and the Soviet Union had nuclear-armed missiles ready to launch plus hundreds of H-bombs in the air aboard target-assigned B-52 bombers. Like millions of others, for decades I lived in expectation of nuclear war caused by miscalculation, error, or madness, and here was America's president joking about it.

I recall an American couple I encountered one Monday morning on my way to work. They were carrying a map of Alkmaar, but looked lost. "Can I help you?" I asked. "We're trying to find a café where we can get a cup of coffee," the man replied. Offering them coffee in the IFOR office just across the street, I explained that nothing was open yet—in those more restful days, Dutch shops and restaurants didn't open before noon on Mondays. Once we were settled down, coffee mugs in hand, they told me a little about themselves. Both were Air Force pilots stationed in Germany.

They were curious about the several antiwar posters hanging on the walls. I told them about the widely supported Dutch campaign to get all US nuclear weapons removed from Holland and other European countries. I was surprised at how positive was their response. "God bless the Dutch," said the husband. "May their efforts succeed!" He told me that he and his wife expected nuclear war in the near future in which they were sure to be among the first casualties. "Our base in

Germany is certainly a primary target for Russian missiles when war breaks out." (I noted he said "when" rather than "if.") "Even if we're in the air at the time, we'll have no place to land and just about everyone we know or care about will be dead."

My guests had arrived in the home country of "Hollanditis," as it had been christened by the international press. It was a way of summing up in one word the vigorous campaigns that were occurring across Europe for the creation of a nuclear-free zone. The initiative had its roots in Holland. The groups and persons responsible were numerous and diverse, with participation ranging from the general in charge of Holland's Army War College to political groups spread from left to right, but the primary source of Hollanditis was the Inter-Church Peace Council (*Interkerkelijk Vredesberaad*). IKV was founded in 1966 by the Protestant and Catholic churches of the Netherlands as a conscience-forming project on issues of human rights, development, and peace. For its first ten years IKV work centered on preparing a Peace Week held in churches throughout the country in late September.

In the mid-1970s, when East–West relations had become more threatening, IKV leaders took a fresh look at their work and saw an opportunity for Holland to play a part in breaking the deadlock in the arms race. As years of negotiations seeking simultaneous reductions by both sides had failed dismally, the option of unilateral initiatives needed promotion: concrete steps taken by states other than the super powers to reduce tension  and mistrust and create an atmosphere in which disarmament agreements could be reached.

In 1977, IKV launched a campaign that was summarized with the slogan: "Help rid the world of nuclear weapons—let it begin in the Netherlands." Its symbol was a drawing of a huge bomb being pushed away by a determined family of five. The message was clear: ordinary people aren't as powerless against the arms race as we usually think. The idea took hold. By 1981 you couldn't walk down a street in any Dutch town or city without seeing nuclear disarmament symbols displayed on posters, clothes, shoulder bags, and living room windows. In four years, a network of four hundred local groups had sprung up, taking the campaign door to door.

Church leaders began to recognize peace efforts as a pastoral responsibility. The general synod of the Reformed Church, Holland's largest Protestant denomination, condemned not only the use of nuclear weapons but their possession. With half the Dutch people opposing all nuclear weapons in the country and two-thirds opposing the stationing of updated NATO weaponry, the political impact was considerable.

Beginning in 1979, part of IFOR's work was to help internationalize the IKV campaign via our European branches and through other groups. I did a lot of writing and interviewing for various newspapers and journals.

Huge rallies were held in European capitals in the fall of 1981—the largest of which was Holland's own—more than 400,000 people filling the streets of central Amsterdam in a protest so festive in spirit that one observer called it "a brief encounter between heaven and earth." There was a still larger turnout—an estimated 550,000—for a similar rally in The Hague in October 1983. The Dutch railway had to lay on extra trains. A member of the royal family, Princess Irene, was a speaker at the rally and shortly afterward was our guest for lunch at the IFOR office.

Anti-nuclear rally in The Hague in October 1983

Tunneling under
the Iron Curtain

I was searching to see in what other ways IFOR might make nuclear war less likely.

In 1981, at the end of a US speaking trip promoting nuclear disarmament, I stopped in Cambridge, Massachusetts, to give a lecture and visit my friend Robert Ellsberg. Together we went to see a film, *Moscow Doesn't Believe in Tears*, a recent winner of an Oscar. Robert had seen it once. It was, he reported, one of the funniest and most touching movies he had seen in a long time.

Moscow Doesn't Believe in Tears is a romantic comedy about social classes in Russia's "classless" society. Centering on three women who arrive in Moscow in the late fifties and, for a time, share a dormitory room, the film follows their struggles to build careers and families. Despite differences in temperament and ambition, they create an enduring friendship. Midway the film jumps to the early seventies, so that we see what has happened after the passage of fifteen years. Their intertwining stories are comic, tragic, convincing, and socially revealing.

The film was an eye-opener for me. Russians became people with whom Americans could identify, not simply cardboard figures imprisoned in the gray world of Cold War journalism. It also brought home the startling awareness that most of us, even in the peace movement, knew far more about weapons of mass destruction than about the people at whom the weapons were aimed. Shouldn't would-be peacemakers be attempting to open doors for face-to-face East–West contact? Would it not help prevent war if we knew by name and had actually met some of the people who would be its fatalities should war break out? Shouldn't this be an element of IFOR's work?

To get things started, I began to look for an opportunity to travel in the Soviet Union, but at the time it wasn't easy to find an opening. The "iron curtain" was more than a metaphor. Obtaining a visa to enter the Soviet Union was hard. The Soviet Union was then at war in Afghanistan, an event sharply condemned by IFOR, which probably explained why a seminar we had arranged in Moscow was abruptly cancelled on the Soviet side. An editor of the Soviet daily newspaper, *Izvestia,* whom I met over breakfast in Amsterdam, candidly explained that there was probably apprehension among the Kremlin's gatekeepers that pacifists from the West might unveil protest banners in Red Square. I assured him that we had no such intentions. "We hope to promote citizen diplomacy, not make a five-minute show of ourselves." "Well," the *Izvestia* journalist said, "try again. Next time you may get a smarter bureaucrat. We are not all so stupid, but neither are we all so smart."

I sought help from Lubomir Mirejovsky, a Czech pastor who led the Christian Peace Conference in Prague. He had connections, I knew, with Russian church leaders. He suggested that representatives of our two movements meet in Moscow for a dialogue hosted by the Russian Orthodox Church with "Violence, Nonviolence, and Liberation" as our topic. A three-sided agreement was reached with visas provided. Metropolitan Filaret of Minsk, then head of the External Church Affairs Department of the Moscow Patriarchate, arranged for us to have the meeting in a small conference room at his office in Moscow, a one-story wooden structure outside the city center—a modest building that bore oblique witness to the fact that the church in those days was still an object of state repression.

Those five days in Moscow in October 1983 went by too quickly. Much of our time was taken up by meetings, which turned out to be quite lively, with a depth and candor that I hadn't anticipated; but our time for sightseeing, unfortunately, was minimal. We had a visit to the cathedrals inside the Kremlin walls. One night we attended a ballet, another, the Russian Circus. The most rewarding experiences of that first trip to Russia for me were not our theological conversations but my own activities on the first and last nights, that is before the other conference participants arrived and after they left. Encouraged by a clear sky and full moon, that first night I walked from my hotel to Red Square a mile or two away. It was amazing to stand in the heart of Moscow after midnight and be almost alone. Two soldiers guarded the tomb of Lenin.

On the last night I explored Moscow's subways. A translator marked stops he especially recommended. I walked to the Kievskaya station, put a five-kopek coin in the turnstile, and went down the crowded escalator. My goal was to visit half-a-dozen stations, but it wasn't always easy to know where I was. My map was in English, the signs in Russian. This proved a fast way to learn the basics of the Cyrillic alphabet.

The stations were everything they were said to be: no two alike, immaculate, free of graffiti. Some had an almost Moorish simplicity; some reminded me of baroque churches. The decoration included mosaics, stained glass, and sculpture. In one station, crystal chandeliers ran the length of the central corridor between platforms and above the train tracks as well. Despite Stalinist propaganda in the decoration, each station was a work of art.

But what stirred me most was simply to be in the thick of ordinary Russian people. While some wore military uniforms, most were in clothing that wouldn't attract special notice in London or New York—nothing fancy, but not threadbare either. As for the faces, I could have found all of them, and the moods they registered, in any bus or tram in Amsterdam. Many were reading books. A round-faced child stared at me—a man with a beard was uncommon in Russia at that time—with an expression divided between shyness and curiosity. Sitting on her father's lap, gripping his hand, her head pressed against his chest, she reminded me of my seven-year-old Wendy.

No less important than people watching was having to ask for help in stations where Metro lines intersect. Each time I found someone who not only would point the way but take me to the right platform. It was encouraging to discover how much could be done despite language barriers.

That first trip in the Soviet Union was like a bike ride through a museum of fine art. I saw wonderful things, but too fast to take them in and with far too little understanding of Russian and Soviet history to make much sense of even those things that weren't a blur. But the trip was enough for me to know that I wanted to come back, see things more slowly, and talk with Russians. I had a particular sense of connection with the Russian Orthodox Church and longed to have the chance to meet believers face to face.

Border Crossing

B ack in Holland, I recalled how Dorothy Day had so often spoken of Russia as "holy mother Russia." She had taken me to Russian Orthodox churches, introduced me to a Russian Orthodox priest, and pressed me to read Dostoevsky and other Russian authors who had helped shape her understanding of what Christianity was all about. Consciously or unconsciously, she had helped prepare me to spend part of my life in Russia.

I wrote to Archbishop Pitirim, head of the publishing department of the Moscow Patriarchate, asking if I might have the cooperation of his department in writing a book about the Orthodox Church in Russia. It would not be, I said, an academic work. Others had done such books, and in any event I was not qualified. But I had spent much of my adult life in journalism, worked for various newspapers and press services, had written biographies and many essays. I felt I could write a book about Russian believers, if the church could provide a translator and open doors to centers of Orthodoxy—churches, seminaries, and monasteries.

It took a year to return to Moscow. When I went back in 1984, I was met by Tanya Tchernikova of the Department for External Church Affairs. "Just tell me what you want to see," she said, "and I'll do my best to arrange it." In the week that followed we visited many of the working churches of Moscow. It wasn't hard—in those days they weren't numerous. We also drove north to the Holy Trinity–St. Sergius Lavra, a large monastic complex and a major center of pilgrimage. Back in Moscow, we spent a day at the Tretyakov Gallery, the most important museum of Russian art, whose collection included icons by Andrei Rublev and other masters of the fifteenth and sixteenth centuries as well as many paintings with religious content from the late nineteenth and early twentieth centuries.

The high point of the stay was simply being present for the Sunday liturgy at the Epiphany Cathedral. By Russian standards, it isn't an old church—perhaps eighteenth century. The icons, done in the Western-influenced style of the eighteenth and nineteenth centuries, were not to my taste. Yet being in this throng of worshipers was

a more exciting experience than I had had in many more beautiful churches. The cathedral became beautiful for me simply because it was such a grace to be there. I mentioned to Tanya that the church was as crowded as a church in the West might be on a major feast day. "Only on a major feast," she responded, "you would have to come many hours early just to get inside."

Orthodox prayer is active. People often cross themselves and then bow, some crossing themselves almost continually. Gazing at the dense crowd surrounding me, I was reminded of the patterns the wind makes blowing across a field of wheat. All the while the most beautiful singing was going on from two choirs facing each other from balconies on either side of the church. During the Creed and the Our Father, the congregation joined with the choirs, singing with great force.

It's the Russian custom to pray standing up. For the noninitiated, this can be painful, as the liturgy runs not less than two hours. "The first hour, you think of how difficult it is to stand," Archbishop Pitirim had warned me. "The second hour you think of nothing at all—if you aren't used to it, it can be torture, but by the third hour you have wings."

At first I stood like a wooden statue. I longed to imitate what those around me were doing, not simply to fit in but because the body language of prayer seemed just the thing to do in church, so much better than just standing still. But I felt embarrassed. I had my hands behind my back, like a museum visitor looking at paintings. Tanya whispered, "Let your hands hang at your side!" Finally I began praying in the Russian style. It was a frontier-crossing moment.

Many of my neighbors were *babushkas*, older, thick-bodied Russian women with shawls or knitted hats whose faces seemed to be carved from potatoes, but there were also many younger women and men plus a sprinkling of children. The babushkas were the majority, but they had a lot of company. Seeing how many young people there were, I could understand the anxieties which, a few days earlier, had prompted the newspaper *Pravda* to call for higher-quality atheist propaganda in order to counter the growth of religious belief among the young.

What cannot be adequately described is the tangible quality of the prayer in the church—as solid as black bread. I felt that if the walls and pillars of the church were taken away, the roof would rest securely on the faith of the congregation below. I had rarely experienced prayer so intense. Was it always so in Russia? I wondered. It must have been solid faith indeed to have survived many hard years of militant atheism. Millions of Orthodox Christians had perished. In the decades since Lenin, the whole of Russia had been stained with the blood of martyrs.

A few months earlier a priest from Leningrad whom I encountered at a meeting in London estimated that the number of practicing members of the Orthodox Church in Russia, far from shrinking, had grown by ten million in the past decade. "I'm not a tall man," he said, "but, short as I am, when it was just me and the babushkas, I was a tree among shrubs. Now I am just one more bush. The young people are the trees." On our way out of the cathedral, Tanya and I found ourselves in a crowd of families waiting to have their children baptized in assembly-line fashion inside an adjacent building.

I learned a great deal during that week, but the book I hoped to write, a project that would require travel far beyond Moscow, was still out of reach. It was obvious that the church was eager to cooperate, but it wasn't the church that issued visas. The Soviet state was still hostile to Christians—indeed there were still Christians in prisons and labor camps, even if the numbers were now far smaller. Some former churches had been made into "museums" of atheism. In whole regions of the country there was not a single functioning church. Where churches had survived, those who attended services, especially men and young people, put themselves at risk of being denied access to higher education or better jobs. Only older women were able to get away with church attendance unpunished. "If you're an old woman," a Russian friend explained, "you're much less likely to be of interest to the security services. They write you off as someone who has lost her wits or never had them."

Pilgrims in the Holy Land

In the spring of 1985, after eight years on the IFOR staff, I had a three-month sabbatical. In April, my father and stepmother, Lucy, came to stay in our house, eager to do a bit of active grandparenting with Daniel, Wendy, and Thomas, while Nancy and I plus Cait and Anne flew to Israel, where I had been offered a three-month teaching post at the Ecumenical Institute—Tantur, as it is usually called. At the urging of Pope Paul VI, the institute had been set up following the Second Vatican Council by Benedictine monks as a place concentrating on inter-Christian and interfaith dialogue. On the border that divides Israel from the occupied territories, Tantur tops a hill on a road leading south from Jerusalem to Bethlehem. Together with a Franciscan nun, Rosemary Lynch, I was teaching two courses, one on "Prophets of Peace" and the other on "Peace Service" (rather than peace *making*, as peace is rarely if ever something anyone can make).

One of the major factors in accepting the invitation from Tantur had been access to its outstanding library plus proximity to Jerusalem, the one city in the world where all segments of Christianity, includ-

ing all Orthodox jurisdictions, are represented. It offered an ideal context in which to better prepare myself for writing a book on the church in Russia. Also we went as pilgrims eager to visit and to be challenged by many of the places that had been important in biblical history.

As the weeks passed, we got to know Jerusalem well, both

Tantur Ecumenical Institute

279

its ancient and its modern quarters. Every week at least one of us if not all four visited the Church of the Holy Sepulcher—or the Church of the Resurrection, as it is called by Orthodox Christians. There were frequent visits to nearby Bethlehem, where we did much of our shopping. Here we often entered the Church of the Nativity. Before our three months were up, our travels by bus and rented car had taken us to sacred sites from the Dead Sea and the Negev Desert to the Mount of the Beatitudes in Galilee. No less inspiring, we formed friendships with many Christians and Jews who were struggling for peace and justice.

One of the significant events that happened during our stay concerned a piece of painted wood about the size of a paperback book. A hope that Nancy and I brought with us was that we might return home with a hand-painted icon from Jerusalem, though our understanding and appreciation of iconography was still shallow.

On our first day in the Old City, in the window of a dingy shop near the Jaffa Gate, a small icon of Mary and the Christ child caught our eye. The price was a hundred dollars, the elderly Palestinian owner told us—a modest price for a hand-painted icon, as we were to discover, but not an amount we could easily afford. We decided not to hurry, yet week after week we paused to gaze at that icon every time we passed the shop. One day it was gone, and then we grieved.

A week later I went into the shop and asked the owner if he might have anything similar. "Similar!" he said. "I have the very icon. But no one wanted it so I took it out of the window and put another in its place." He took it down from a dark shelf behind him and laid it in my hands. Asking him to keep it for me, I gave him a ten-dollar bill. The next day I paid the balance, wrapped the icon in a tea towel, and brought it back to Tantur.

Graced by that small icon, our apartment instantly became a different place. I carefully unwrapped it and placed it in an empty spot on a bookshelf. Meanwhile Nancy lit a candle. What better way to receive an icon into one's home than to pray? That was clear. But what prayers? Improvising, we recited the *Te Deum* from the Anglican *Book of Com-*

mon Prayer, then read Mary's *Magnificat* from the Gospel of Luke. Just a few days before, we had bought a Jewish prayer book and quickly found several prayers addressed to the Creator of the Universe. We recited the text of the Great Litany of Peace used in the Orthodox Liturgy of St. John Chrysostom. We sang a Protestant hymn that Nancy had learned as a child growing up in the Dutch Reformed Church. Never was there a more hodge-podge service, such an awkward, Marx Brothers beginning. Our guardian angels must have had a good laugh. But whatever the moment lacked in polish was more than made up for in gratitude for the icon that now graced our home. It brought us closer to Christ and his mother and at the same time was a school of silence and prayer. It proved to be a school of theology as well.

The next day we showed the icon to a Maryknoll priest in residence at Tantur who was a specialist in Eastern Christianity and well versed in icons. Ours was Russian, he told us, and had the name *Vladimir-skaya*—the Vladimir Mother of God. Its prototype, more than a thousand years old, had come from Constantinople to the Russian city of Vladimir in the eleventh century and later made its way to Moscow. Indeed, it dawned on me, I had seen the original in a protective glass case at the Tretyakov Gallery in Moscow. Our icon, he guessed, was three or four hundred years old. "Tens of thousands of Russian pilgrims came to Jerusalem in the nineteenth century, many of them walking most of the way," he said. "Probably one of them carried this, and it never found its way back to Russia." On the commercial market, he told us, it was worth far more than we had paid for it and could only have come to us as a gift of the Mother of God.

Whether he was right about the age of the icon, its provenance, or its material worth to collectors, I make no claim. If one's main interest is prayer, it doesn't matter. What he was certainly right about was that it was Mary's gift to us. We had come to Tantur, in part, to study our way closer to Orthodox Christianity in general and the church in Russia in particular. This small icon provided a wider gateway than any book. We had not found the icon—the icon had found us.

Whenever either of us went to Jerusalem, we visited the maze-like Church of the Resurrection to pray. My most memorable experiences inside that ancient building occurred at Easter. I was fortunate. It's all but impossible to get inside the Church of the Resurrection on Pascha—one must have an invitation. Providentially, George Hintlian, a leader of Jerusalem's Armenian Christian community, had obtained one for me—a precious gift. Each of the several Christian communities in Jerusalem is allotted only so many passes. Once the guests are inside the church, the doors are bolted. No one can enter or leave. I don't recall how many hours we were locked inside—time stopped. The area immediately around the tomb in which Christ rose from the dead was densely crowded on all sides.

At a certain moment the Patriarch of Jerusalem, having entered the tomb and been locked inside, lit the "holy fire," or, some say, the fire is lit miraculously. Flame burst out of the tomb's small windows. The sealed doors were opened, and the patriarch came out bearing two candles which he then used to light the candles everyone was holding. No one held only one, rather ten or twelve—each candle becomes a gift to a friend or relative who couldn't be present. Meanwhile, those present utter cries of joy not unlike those one might hear in a crowded sports stadium at the moment a winning point is scored in a crucial game. Some exultant young men rode on the shoulders of friends. It was an amazing sight. The space around the tomb became uncomfortably hot—so many candles burning, so many people packed so tightly. Anyone who suffers from claustrophobia will find it slightly terrifying. During the hours we were locked inside the church, I twice retreated to Golgotha, the nearby place of the crucifixion. It is a rare blessing to be entirely alone at the exact spot where Christ gave himself for the life of the world. I didn't get back to Tantur until the early morning.

Another event of great significance during our three-month sabbatical was the result of Nancy's being prodded to answer a tough question.

One day, leaving Cait and Anne in my care at Tantur, Nancy went to the studio of Elie Schwartz, a retired German art teacher living near the Western Wall in the Jewish Quarter of Jerusalem. It was mid-June. We were nearing the end of the sabbatical.

We had passed by Schwartz's studio several times, always pausing to admire the artwork displayed near his front door and to listen to recorded classical music that he seemed to play throughout the day. He had a sign set up on the sidewalk in front of the studio—"Draw your portrait, half an hour, ten thousand shekels"—about ten dollars at the time. This was obviously his way of making some extra cash and getting to know people. Without telling me, Nancy had decided to have him draw a portrait of herself—it was, she explained to Elie Schwartz, to be given to me for my birthday in November. Half an hour ended up being a two-hour session. Schwartz was intrigued not only by Nancy's face but by her past. As he drew, he asked her a wide range of questions. "Tell me about your family. What does your father do?" Nancy no longer remembers everything about their conversation except that the questions got deeper and deeper. Finally he asked, "What is the thing you fear most?" Without hesitation, Nancy replied, "Nuclear war." This was 1985, after all—the height of the Cold War; during the previous year or two Nancy had suffered repeated nightmares of atomic apocalypse. "No, I don't believe it," Schwartz said emphatically. "What do you *really* fear the most?" It took Nancy several minutes before she realized that, as terrified as she was of nuclear holocaust, Schwartz was right—she had an even deeper fear. "My biggest fear is getting to the end of my life and not having made use of the talents I've been given."

Portrait of Nancy by Elie Schwartz

It was, for Nancy, a lightning-bolt moment. She felt her compass had been reset. As for the portrait Schwartz made, Nancy couldn't wait for my birthday. She gave it to me that evening, as she had to tell me without delay about her conversation. In some way, she knew she had to do something vocationally with her love of language. How she was going to do that wasn't clear, but language and literature had been the focus of both her undergraduate and graduate studies. That part of herself needed to be put to use.

Nancy's lightning bolt struck me as well as her. I had been increasingly frustrated that my life as a writer was relegated to the margins of my working day, much of which was focused on administration and fund-raising. In my eight years with IFOR, the only book I had managed to write, using scraps of time at night and on weekends, was a hundred-page introduction to the life of Thomas Merton, more a sketch than an actual biography. I yearned to revise and expand it. I also longed to work on a biography of Dorothy Day.

As the sabbatical drew to an end, we both knew we had arrived at a critical moment in our lives: we had to make a change. The question was staring us in the face: What comes next? And how could we pay our bills if we had no steady income? It took several years to answer these questions.

Standing on Cracking Ice

In March 1985 a political event occurred in the Soviet Union that was to make the world a less dangerous place: Mikhail Gorbachev became general secretary of the Communist Party and thus head of state of the Soviet Union.

He was seen from the start as a reformer, but at the time of his appointment few imagined how radical a reformer Gorbachev would prove to be. He was convinced that major change was needed and also that relations with the United States and Western Europe had to become constructive rather than confrontational.

Gorbachev began using the words *perestroika*, meaning restructuring, and *glasnost*, meaning openness and frankness in government affairs, a favorable climate for political debate in the press and greatly reduced censorship. What used to be unsaid was being said. Books that had been banned began appearing in bookshops. Films that had been locked in vaults were suddenly on cinema screens. What used to be thought hopeless was being eagerly awaited. The jamming of radio broadcasts by the BBC and Voice of America was stopped. Despite all the blows religious believers had received in the past, a remarkable sense of expectation had begun to flourish within churches. Antireligious repression ground to a halt. Outspoken radical Christians who had been imprisoned were freed. While Gorbachev had as yet said nothing about a new religious policy, the weather was changing. One smelled it rather than touched it.

In December 1986, I received an unexpected invitation from Metropolitan Filaret of Minsk, head of the Church's External Affairs Department, to come to Moscow in mid-February to participate in a three-day conference, "For a World without Nuclear Weapons, for Mankind's Survival," at which Gorbachev was to give an address.

Upon arriving in Moscow six weeks later, I was welcomed with the astonishing news that the obstacles to my writing a book on the Russian Orthodox Church—no doubt KGB-imposed—had been removed. After the conference ended, I could stay on in Russia to begin the travel and interviews I had proposed. An Oxford-educated priest from Kiev, Father Boris Udovenko, had been assigned to travel with me.

Meanwhile, a thousand people, all prominent in their fields, had come to Moscow for the conference. We were divided up into various sections—religious, scientific, medical, literary, artistic, business, ecological, and military.

That first afternoon, the conference not having begun, I waded through the snow to a multifloored bookshop on Kalinin Prospekt. While in the arts section, I got into conversation with an English-speaking economist who, I told him, had a striking resemblance to Russia's last czar, Nicholas II. "Yes, people say that," he laughed, "but I hope my life will not end the way his did." We talked about art books—I had just bought a handsome volume on Ilya Repin's paintings. I asked him about *glasnost*, wondering whether he would dare to talk politics in a crowded shop in central Moscow. Without hesitation he did some quick pantomimes of the last few Soviet leaders prior to Gorbachev. He showed Leonid Brezhnev as a man with head tilted heavily to one side, eyes half-closed, snoring. "Corruption prospered," he said. "It was worse than you can imagine. And then came Brezhnev's successors, corpses even while still in office, and nothing changed." He played the part of one dead body, then another, eyes now entirely closed. Then, springing back to life, "But Gorbachev, now he is alive and he is a clever man. Finally we have someone who is alive and can think."

He talked about the impending publication of Pasternak's long-suppressed novel, *Doctor Zhivago*, and mentioned various films I should see, especially *Repentance*, which had escaped from a long hibernation in the vaults of the censors and was now showing in cinemas all over the country, including seventeen screens in Moscow. "It's a black comedy, a parody," the economist said. "It's the first time that the Stalin era has been the object of a critical movie. For decades Stalin simply disappeared. For years his picture had been on every wall—and the next day it was gone. Until Nikita Khrushchev, nothing was said about Stalin or what he did or how many died or where they died, and after

Khrushchev, the silence returned. Now research into the Stalin period is finally being allowed." Our conversation drifted on to the topic of used bookshops in Moscow. We parted company after exchanging addresses.

There is a Russian phrase—*bytovoe blagochestie*—which means "the art of ritual living." Stopping to visit a church on a busy Moscow street, I thought of the art of ritual living while noticing how some of the people walking by paused, bowed, and crossed themselves. I had not seen such public gestures of piety before. Change was in the air.

The next morning, the conference was off and running. Metropolitan Yuvenali, the bishop of Moscow in all but title, was chairing the religious section. About two hundred people were taking part, mainly Christians, but also a good many Jews as well as Hindus, Buddhists, Shintoists, and Muslims. Most of the speeches were made off the cuff and, on the whole, either interesting or mercifully brief. Several speakers touched on hot subjects, including Afghanistan, where what the Soviet Union was doing was compared to what America had done in Vietnam.

After supper I had a long talk with a translator assisting in the business section of the conference. A Muscovite, he talked about the struggle in the city to save and restore surviving old buildings. Then we switched gears to Russian literature, starting with Dostoyevsky and working our way to Valentin Rasputin, a contemporary author whose stories often have a religious note and who was well known for his struggle to protect the environment from industrialism. Then he asked if I knew the books of Thomas Merton. It turns out he was an avid reader of Merton and had a number of Merton books in his library. He was astonished that I actually had known Merton, but not nearly as surprised as I was that Merton's books could be found on any bookshelf in Russia.

The next morning, those of us in the religious section were off to the Danilovski Monastery, a few miles south of the Kremlin, to take part in the Holy Liturgy. A community of twenty-one monks was now living there, the youngest monastic community in the Soviet Union. Among those buried in its cemetery in pre-Soviet times was Gogol, author of the comic novel *Dead Souls*. After the Revolution, the Danilov Monastery became an orphanage, then a prison, and more recently a factory. In an unanticipated gesture by the state, the compound had been returned to the Russian Orthodox Church. The church and the surrounding derelict buildings within the walls were experiencing a resurrection. Tons of rubble and mud had been carted away. The hard labor was mainly being carried out by devout volunteers.

During the liturgy a nearby family caught my eye. I was enchanted by two young sisters, perhaps five and seven years old, and their young brother, about four. The boy was sitting on the floor, back resting against the iconostasis, sucking his thumb. The girls were deeply absorbed in the service, watching everything attentively, crossing themselves solemnly, all without a trace of self-consciousness. At times the younger girl leaned against her older sister, who in turn had her arms around the younger one. At other times they were holding hands. A short distance away I noticed a lean, bearded man about my age with his wife and their son, about nine. The intelligence in the boy's face and his attitude of deep devotion were impressive. He often rested against his father. All the while the singing fell on us as if we were standing under a waterfall.

Wanting to buy a few icon cards, I went into a small shop built into the wall surrounding the monastery where I was waited on by a lean, grizzled elder wearing patched clothing, something of a human cactus—a man who had seen many hard years. As he gave me change for a twenty-ruble note, he was quietly whispering not numbers, it dawned on me, but a short form of the Jesus Prayer: "Jesus, have mercy, Jesus, have mercy, Jesus, have mercy. . . ." After putting the change in my pocket, I lingered, pretending to look at other items for sale, but really only to see if his whispered prayer ever stopped. If it did, it was not while I was there.

At lunchtime at a restaurant in the city center, I happened to be placed along the path of Patriarch Pimen, a former Gulag prisoner. He had aged since I last saw him two years earlier—now he had difficulty walking. Two people helped him make his painful way to a table, yet his lively eyes were darting around with great attention, not missing a thing.

Participants in the religious section of the conference met in the afternoon to hear the draft text of a proposed common statement, the work of a panel that included Dwain Epps from the National Council of Churches in New York. The committee managed to catch the spirit of the meeting, neither accusing nor praising but concentrating on positive steps to be taken. "People of religion have special roles to play, among them: promoting unity among the peoples; increasing contacts across lines of division; helping to eliminate prejudiced enemy images; and intensifying education for peace." Leaders of the nuclear states were urged to renounce nuclear deterrence and to conclude new treaties leading toward a nuclear-free world. It was a simple text, but not lacking in a sense of urgency: "We appeal to all to commit themselves unalterably to the task of building the basis for common security today. The time has come for us to ask the ancient questions: If not me, who? If not now, when?"

The next and last morning all the conference participants came together for a plenary meeting at the Kremlin. Our first stop was the Palace of Facets in the oldest part of the Kremlin, where we were taken to what had once been the throne room of the czars. It was decorated with biblical scenes depicting the creation of the world as described in Genesis—suitable images for a meeting preoccupied with threats to creation.

After an hour of informal conversations, we were ushered into the Supreme Soviet, a large hall that was the meeting place of the most authoritative legislative body of the Soviet Union. There was nothing hierarchical about seating arrangements. More than halfway back in the hall, I found myself sitting directly in front of a member of the Central Committee of the Communist Party, Georgi Arbatov, a key figure in the Gorbachev inner circle and architect of Soviet foreign policy. He had recently told a *Time* magazine reporter, "We are going to do something terrible to you. We are going to deprive you of an enemy." Over to the side I noticed Kris Kristofferson, the American singer, songwriter, and actor who had recently played the leading role in a film dramatizing a Soviet takeover of the United States. He looked rather sheepish. Most surprising, a few rows in front of me, was the renowned nuclear physicist Andrei Sakharov, around whom the press gathered as if he were Albert Einstein risen from the dead. Truly it was headline news that the country's most famous dissident, long kept in internal exile, a man who had paid a heavy price for his advocacy of human rights, was now was a guest of honor in the Kremlin.

Sitting at a podium in the front of the hall was a representative from each section of the conference plus Gorbachev.

A highlight of this final session was a speech by Graham Greene, representing the writers' section. He apologized that he would be speaking just for himself but, he commented, "no writer can possibly represent more than one writer." Then he explained, without ever mentioning his latest novel, *Monsignor Quixote*, what that book was all about: religious people opening their ears to Marxists about a more just social order, and Marxists discovering that God not only exists but is far more radical than they are. General Michael Harbottle from Britain spoke, as did Dr. Bernard Lown of Harvard, one of the initiators of Physicians for the Prevention of Nuclear War. Metropolitan Paulos Mar Gregorios from India, a president of the World Council of Churches, spoke on behalf of the religious section of the conference. There was an Italian businessman, a political scientist, an ecologist. The speeches, broadcast live on Soviet television and rebroadcast in the evening, were all quite good.

Gorbachev came last and gave a major address. He argued that the fact that we had survived forty years with nuclear weapons is not something to count on forever. "We are," he said, "the lucky survivors of many war-risking games of chance. Nuclear deterrence is a policy based on intimidation and threat. It must always be backed up with definite action, and this actually increases the chances of military conflict. If we continue in the direction we are going, living in a constant state of high alert with enormous stocks of such weapons, then catastrophe is highly likely. . . . Eventually we will terminate our own existence, and there will be no second Noahs." He didn't agree with those who argue that war is part of human nature. "Many say so. If so we are doomed. I cannot accept such a dogma." His basic message was that the responsibility is in our hands to make an unprecedented break not only with weapons of mass destruction but with militarism. Everything that matters depends on this. Gorbachev was no pacifist, but he seemed to be an abolitionist: someone who believes in a future without doomsday weaponry and even a future in which war is as unthinkable as slavery. "The immortality of the human race," he said, "has been lost and can only be regained by the elimination of nuclear weapons. The nuclear guillotine must be broken and with it the alienation of politics from ethics."

He spoke about democratization and the "revolution now in progress" in the Soviet Union, which he said was unstoppable and which shouldn't be seen as simply a response to Western pressures or criticisms but as an event with local roots. "We want a democratic society. We want more socialism and more democracy." The main problem with politics, he said, "is that it has become soul-less." Gorbachev's own view seemed to be summed up in the words, "Life will have its way."

Outside the hall, an American journalist asked me what I thought of Gorbachev's speech. I said that words on a page or a face on a television screen just aren't the same as hearing someone speaking at length, unedited, and in the same room. I hoped she could find a way to communicate the possibility that what he said isn't a propaganda charade. His speech reminded me, I said, of Pope John XXIII's encyclical *Pacem in Terris*.

Sandwiched between two old enemies, Norman Mailer and Gore Vidal, I made my way to a buffet lunch on the top floor of the Palace of Congresses, one of the few modern buildings within the walls of the Kremlin. For the first time that week, we had wine with our meal. Given the small crowd gathered around him, I wasn't able to speak with Gorbachev but was close enough to take a photo of him, as requested by two of my daughters.

I sought out Graham Greene, now 82, who recalled we had occasionally exchanged letters. He had watery, pale blue eyes and a ghost-like handshake, but there was a strong pulse in his words. He worried that he had let rhetoric get the best of him during his speech. I also talked with actor Gregory Peck. We spoke about Dan Berrigan's play, *The Trial of the Catonsville Nine*, the movie version of which had been produced by Peck. It was a box-office disaster, he said, but had won a film prize. Peck predicted that one day it would come into its own. I noticed Yoko Ono standing quietly by herself and saw Marcello Mastroianni, looking venerable and tired, cheerfully signing autographs.

In the afternoon I was one of several people accompanying Metropolitan Yuvenali to the US Embassy. We were received in a small room on the ground floor. I was impressed by how warm and unpretentious Yuvenali was. He asked the embassy staff to forward to President Reagan a copy of the final statement of the religious section of the conference as well as the same medal that had been presented to Gorbachev in the morning: an enameled medallion with a view of the earth from space.

To be in Moscow in 1987 was to hear the loud crack of Cold War ice breaking under our feet. Who would believe that former cold warrior Ronald Reagan, of all people, would embrace the moment? To his undying credit, Reagan played a decisive role in greatly reducing the number of US and Soviet nuclear weapons and their delivery systems. In December 1987, Reagan and Gorbachev signed the proposed treaty, and six months later, again in Moscow, signed the final text, now ratified by the US Senate, of the Intermediate-Range Nuclear Forces

Treaty. Reagan told reporters that he no longer considered the Soviet Union an "evil empire," a phrase he had often used in his first term as president. The climate between the two superpowers had changed so dramatically that Reagan described his relationship with Gorbachev as one of friendship.

While Reagan and Gorbachev were shaking hands in the Kremlin for another treaty signing ceremony in 1988, I was also in Moscow and nearly crossed paths with First Lady Nancy Reagan. My translator and I had gone to Peredelkino, a village on the edge of Moscow made famous by the writers who had lived there, most notably Boris Pasternak, whose burial place is next to the Transfiguration Church. Three older women were sitting on a stone bench at the foot of Pasternak's grave. One of them pointed to a branch of pale lavender orchids lying in front of the tombstone. "Nancy Reagan put them there! I saw her do it with my own eyes," one of them told me. What surprised the women as much as meeting so famous a person was that she came only with her driver—"She was alone. There were no journalists, no photographers!" Apparently I was not the only pilgrim that day. On my return to Holland, I sent Mrs. Reagan a photo of Pasternak's grave and her orchids. She responded with a note of thanks.

A Change of Address

When I first went to Russia, I hadn't anticipated the impact the Orthodox Church would have on my inner life, and not only mine but Nancy's. Neither of us was window shopping for a different spiritual home. All I was hoping to achieve was to help open a few East–West doors for encounter and dialogue in order to make war less likely. As for a spiritual home, we already had one. For all the complaints one could list about the shortcomings of the Catholic Church, neither of us was in the market for a "better" variety of Christianity. It's only in the distance that the grass looks greener. Every church falls short of the gospel of Christ.

Just after Easter 1987, Metropolitan Filaret of Minsk, head of the External Affairs Department of the Moscow Patriarchate, asked me about my family and the effect of my Russian travels on our home life. I mentioned that Nancy, following the Russian example, had been observing days and periods of fasting. More important, each night we were praying before our icons, standing as Russians do and using prayers from the Orthodox liturgy. "Your wife is part of what you are doing," said Filaret, "just as the wife of a priest shares in the priesthood. Your wife is a *matushka*,[1] and she should come with you to Russia. Why does she never travel with you?" I laughed. "Simple! We can't afford it." "You should have told me," Filaret responded. "I am inviting you and Nancy to come this summer. It isn't just a polite word. You will be my guests once you arrive in Moscow. I'll arrange everything. You haven't yet seen my part of Russia—Belarus, White Russia, the real Russia." He gave me a final blessing and an Easter egg to bring home to Nancy.

---

1. The intimate form of the Russian word for mother, the honorific title of a priest's wife.

As a consequence, Nancy and I spent much of June in Russia and Belarus. Parts of the journal she kept were woven into the last section of my book *Pilgrim to the Russian Church*.[2]

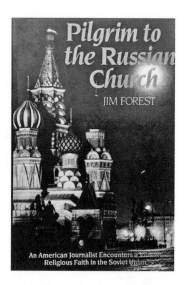

In June we set off for Russia by rail, a fifty-hour journey, beginning in the Dutch city of Amersfoort, with seats in the train's only Soviet carriage. A hammer-and-sickle emblem was on the sides. Most of the other carriages were going to Copenhagen and Stockholm. Along the way the train picked up new cars, dropped off others. By the time we crossed the Russian border we were part of a lengthy column of Soviet carriages all bound for Moscow.

What impressed Nancy most in Russia, as it had me, was the church's worshiping life. "I have never been in congregations of such unqualified religious concentration," Nancy wrote in her journal. "At the very first liturgy I attended, I had a sudden sense of being at the center of the universe and knew that each of us had this in common. The fact of standing rather than sitting may have something to do with remaining attentive to the activity in the church rather than slipping into private daydreams or plans for the rest of the day. You can't help but pay attention to the sensuous drama going on, the brilliant iconostasis, the constant singing, the incense. All these things pulled me again and again to the business at hand, the eternal present, with its music. I had such a deep sense of spiritual connection."

One of the things that especially impressed Nancy was the freedom children had to move about and sit or stand as they pleased during services, a mobility made possible by the absence of pews as well as understanding parents and church tradition. "No one shushed the children," she commented.

Back in Holland three weeks later, we were overflowing with gratitude for what we had witnessed together, but still it hadn't crossed our

---

2. *Pilgrim to the Russian Church* was published in 1988 by Crossroad Publishing Company; the book is now out of print, but the full text is online: http://jimandnancyforest.com/2019/04/a-pilgrim-to-the-russian-church/.

minds to become Orthodox. What finally tipped the scales wasn't the various aspects of Orthodoxy that we found admirable but a specific Orthodox parish, St. Nicholas of Myra in Amsterdam. Thanks to a mutual friend, a co-worker at IFOR, Joe Peacock, I had come to know the rector, Alexis Voogd, also professor of Russian language at the University of Amsterdam. In the first stage of our relationship, he had suggested a number of places to visit and people to interview in Russia. His guidance made *Pilgrim to the Russian Church* a better book than it might have been.

In December 1987 Father Alexis phoned me at the IFOR office with an invitation: "Jim, you've been to so many Orthodox churches in Russia but never to the church in Amsterdam! How about you and Nancy taking part in an ecumenical gathering we're having in January to mark the thousand-year anniversary of the baptism of Russia?" He went on to explain that in the year 988, Prince Vladimir called on the people of Kiev to be baptized in the River Dnieper. Before the year ended, Christianity had quickly taken root in much of what today is eastern Ukraine and areas farther north that in time became Russia and Belarus. I said yes.

On Saturday, January 9, Nancy and I took the train to Amsterdam. The parish at that time used a rented Catholic chapel barely big enough to hold forty people. I was surprised that the majority of parishioners were Dutch—I had imagined we would find mainly Russians in exile.— The event itself was something of a hodge-podge. There was a welcome from Father Alexis in which he briefly described the Christianization of Ukraine and Russia in the late tenth century. Both the local Catholic archbishop and the head of the Dutch Council of Churches spoke about the exciting developments occurring in the Soviet Union, especially the end of religious repression. The parish choir, perched overhead in a loft reached by a steep flight of stairs, sang a few pieces that were normally heard during the liturgy.

The gathering was followed by a reception in a building not far away. Wine and vodka flowed freely. We found ourselves in a surprisingly multinational, intellectually engaging, welcoming community. One of the people we met was another American, Margot Muntz, who in her younger years had been a dancer and was now a Dutch-to-English translator. Amsterdam had become her home in 1946, just after the war. She was now a widow; her husband had been a Russian. They had been among the founders of the parish. Walking back to the train station,

Nancy and I decided to come back as soon as possible to see what the parish was like on a normal Sunday. Would the aspects of worship that we both had so admired in Russia be diluted in a Western setting?

The following week we returned. It happened to be a Sunday when Dutch was the main liturgical language—week by week the language balance see-sawed back and forth, one Sunday mainly Dutch, the next mainly Russian, with the Epistle and Gospel readings always in both. We found the climate of worship was no less intense than we had experienced in Russia.

Back home we talked about perhaps returning on alternate weeks, attending Mass at our Catholic parish on the Sundays in which the Latin choir, to which we belonged, was singing. But we quickly found that a religiously divided life was no solution. By mid-February we were on the train to Amsterdam every Sunday. The parish of St. Nicholas had become our home, even though we were not receiving communion there. Finally on Palm Sunday, following chrismation, I crossed the border. Nancy did the same at Pentecost. We had become Orthodox communicants.

Several friends afterward spoke of my "conversion" to the Orthodox Church, but I didn't regard the move as a conversion. It was simply a change of address in the same neighborhood I had been living in since I was eighteen. Orthodoxy and Catholicism have so much in common, far more than what separates them. I have never embraced the label "ex-Catholic."

Among the most distressed by my "change of address" was Henri Nouwen. He sent us a letter full of anguish. I responded:

> *Your letter touched both of us. . . . While I was Catholic (I feel very odd putting it in the past tense, because I am still Catholic; but I am speaking about where I stand among the lines of division that scar the Body of Christ), I was hesitant to express or even think about criticisms of the Catholic Church. Like yourself, I am not a person especially drawn to criticism. Anyway, I have so much to be critical about in regard to myself that it seems absurd to get fussy about the flaws of others. Also, when criticism is of a church, the criticism implies that the critic stands in a place where criticism has little or no local application; and that is never true.*
>
> *As a Catholic I always tried to center my awareness on what was good in the church, of which there was plenty. There is a great deal to*

notice in that regard even here in Holland, despite the aridity, the social reticence, the head-centeredness, the lack of a penitential dimension (how rare to encounter confession in Dutch Catholic parishes!), and the awful polarization. Yet the Dutch Catholic Church still has the sacraments and still listens to the Gospel. It has been and continues to be one of the most committed to the poor and among the most thoughtful about the structures that cause suffering. It has been one of the most serious about trying to overcome historic divisions between Christians. In Dutch Catholicism there is a great deal that is outstanding.

It is always a problem that, whenever one makes a move, he feels freer to criticize his former place—or, in the case of a broken marriage, his former partner. But however long I make my list of complaints about Catholicism, and however serious the items listed, in fact these have little to do with why I have become Orthodox—about which one could make some other long list of faults, though being rather new to Orthodoxy, I cannot be so detailed. In another few years no doubt I will be able to write at length about what is wrong with Orthodoxy.

I think what has mattered to me most about Orthodoxy has been the way the Orthodox pray and the fact that the Eucharist is at the center and there is an overwhelming sense of Jesus being present, in bread and wine and word and in each other. In fact this had much to do with my attraction to Catholicism nearly thirty years ago. But in Catholicism much that I treasured has been moved to the attic. The awe seems gone. And Latin, a language of transgenerational and borderless worship, is mainly gone, wherein I found a beauty that hasn't nearly been matched in the current Catholic liturgy. Where Latin survives, it is either because the local congregation is elderly (that's the case for our parish in Alkmaar) or because of Lefebvre-ism, which seems to represent a grim nostalgia for fascism and the Holy Inquisition. The impressive thing is that Orthodoxy makes no attempt at producing an updated "relevant" liturgy. Far from keeping up with the times, the Orthodox liturgy has hardly changed from ancient times. The Orthodox seem to realize that liturgy itself is the touchstone of relevance.

You expressed the hope that we would be bridge builders. I share that hope. I have brought with me everything that was dear to me in Catholicism. On Easter night, I was moved that one of the hymns we sang was a traditional Latin Easter chant, "Christus resurrexit." No hymnal was needed to sing it.

I reminded Henri of a passage from Merton:

If I can unite in myself the thought and the devotion of Eastern and Western Christendom, the Greek and the Latin Fathers, the Russian with the Spanish mystics, I can prepare in myself the reunion of divided Christians. From that secret and unspoken unity in myself can eventually come a visible and manifest unity of all Christians. If we want to bring together what is divided, we cannot do so by imposing one division upon the other. If we do this, the union is not Christian. It is political and doomed to further conflict. We must contain all the divided worlds in ourselves and transcend them in Christ.[3]

I write these pages after more than thirty years of centering my eucharistic life in the Orthodox Church. In the course of these decades, I've found that the walls dividing our fragmented Christian world are fewer than the bridges connecting Christians. There is no Catholic Jesus, Orthodox Jesus, Protestant Jesus. There is only Jesus.

Every now and then I am given a vivid reminder of our underlying unity. One such moment occurred several years ago while I was reciting my morning prayers while walking in the park that circles the oldest part of the town of Alkmaar. Following advice from one of the priests of our parish, I was saying each phrase in each prayer again and again as a way of keeping my prayers from becoming too mechanical. Instead of simply reciting the Our Father straight through, I was saying "our Father . . . our Father . . . our Father. . . ." When I had reached the words "give us this day our daily bread" and had repeated them several times, a slice of very ordinary bread fell from the blue sky, hitting the asphalt path with a thud directly in front of me. For half a minute I stood stone still, gazing at the bread in astonishment, then walked on a few paces before coming back to take a photo of the bread. I wanted to show it to Nancy as proof it wasn't a hallucination. And I laughed. It was as if God decided to remind me that the silence of heaven doesn't mean no one is listening.

One piece of bread. One Jesus Christ.

---

3. Thomas Merton, *Conjectures of a Guilty Bystander* (New York: Doubleday, 1966), 12.

Miloserdia

In June 1988, two months after my chrismation, I returned to Russia once again, on this occasion with Father Alexis Voogd. We both had been invited to participate in the thousand-year anniversary of the mass baptism of the Kievan people—thus the foundation of Christianity in what eventually became Ukraine and Russia—and also to attend the church council that would be meeting for several days at the Holy Trinity–St. Sergius Lavra Monastery north of Moscow.

The millennium celebration provided the perfect starting point for my next book, *Religion in the New Russia*,[1] a portrait of the changes occurring in religious life not only for Orthodox Christians but for Catholics, Protestants, Jews, Muslims, and Buddhists. Traveling by train and air, my journeys in the months that followed would take me from Moscow to Kiev, from Samarkand to Irkutz, from the White Sea to Lake Baikal, from Petrozavodsk near the Finnish border to Ulan Ude in the southeast of Siberia near the Mongolian border.

The main public event in Moscow was an outdoor liturgy at the Danilovski monastery, where a crowd of ten thousand filled the large space within the walls. It was my first occasion of receiving communion in Russia.

In its surprises, each day of that June visit seemed to outdo the day before. One of these was the Vatican's participation, an impressive witness of ecumenical solidarity. Nine cardinals had been sent to Moscow by Pope John Paul and all were present that day. One of them was the archbishop of New York, Cardinal John O'Connor, whom I found staying in the same hotel where I was. After meeting in an elevator, we

---

1. *Religion in the New Russia* was published in 1990 by Crossroad Publishing Company; it is now out of print but the full text is online: http://jimandnancy forest.com/2019/04/religion-in-the-new-russia/.

talked in the lobby discussing the breakthroughs occurring in Russian religious life, and also the possibility of Dorothy Day's canonization, a process that in fact O'Connor initiated a decade later.

Following the council, Father Alexis and I attended the celebrations in Kiev, where we stood in heavy rain among the throng that carpeted the west bank of the Dnieper River. The downpour seemed choreographed by heaven. What appropriate weather for commemorating a mass baptism! Like a special effect in a cast-of-thousands Hollywood film, there was a sudden opening of the rain clouds midway through the liturgy, with rays of sunlight illumining the outdoor altar and the nearby statue of Prince Vladimir.

But the most impressive event was yet to come and went unnoticed by the world press. On June 20, after the end of the formal millennium celebrations, Moscow's evening television news program included a minidocumentary about the rebirth of *miloserdia*—the works of mercy—in Russian church life. For the first time since Lenin, Christians were being allowed, even encouraged, to openly play a role in the relief of suffering. The program's focus was on the patriarch's own church, the Epiphany Cathedral in Moscow, which was now in partnership with a nearby hospital. An agreement had been signed making it possible for church members to serve there as volunteers.

"The Christian religion teaches care of neighbor," hospital director Anatoly Soloviev explained. "This is a concrete way of doing it. Now we have our first contact with a religious group. We think it can help with problems we have offering health care. Some of the patients need constant care, and we don't have the staff to offer that. The feeling you get from believers is compassion. Patients need that. They need the support of faith and love."

Father Matvei Stadniuk, dean of the Epiphany Cathedral, was also interviewed. "What led the church to help in this way?" he was asked. "Our Orthodox people are part of society," he answered, "and I'm very glad that now the opportunity has come to help people. It is *perestroika* and democratization at work. The time has come for common feeling. It means seeing what you can do today. Tomorrow may be too late. This work is a moral reward for the people. The way people respond already shows that the conscience of our people has not been destroyed. We expect that many in our church will take part. The hospital is our neighbor. We hope to give help every day. After all, to have any success in healing you have to have love."

"If you have a feeling of mercy in your heart," said one of the volunteers, "you will do this." A priest was shown making the sign of the cross over a woman too ill even to raise her head. In another room a nurse was standing next to a frail patient. "Do you feel pushed aside by these volunteers coming from the church?" the nurse was asked. "Oh no," said the nurse, crossing herself, "I am a believer myself!"

"It is the first time," said an astonished Orthodox priest who was watching the news with me, "that anything like this has been permitted since Lenin! In the past it has been said that the state provides all social services and needs no help from religious believers in doing it. But that's far from true. At almost all hospitals the nursing staff is far too small. Many patients are suffering for lack of adequate care."

Assisted by a Muscovite English teacher, three days later I visited Clinical Hospital Number Six, a few blocks west of the Epiphany Cathedral. We searched through several buildings surrounding a small park until we found the director. I asked how many hospitals were involved in the volunteer initiative. "So far this is the only one," said Soloviev, "but I think many more will quickly do the same." "What sort of volunteers are coming?" "Ordinary people. There is no pay for it and there are no qualifications needed except the willingness to help."

He laughed when I asked about the history of the hospital's engagement with the local church. "It is so new that it is hard to say there is any history! We began just ten days ago during the celebration of the church's millennium. There were talks between the hospital staff and representatives of the church. Then it was announced at the cathedral during morning prayer June 8 that we would welcome volunteers. The first one to show up was a man named Sergei Leonidovitch Timofeev. Then came a nun, Mother Marianelle, who brought a group of believers with her. We can say these people are the founders. So far, except Sergei, they're all women. They come when they have time. There is no schedule."

"What do they do?" "They clean wards, change linens, take care of bed pans, talk to the patients, sit with them, read the newspaper or a book aloud. They make contact with the believers among the patients, and, if a patient asks, they invite a priest to bring the sacraments or to come and pray with them."

How is it going? "We are happy about it. We see how much it means to the patients, and it is good for the staff also. One of the patients, an old man who has had five heart attacks, asked if he can give his money to the hospital to help others. This is something we never heard from a patient before. You are seeing the very beginning. We don't know where it will lead. I have no prognosis. But I have hope. We are in a new period of our history; we are starting a new life. Both the clergy and the doctors have hopes that this will develop. From our side, we are ready to do our best. But we have no experience in it and are learning as we go."

The next day I went to Patriarch Pimen's residence near Arbat Street to meet Father Matvei Stadniuk. His desk was covered with papers and books. There were several icons on the wall. He had a short white beard and a shy manner. No translator was needed—he spoke English fluently.[2]

"Our Russian word for acts of care is *miloserdia*—works of a merciful heart," he explained. "It means any action done for others out of Christ's love. In her long history the church was always taking care of people. There is nothing new in this, but the possibility in our situation is new. We are just starting to put seeds in the ground. It is too early to say what will come from them. But the church should do whatever she can for those who are in need. We hope that the possibilities to do this will improve, especially now that we have a good relationship with the government. As you know, *perestroika* is going on. Thank God! This renewal of structures comes from *dukhovnost*—the spiritual life of the people. Our country and every country need *dukhovnost*. In fact I think America may need

---

2. For a more detailed account of my interviews with Father Matvei Stadniuk, see my book *Religion in the New Russia* (New York: Crossroad, 1990), 35–41.

it even more than we do. *Dukhovnost* is the reason the church has survived so many centuries and difficult times."

How are members of the congregation responding? "One person asked me whether it was more important to go to the church for services or to go to the hospital to volunteer. Well, normally we don't have to choose between one and the other, but I said sometimes it may be more important to go to the hospital. Sometimes the needs there may be the most urgent."

We talked about forgiveness. "To live in Christ," said Father Matvei, "is to forgive, but this is very hard sometimes. If someone killed your brother, it is not easy to forgive the killer. We have to take the example of our Savior who said, 'Father forgive them, they don't know what they are doing.' Forgiveness is at the heart of the transformation happening in our country. This rejuvenation is impossible without forgiveness. *Perestroika* cannot happen by itself, without a spiritual life. We know from our history how much evil one man can do. With one small match you can burn down a huge building, but with the light of forgiveness you can do even more. With spiritual fire you can heal."

In the hour we were together, Father Matvei spoke repeatedly of gratitude: "We are grateful. . . . We should give thanks. . . . Thanks be to God! . . . We should say thanks to God!" It was his deep gratitude that I felt even more than his words.

When leaving, I gave him a copy of my biography of Dorothy Day.[3] He was amazed at the gift. "Dorothy Day! Did you know her?" I said I had worked with her on the Catholic Worker staff in the early sixties and that it was she who first brought me to visit a Russian Orthodox cathedral, the church on East Ninety-Seventh Street in New York. Father Matvei clapped his hands and laughed. "Jim, I thought you were familiar! We have met before! I remember you when you were a younger man! I was serving in that church—I was the dean. Dorothy used to visit me and I once went to the Catholic Worker farm. I remember her bringing you to our church. I believe that there are no accidental meetings. Please come and see me again when you return to Moscow."

---

3. It was the first edition, *Love Is the Measure*. A revised, expanded biography was later published by Orbis Books: *All Is Grace: A Biography of Dorothy Day* (Maryknoll, NY: Orbis Books, 2017).

The Family Farm

There was another border that Nancy and I crossed in 1988. Ever since our Jerusalem sabbatical in 1985, we had been preparing the transition to home-based work. Now, we decided, that time had come. When I cleared my desk at IFOR, I had been on the staff nearly twelve years. During a meeting of IFOR branches that summer in Assisi, Italy, some kind words were said about what I had done and several parting gifts were presented. The one that I treasure most was a specially decorated Dutch wooden shoe painted by my French co-worker Françoise Pottier. On one side was the main Dutch symbol of nuclear disarmament—several people pushing away a huge bomb; on the other an icon of St. Francis; and on the front the silhouette of an onion-domed Russian church. This trinity of images touched on key aspects of what had shaped much of my work and life since departing from America.

Returning to Alkmaar from Assisi, I felt as if we had just jumped off a diving board and were about to find out if we could walk on water. With very little predictable income and almost no money in the bank, we were economically dependent on freelance work—editing and translation jobs in Nancy's case, a mixture of writing, editing, and speaking in mine.

We saw ourselves as re-inventors of the family farm—an economic partnership in which husband and wife shared equally in the labor and made decisions by talking them through as equal partners. Metaphorically, how our "farm" fared economically depended on a good balance of rain and sun. During the first two or three years, we had many sleepless nights—farmer Jim and farmer Nancy did a lot of praying for tolerable economic weather.

By the fall of 1988, I had three part-time jobs besides trying to find islands of time for my own writing projects. To do more book work was the reason I had ended my IFOR work, but writing income is unpredictable and occasional and royalty payments come only twice a year.

My most demanding job was writing, editing, and producing a monthly collection of news reports for Peace Media Service, a project I had envisioned while still on the IFOR staff and that came with me when I departed. It provided me with a modest but dependable monthly salary for seven years. The first edition of PMS was posted in October 1988, the last in June 1995.

Peace Media Service met a pressing need. An adage of journalism declares: "If it bleeds, it leads." Just look at any newspaper. Reports of

murder and war win first place on the front page—killing someone gets bigger headlines and more prominence than saving lives. The idea behind Peace Media Service was to attempt to change the balance, even if only slightly, by distributing readable, reliable reports of nonviolent peace efforts that deserved attention but were generally ignored by the mass media. PMS also provided subscribers with first-rate political cartoons by the Dutch illustrator Len Munnik, familiar to the Dutch public (he continues to be seen several times each week in the pages of the newspaper *Trouw*), but unfamiliar to the rest of the world.

A Quaker-associated foundation in New York gave PMS significant support. We also had a number of enthusiastic private donors, including folk singer Pete Seeger, violinist and conductor Yehudi Menuhin, Muppeteer and film director Jim Henson, and Arthur C. Clarke, whose science fiction stories had inspired me as a kid. PMS kept going and even growing for seven years, with subscribers from a wide variety of publications and news outlets, including the BBC and *Time* magazine, but in the end we were done in by economics—the dollar, the currency of most of our income, had been worth 3.5 guilders when we started but had sunk to 1.5 guilders seven years later.

Another worthwhile job that came my way in 1988 was editing *Forum*, the quarterly publication of the Program for Justice, Peace and the Integrity of Creation for the World Council of Churches. The journal, in tabloid newspaper format, was issued seasonally, which meant four visits a year to Geneva to consult with the WCC staff. It was exciting to play a part in this major WCC undertaking.

My third commitment, one that continues to the present day, was to help develop the Orthodox Peace Fellowship. In 1988 OPF was more a dream than a reality. The concept owed its genesis to a poet and playwright living in New York, Mariquita Platov, an elderly member of the Fellowship of Reconciliation who had found her way to the Orthodox Church. Even before becoming Orthodox myself, while still IFOR's general secretary, I had cheered Mariquita along with her vision. I knew quite well that Orthodox Christians were as likely as Christians in other churches to be nationalists first, Christians second. How often the cross has been made to serve as a flagpole! Thanks to Mariquita and another volunteer, Jim Larrick, a mailing list began to take shape. Several two- to four-page newsletters had been sent out.

Once I became Orthodox myself, I began helping bring OPF to life. As a first step I set about enlisting a board of advisors made up of respected Orthodox theologians from various jurisdictions while at the same time, in consultation with advisers, drafting a statement of purpose.

While over the years there have been OPF conferences and retreats both in America and Europe, our major continuing project from 1989 onward has been a quarterly journal that we christened *In Communion*. I was its editor for more than twenty years; today the editor is Nicholas Sooy. For many it has become a publication not just to read but to save. In its early years it existed only on paper, but as the internet began to take shape, we created a related website as well—incommunion.org. Here the contents of every issue of the journal are available without charge to any interested person. The website has become a much-used online library of articles, essays, books, and other resources that is visited by thousands of people each month, Orthodox and otherwise, from all over the world.

Through the journal and website, OPF has played a part in making Orthodox Christians, from bishops to young converts, more aware of the radical challenge posed to Christians today by the early church, in which participation in war was definitely not encouraged and when the practice of the works of mercy was a normal aspect of ordinary Christian life. Like the church of the early centuries, OPF has been an advocate of what has now been termed "the consistent pro-life ethic," opposing war, abortion, capital punishment, assisted suicide, and euthanasia.

The Orthodox Peace Fellowship played a role in making better known and speeding the canonizations of two martyr-saints of the twentieth century, Mother Maria Skobtsova,[1] who founded a house of hospitality in Paris at the time Dorothy Day was doing the same thing in New York, and Alexander Schmorell,[2] one of the initiators of the White Rose, a movement of student resistance to Hitler and Nazism in Germany. Both died martyr's deaths.

Because I had so much else to do, my own writing often had to fit into crevices of time, mainly nights and weekends, but by the end of the nineties I had a surprising number of books in print: *Pilgrim to the Russian Church*, *Religion in the New Russia*, *Love Is the Measure* (a biography of Dorothy Day, since expanded to become *All Is Grace*), *Living with Wisdom* (a biography of Thomas Merton, since expanded into a revised edition), *Making Friends of Enemies* (later enlarged to become *Loving Our Enemies: Reflections on the Hardest Commandment*), *Four Days in February* (on a nonviolent revolution in the Philippines, a book coauthored with Nancy), and the first of two children's books, *The Tale of the Turnip* and *The Whale's Tale*, both illustrated by Len Munnik.[3]

Little by little Nancy's translation work began to gain traction. In 1989 she founded her own business, Forest-Flier Editorial Services. Her first major commission grew out of one of my occasional visits to the World Council of Churches headquarters in Geneva. Over lunch one day, Jan Kok, a Dutchman who then headed the WCC Publications Department, was impressed when I told him how much more fluent

---

1. For more about her life, see "Mother Maria Skobtsova: Saint of the Open Door," at http://jimandnancyforest.com/2006/08/mothermaria/. There is also a collection of her essays, *Mother Maria Skobtsova: Essential Writings*, ed. Helene Klepinin-Arjakovsky, trans. Larissa Volokhonsky and Richard Pevear (Maryknoll, NY: Orbis Books, 2003).

2. For more about his life, see "Alexander Schmorell: A Witness in Dark Times," http://jimandnancyforest.com/2011/02/alexander-schmorell-a-witness-in-dark-times/.

3. For a complete list of books in print, see www.jimandnancyforest.com/books/.

Nancy's Dutch was than my own. Jan's eyebrows lifted. "Do you think," he asked, "that Nancy might consider translating a Dutch theological study we want to publish into English?" Nancy welcomed the job. "I wore out my first Dutch–English dictionary on that project," she recalls. Another WCC book commission quickly followed.

Translation commissions also started coming from the Anne Frank House in Amsterdam. We had developed friendships there with several staff members, in part thanks to the Orthodox Peace Fellowship's collaboration in bringing Anne Frank-related traveling exhibitions to Kiev and Moscow. Nancy's work with the Anne Frank House continues to the present day.

Nancy's client list has developed to include the Royal Library in The Hague, the Kröller-Müller Museum in Otterlo, the Van Gogh Museum in Amsterdam, Lemniscaat Books in Rotterdam, Canongate Books in Edinburgh, and several US-based publishers: World Editions, Tor/Macmillan, New Directions, and the MIT Press. It has become a challenge finding storage space in our small house for all the volumes Nancy has translated in the past thirty years.

Nancy especially credits Margot Muntz with making her aware that translation could be the vocation her love of language had long been edging her toward. By the time we met her, Margot was one of the principal translators for Amsterdam's Stedelijk Museum, a major Dutch repository of modern art. Margot introduced Nancy to professional organizations, giving her tips and ideas, and was an enthusiastic cheerleader and friend until her death in 2005.

The family farm is still functioning. The wheat is growing, the cows are being milked, and apples are ripening.

A Pilgrimage of Illness

One of my favorite writers is Flannery O'Connor, who died young, age thirty-nine, after years of being afflicted by lupus. Her short stories and novels never fail to surprise. Her letters are no less remarkable—some hilarious, some profound, many both. As her letters bear witness, she was as much a theologian as a storyteller. Eight years before she died, she wrote to a friend, "I have never been anywhere but sick. In a sense sickness is a place, more instructive than a long trip to Europe. . . . Sickness before death is a very appropriate thing and I think those who don't have it miss one of God's mercies."[1]

My only experience so far of life-threatening illness began in 2003. Routine blood tests arranged by our family doctor suggested that my kidneys might not be working as well as they should. I was referred to the local hospital. About a week after a round of tests, Dr. Willem Bax, an internist, told me that my kidneys were failing, that the condition was irreversible, and that probably within six months I would need to begin dialysis in order to stay alive. "We will be seeing a great deal of each other," he told me, and indeed we have. I've been in his care the past sixteen years.

Dialysis didn't sound inviting—an alternate method of filtering the blood when kidney function has either dropped below 10 percent or the kidneys have altogether stopped working, an event that can happen suddenly. Without an alternate method of getting rid of the wastes that are filtered out of our bloodstream by the kidneys, the condition is a death sentence.

Things moved more slowly than Dr. Bax had estimated—six months became a year, one year became two, but at last the day came when

---

1. Flannery O'Connor, *The Habit of Being: Letters of Flannery O'Connor* (New York: Farrar, Straus & Giroux, 1999), 163.

Dr. Bax, after reviewing the latest blood test, said dialysis had to begin tomorrow.

I became a traveler in the world of chronic illness, a pilgrimage route far more trafficked than the roads to Canterbury, Santiago de Compostela, and Jerusalem combined.

Sickness is time consuming and limiting. With three long sessions of dialysis a week, each about four hours long, more than ever I was anchored in Holland. This is not to say that travel was impossible. I've had dialysis care in France, England, Greece, Spain, Canada, and the United States. It just requires a lot of planning.

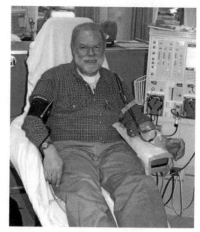

In my third week of dialysis, January 27, 2006

Like anyone with a prolonged illness, I had to rethink how to make the best use of each day. My available time for activity had been cut dramatically. Where should the adjustments be made? The decisions involved economies in almost every area of life—less correspondence, less walking, less biking, less household work, less recreational time. Only family time and time spent at our parish church were untrimmed.

Then there was the question of how to make the best use of all those hours spent at the hospital. My first solution was to watch films. Shortly before dialysis began, Nancy gave me a compact DVD player. For the first few months at the dialysis clinic, I watched films, from old Charlie Chaplain comedies to the Harry Potter series, from Orson Welles's *Citizen Kane* to a movie version of Shakespeare's *Hamlet*. I would have preferred books, but they seemed ruled out because I didn't dare move my left arm due to the two long needles inserted in it, one outgoing, one incoming, with the blood-filtering mechanism in between. It seemed obvious that holding a book and turning pages was a two-hand operation. Only my right hand was free. However, as the weeks passed I found I could, with care, safely shift my left arm a little to the right and make a slight turn of the wrist, with the result that I could hold a book, using my right hand to turn pages. A breakthrough! I felt like a prisoner who had been given permission to work in a garden outside the walls.

From then on, dialysis became a time mainly given over to reading. I can honestly speak of dialysis as a period of major blessings. There were so many books I had long wished I had time to read, plus many other books I wanted to read again. Now I had acres of time to read and could do so with no sense of neglecting anything else. Some clouds really do have a silver lining.

My reading was far ranging, from Garrison Keillor to Dostoevsky, from art history to travel books. At the time I was working on a book about pilgrimage, thus much of my reading was on that topic: journals kept by pilgrims, interviews with pilgrims, books on major centers of pilgrimage, books on the history and theology of pilgrimage.

It was reading about the theology of pilgrimage that proved most helpful. The more I worked on the book, the clearer it became that the most crucial element of pilgrimage isn't walking along traditional pilgrim routes, great blessing that such journeys can be. The essence of pilgrimage is becoming more aware of the presence of God no matter where you are. This could happen in the most ordinary location—at the kitchen sink, in a bus, in a supermarket, or in a parking lot. It could happen in a hospital dialysis ward. Pilgrimage is a way of living daily life wherever daily life requires you to be. For those on a quest for the kingdom of God, no passport is required. If you happen to be sick, the best place to meet God is here and now in that sickness.

What a laugh! I had been writing about pilgrimage without being aware that the situation I so desperately wanted to avoid and whose demands on me I so deeply resented and resisted could do more for me than walking a thousand miles in prayer.

I recalled an encounter that my friend Mel Hollander had with Dan Berrigan. Dan was giving a lecture on pastoral care of the dying, and Mel, a cancer patient whose condition had been judged terminal, decided to attend. In the classroom Dan immediately noticed Mel's bruised skin color and dark, sunken eyes. His first words to Mel were, "What's the matter?" Deciding to respond with the same directness, Mel said, "I'm dying—I'm dying of cancer." To which Dan replied, without hesitation or embarrassment and just as briefly, "That must be very exciting." Mel later told me how Dan's few words instantly cleared the dark sky he had been living under. What had until then been a grim journey on a short road to the graveyard suddenly became the most exciting event of his life.

Looking at what was happening to me through the lens of pilgrimage, I came to understand that worse things could have come my way than having to spend so much of my life in a hospital, a place where nearly everyone is either sick, caring for the sick, or visiting the sick. Holy ground.

God bless everyone with good health, who see doctors rarely and have no prescription medications at home. Would that I were one of them. But good health is a condition that can give rise to its own illusions. So much is taken for granted. Having been deprived of good health, the sick are well aware that they are unable to survive on their own.

The pilgrimage of illness made me more conscious than ever before of a basic reality in everyone's life: my dependence on the care of others, Nancy first of all. Raised as I was in a culture that prizes individuality and independence, I had been slow to realize just how much I relied on others, though actually there had never been a day of my life when this wasn't the case. That dependence started the instant I was conceived, and it will continue without interruption until I draw my last breath. I depend on others for love, for encouragement, for inspiration, for food. I depend on others for the words and gestures that make communication possible. I have others to thank for all the skills I have acquired. Whatever wisdom I have is borrowed from others. Sickness makes it all but impossible to nourish the illusion of being autonomous.

In the community of the sick, all patients are aware of how much they depend on the doctors and nurses who care for us, or all those who do such hidden tasks as laboratory analyses and keeping the hospital clean. I recall a young scarf-wearing Muslim woman, mop in hand, who always gave me the warmest smile when we happened to pass each other in the hospital hallway.

Each visit to the hospital reminded me that the journey being made by others was often far harder than mine, and more difficult to bear—children who were gravely ill, people in great pain, faces collapsing with discouragement and grief. Being among the sick is being among those who include the dying. During a dialysis session one day, I happened to witness a frail man in his eighties die before my eyes. I thought he had dozed off.

In fact all pilgrimage routes are lined with graves, most of them unmarked.

I recently got a letter that began "Dead Jim." I haven't taken my last breath yet, but I'm well aware it will happen. Nancy and I often joke about the hand-in-hand walk we're taking down Cemetery Road.

But for the time being I'm one of the escapees. Today, kidney illness is treatable. It's possible to live a long and, for many, a full life on dialysis. It's also an illness that, for many patients, can be reversed by a kidney transplant. I am among the extremely fortunate. Not only am I living in a country in which intensive medical care is not financially devastating (thanks to the Dutch health care system, we've never had to worry about access to treatment or its costs), but Nancy offered me one of her kidneys. I hadn't sought such a gift or even imagined it.

It was far from an easy decision, as Nancy makes clear in an entry she wrote for our blog, "A Tale of Two Kidneys."[2]

People have told me how brave I'm being, but believe me, the bravest part of this whole process is getting yourself to that point where you overcome all your excuses and fears. I kept thinking of Frodo in The Lord of the Rings, *who finally makes the decision to carry the ring in order to destroy it in Mount Doom. He must make this decision on his own, and when he finally says, "I'll carry the ring," that becomes the organizing principle for the entire story.*

I have always believed that Tolkien was very deliberate in naming Frodo, and that his name could easily fit into the long etymological entry for the word "free" in the Oxford English Dictionary. *Frodo—one who acts out of freedom. Freedom doesn't mean doing whatever you feel like if it's in your interest, because sometimes you do things that you think are in your interest only to discover later on that you did them under some kind of compulsion—peer group pressure, fear of rejection, fear of loss. Acting under compulsion isn't freedom. But acting out of love, sometimes doing something that's downright dangerous, is what freedom truly is. (Interestingly enough, the word "free" and the word "beloved" and "friend" are related, as the* Oxford English Dictionary *makes clear.)*

So I said yes. And when I did, I suddenly felt as if all the winds were blowing in the right direction, as if I had made a free decision that was somehow in line with a kind of cosmic truth. I realized that for all the months that I had been saying I couldn't donate a kidney due to economic worries, I had made myself responsible for a kind of self-wrought logical argument that had to be constantly reinforced with my own insistence in order to stay in place. But the yes floated freely. The yes was borne up by something beyond me and my own logical arguments.[3]

---

2. Our daughter Cait created a blog for us to record our transplant experiences: www.ataleof2kidneys.blogspot.com.

3. Nancy Forest, "Saying Yes," http://jimandnancyforest.com/2009/07/saying_yes/.

It wasn't just Nancy who was a rescuer. Our kids were deeply embedded in the transplant process. One of the high points in our memories of that period was a family gathering initiated by the nurse heading the transplant unit at the Amsterdam Medical Center. All of us, plus our parish priest, Father Sergei Ovsiannikov, met in a small conference room to discuss with the nurse what was going to happen and to explore questions anyone might have, including what are the operation's risks and what happens if my body rejects the transplant.

Crucial support also came from our parish, St. Nicholas of Myra Russian Orthodox Church in Amsterdam. At the end of the liturgy the Sunday before the surgery, Nancy and I were given a special blessing by Father Sergei in front of the whole congregation. The anointing reminded me of our marriage in the church. There was a similar sense of standing in a radiant circle of pure grace. On the transplant day itself, the last day of October 2007, a prayer vigil was held in our church throughout the hours our two operations were in progress.

Finally, after a year of tests and interviews, one of Nancy's kidneys was removed from her body and placed in mine. It has thrived there ever since, as eager to work for me as it had been for her. With family and friends, two days after the surgery we celebrated our twenty-fifth wedding anniversary at the University of Amsterdam Medical Center.

One detail: Shortly before the transplant, we were given a postcard reproduction of a thirteenth-century illumination of Eve's emergence from Adam's body. Adam is sleeping peacefully while Eve is wide awake. Jesus is standing beside them, his left arm grasping Eve's wrists in a gesture similar to a midwife pulling a child from the womb, while his right arm is raised in a gesture of blessing, suggesting his power to create.

The source of the image is the book of Genesis. It is part of a series of scenes that begin with the creation of the cosmos, a favorite subject of Byzantine and medieval art. In each panel, Christ is the key figure. The Second Person of the Holy Trinity, though not yet incarnate, is portrayed as the human being he is to become. This is a way of illustrating the biblical affirmation that each of us is a bearer of the image of God.

Images having to do with Adam and Eve have always fascinated both of us. One of them hangs over our bed. Such stories have almost nothing to do with what, these days, we think of as history. In fact we know very little about the first human beings. But the Adam and Eve story is profound. It stresses an original oneness in Adam and Eve, the two of them mysteriously one being until the body of Eve is drawn out of the body of Adam.

There is an ancient Jewish commentary that responds to the question why was there only one Adam and only one Eve? The answer is so that no human being can regard himself or herself as being of higher descent than anyone else. The basic fact about human beings is that we all belong to the same family tree.

At the same time there is the elusive but compelling memory that still haunts the human mind of a primordial, womb-like Eden: a paradise in which there was no war, indeed no enmity. The first murder, the first splinter of war, occurs only after Adam and Eve have been expelled from Eden.

For Nancy and me this particular image of Adam and Eve has another level of meaning. This icon seems to foresee two-way traffic—in kidneys, for example—between the sons of Adam and the daughters of Eve.

One final note: Several weeks after the transplant, Nancy went back to the hospital for her first check-up. When asked by the doctor how

she felt, she said that far from feeling weak or depleted, she felt in tip-top shape, glowing with energy. The doctor wasn't surprised. He said this is common with kidney transplants between spouses—all they need is the same blood type. In fact, he said, a study had been done in Sweden on this very phenomenon, and that while one would expect a low rate of success in transplants between people who are not blood-related, in the case of married people just the opposite is true. The success rate is very high. There is still no scientific explanation for this, although to us the reason seems patently clear. Love. Nancy says she is convinced that the reason her kidney is so happy in my body is that it knows its partner is never far away.

We realized we had been made aware of new meaning to the passage from Genesis: "and they shall be one flesh."

Peace Activist?

Ihave no idea how many lectures I've delivered since the first one
that I gave while a high school student in Hollywood. "Generation
in the Shadow" was the theme, a reference to living beneath the mushroom clouds generated by nuclear explosions. Hundreds and hundreds,
certainly. In the introductions that have preceded each lecture, I've
almost invariably been described as a "peace activist." It's a label that
always makes me uncomfortable. I am tempted to look around and see
if there is someone standing behind me who really is a peace activist—who never misses demonstrations, never fails to sign petitions, is
arrayed with protest badges, and feels troubled if not currently in jail
for another act of civil disobedience.

The problem is that I'm not by nature an activist. Perhaps there is
something of Thomas Merton's monastic temperament in me. I feel
uncomfortable in crowds—masses of people drawn together by a common objective generate powerful currents and undertows that often
scare me. I'm not an automatic participant—discernment is needed.
When it comes to taking part in protests and demonstrations, I have
to convince myself that this specific act of protest or witness really is
worth taking part in and then push myself by brute force out the door
while wishing my conscience would leave me alone. I would much
rather walk in the woods than walk in a march. There is a part of me
that would have preferred that the Milwaukee Fourteen had been the
Milwaukee Thirteen. I don't enjoy disputes. This aspect of my character has been a constant since childhood. And yet there is my sometimes
pushy, problematic conscience that every now and then manages to
prod me into doing troublesome things. If I am some sort of activist, it
is a reluctant activist.

Nor can I, in all honesty, glibly call myself a Christian. Rather I'm someone *attempting* to become a Christian. It's a lifelong project with lots of reverses.

I'm now nearing eighty, more than five decades older than I ever expected to live when I left the Navy and joined the Catholic Worker. At the time, nuclear Armageddon seemed inevitable and near. Part of my endeavors all these years has been to be among those working to prevent such a catastrophe. What has almost happened time and time again hasn't happened yet, thank God, and thanks in part to all the people who in various ways have sought peace.

If I have made a particular contribution, it has mainly to do with looking for ways to overcome enmity. To love an enemy, first you need to meet the enemy and try to find in him or her a bit of the divine likeness.

Perhaps the most important thing I've learned is that if I cannot find the face of Jesus in the faces of those who are my enemies, if I cannot find him in the unbeautiful, if I cannot find him in those who have the "wrong ideas," if I cannot find him in the poor and the defeated, how will I find him in bread and wine or in the life after death? If I do not reach out in this world to those with whom he has identified himself, why do I imagine that I will want to be with him and them forever in heaven? Why would I want to be, for all eternity, in the company of those whom I avoided every day of my life?

I've learned that there is no way to cleanse the world of "the bad guys" because the bad guys include us. As Solzhenitsyn wrote in *The Gulag Archipelago*:

> *The line separating good and evil passes not through states, nor between classes, nor between political parties either—but right through every human heart—and through all human hearts. This line shifts. Inside us, it oscillates with the years. And even within hearts overwhelmed by evil, one small bridgehead of good is retained. And even in the best of hearts, there remains . . . an un-uprooted small corner of evil.*[1]

---

1. Aleksandr Solzhenitsyn, *The Gulag Archipelago*, abridged edition (New York: Vintage Classics, 2018), "The Ascent," 312.

Mentors

During a conference I was attending with Thich Nhat Hahn, Thây reached over for the journal in which I was taking notes and drew a simple diagram on a blank page: four small circles arranged as if they were the corners of a square with a fifth circle in the center. The arrangement was similar to the dots on the five-side of a gaming die. Next to one of the outer circles he wrote Thomas Merton, next to another Dorothy Day, next to the third Dan Berrigan, next to the fourth Al Hassler. Next to the central circle he inscribed Jim. Underneath the five circles Nhat Hanh wrote: "Jim admires Thomas Merton, Dorothy Day, Dan Berrigan, and Al Hassler, but Jim is not any of the people he admires. Jim is only a name. I is only a pronoun. Who is Jim Forest?"

This last sentence was, for me, a *koan*—a Zen question that is something like an arrow shot into one's back just out of reach. I struggled with that question for a long time, slowly coming to realize that I had long been trying to create a self that was a weaving together of people I especially admired, and not only the four whom Nhat Hanh had singled out but himself and several others. While I could easily have developed a worse method of shaping my identity, the best I could achieve from it was the construction of a strange mask. Whoever God had in mind in calling me into existence, it was not a mish-mash of others, however admirable. Finding mentors and learning from them was essential, but finally I had to discover my own true face. It's a work in progress.

I look back on my mentors with speechless gratitude. If in so many ways I haven't come close to their examples, still they have helped me discover who I am without a mask.

My parents were my first mentors, especially my mother. Hers was a

317

gift of selfless commitment, to her sons and her community. She was a model of stubborn resistance to injustice. If my father was, in my childhood, too absent, he was a model of courage, integrity, and care for the well-being of others.

Dorothy Day became a second mother. Had I to choose one word for what her life was all about it would be hospitality. If I were an iconographer, I would paint Dorothy standing before an open door. She was occasionally in jail, but most of her life by far was spent welcoming those whom many others had made unwelcome. Every time I open our front door to a stranger wholeheartedly, it is partly thanks to Dorothy. She also represents the importance of what she called voluntary poverty—having less rather than more, sharing, making do. Every time I manage not to buy something I can get along without, it is partly thanks to Dorothy. Her acts of protest and resistance were rooted in her opening the door to strangers. I also witnessed in her the importance of a disciplined spiritual life.

Dorothy Day

Thomas Merton

Thomas Merton was a second father. He taught me a great deal about friendship. I remain astonished at his finding time to write to me so often, helping me see the way ahead and also cheering me along when I had fallen flat on my face. I learned from him not to allow myself to be dragged along by peergroup pressure, the most powerful of social forces. I learned from him both the power of words and the limitation of words. As he once said, "He who follows words is destroyed." I learned from him the importance of creating and safeguarding periods of attentive silence and prayer.

Thich Nhat Hanh with young Daniel

I owe so much to Thich Nhat Hanh—traveling with him, living with him, talking and working with him. Early in our friendship he taught me how to climb six flights of stairs without arriving at my front door out of breath, but really what he was teaching me each day we were together was how to live minute by minute in a refreshed condition. He helped me find the baby Jesus in a sink full of dirty dishes.

And then there is Dan Berrigan, who taught me a great deal about the love that has to be at the heart of protest. His protest activities were, to use a phrase of his, shaped by "outraged love." "Outrage" is only an adjective that sharpens the edge of the key word, "love." "Where there is no love," said St. John of the Cross, "put love and you will find love."

Thank God for Henri Nouwen. The hardest events of my adult life have been my three failures in marriage. Henri helped me get through a time when I could see no light at the end of the tunnel. His wedding gift to Nancy and me was a reproduction of St. Andrei Rublev's icon of the Old Testament Holy Trinity. In explaining that gift to us, he helped me see icons with more understanding and appreciation.

Daniel Berrigan

It was a privilege to work side by side with A. J. Muste for a year. This foe of war was among the kindest and most patient human beings I've ever known. No one was his enemy. His day-to-day life bore witness to a proverb he often repeated: "There is no way to peace. Peace is the way."

Henri Nouwen

I learned from another mentor, Al Hassler, that peacemaking is not just living in a continuous state of reaction to current crises. Al was among the first to see how intertwined are peacemaking and care of the environment.

One Russian friend I must especially single out is my longtime pastor, the late Sergei Ovsiannikov. He too had Communist parents, and he too had been a prisoner. He rarely gave a sermon in which the word *svoboda* (freedom) wasn't used. Born in what was then called Leningrad, he died last year in Amsterdam. Eternal memory!

My six children—Ben, Dan, Wendy, Thom, Caitlan, and Anne—have been among the most influential of my mentors. While I made a slow and awkward start in becoming a full-time father, at last I learned to make decisions that were shaped by the truest answer I could give to the question, "What would be best for them?"

Al Hassler with Joan Baez

And now my ten grandchildren play a major role in shaping my life. I do a lot of grandfathering these days. It is an awesome thing to watch a child growing up and to play a supportive role in that process. They make me think more and more deeply about what needs to be done, what choices need to be made, to make the world safer for them.

One last mentor is the mentor I live with: Nancy. A friendship of long standing blossomed into the most intimate partnership I've ever known or imagined. So far, forty-two years of friendship and thirty-seven years of marriage. . . .

Thank you, God. Amen.

ACKNOWLEDGMENTS

A Few Words of Thanks

Thanks to all those people who encouraged the writing of this book, a project about which I had many doubts. I found it much easier to write about such people as Thomas Merton, Dorothy Day, and Daniel Berrigan than about myself.

Writing a memoir was first suggested more than twenty years ago by John Dear. Here it is at long last, John!

Another of the book's most persistent advocates has been John Williams, who also went to prison for burning draft files and for years was part of the Catholic Worker community in Seattle. John read draft after draft as these pages were being written and made countless helpful suggestions. John followed the evolution of the manuscript more closely than anyone except Nancy. It was while staying with John and his wife, Kathleen O'Hanlon, that this book was completed.

Tom Cornell, among my oldest friends, helped sharpen my memory of our days working together at the Catholic Peace Fellowship.

Carolyn Zablotny helped refresh memories of the Emmaus House period of my life.

Shawn Storer and his co-workers with the Catholic Peace Fellowship in South Bend, Indiana, found CPF documents I needed in the archive at Notre Dame University.

Tim Schilling, another American writer who landed in the Netherlands and put down roots here, read this book as a work in progress, asked many helpful questions, and laughed at all the right places.

Lyn Isbell, a friend since she was a young mother and who is now a retired teacher of American and English literature, applied her stethoscope to these pages and gave the book a stronger heartbeat.

Willy Eurlings, who translated my biography of Thomas Merton into Dutch, had a special talent for finding textual redundancies and correcting historical inaccuracies.

I owe Maria Angelini and Paul Kobelski each a bottle of champagne for their hard work in laying out this book.

Nancy has been one of my editors long before it ever crossed our minds that we might marry each other. She urged me to write this book and listened to me read aloud each chapter as it was written, raising questions, making suggestions, offering criticism where criticism was needed, and occasionally rewording clumsy sentences and paragraphs. This book is better joined than it would have been without her verbal carpentry.

Last but far from least comes my editor and publisher Robert Ellsberg, without whom much of my writing these past thirty years might not have happened and certainly wouldn't have been as attractively published. We first met in 1972, when he was in his teens; with his father, Daniel Ellsberg, he had come to attend the trial of the Harrisburg Seven. Meeting again at Thich Nhat Hanh's apartment in Paris a year or two later, together we climbed to the roof of Chartres cathedral. Through thick and thin, happiness and sorrow, we have long been the closest of friends.

Jim Forest
July 30, 2019, the feast of St. Martha

Index of Names

Abbot, Berenice, 176
Arbatov, Georgi, 288
Artyushkin, Yuri, 208
Asimov, Isaac, 44
Attenborough, David, 264
Auden, W.H., 107
Augustine, St., 108
Autherine, Lucy, 214

Baez, Joan, 125, 246, 257, 320
Baker, Jack, 83, 92, 102
Baldwin, James, 133
Baldwin, Roger, 248
Bamberger, Dom John Eudes, 267
Bartelme, Betty, 176
Basie, Count, 25
Baskin, Dorothy, 18, 23, 48, 55-56, 58-59, 61-62, 72-74
Baskin, Jack, 48, 55, 67
Batterham, Forster, 123
Batterham, Tamar, 102, 123
Bax, Willem, 308
Bea, Cardinal Augustin, 142
Berrigan, Daniel, 107-8, 140, 146, 148, 151, 154, 159, 165-66, 172, 175, 187-89, 196, 217, 227, 232, 238, 242, 257, 280, 290, 310, 317, 319, 321

Berrigan, Philip, 144, 156, 158-59, 174, 196, 257
Bloy, Léon, 215
Bly, Robert, 209, 246
Boyle, Kay, 133
Bradbury, Ray, 44, 55
Britten, Benjamin, 135

Camus, Albert, 134
Cao Ngoc Phuong, 221, 224-25, 228, 239, 256
Capell, Frank, 138
Capp, Al, 233
Cardenal, Ernesto, 231-32
Castro, Emilio, 256
Castro, Fidel, 84
Chavez, Cesar, 231
Chesterton, G.K., 82
Clarke, Arthur C., 304
Collins, Michael, 207-8
Cooke, Cardinal Terence, 231
Cooper, Bob, 238
Corbin, Marty, 144, 157
Cornell, Tom, 144, 148, 152, 157, 159, 161-62, 164, 166. 188, 246, 331
Corrigan, Mairead, 240, 258
Cotton, Don, 189
Cox, Harvey, 215
Cullen, Michael, 189, 193, 195

Cunnane, Robert, 148, 189

Dahl, Roald, 28
Daniélou, Jean, 141
Davis, Mina, 16
Day, Dorothy, 48, 82, 88, 90-112, 114, 118, 123-25, 127-29, 131-34, 144, 148, 153, 156, 161-63, 168-70, 176, 187-88, 209, 214, 231, 246, 276, 283, 299, 302, 306, 317-18, 321
De Beer, Patrice, 245
Deats, Richard, 246
Dellinger, Dave, 133-34, 247
Deming, Barbara, 133
Desai, Moraji, 263
Dickens, Charles, 13, 29
Digia, Ralph, 152
Disney, Walt, 33, 112
Dostoevsky, Feodor, 106, 276, 310
Douglass, Jim, 140, 142-43, 187, 246
Dozier, Bishop Carroll, 246
Drown, Fred Allen, 13-14, 16
Drown, Margaret Loretta, 13
Duffy, Thomas, 81, 83, 88

Duncan, David, 117
Durso, Jim, 83
Dylan, Bob, 123, 139

Egan, Eileen, 115, 132
Elbert, Jean, 147
Ellsberg, Daniel, 246, 322
Ellsberg, Robert, 169, 246, 248, 273, 322
Epps, Dwain, 287
Epstein, Louis, 60
Esquivel, Adolfo Perez, 258-61
Esquivel, Amanda, 258
Eterman, Peter, 250
Evans, Hermene, 140, 152

Ferlinghetti, Lawrence, 60
Ferry, W.H., 147
Filaret, Metropolitan of Minsk, 274, 284, 292
Flanagan, Raymond, 118
Flynn, Elizabeth Gurley, 95-96
Forest, Anne, 21, 269, 279, 282, 320
Forest, Ben, 10-11, 136, 139, 153, 158, 168, 191, 205-6, 212, 229-30, 232, 244, 250-51, 253, 266-67, 269, 320
Forest, James Frederick, 6, 12-24, 40, 46-48, 51, 54-57, 59-65, 67, 114, 191
Forest, Jean (nee Morton), 129-32, 136, 139, 153-54, 158, 168, 129-32, 136, 139
Forest, Lucy, 20, 67, 279
Forest, Marguerite, 2,

10-11, 17-18, 22-26, 29-30, 32, 35-36, 39-42, 46, 49, 51-52, 56, 153, 191, 206, 212, 269, 317
Forest, Nancy, 236, 254, 268-69, 279-83, 292-95, 297, 303, 306-7, 309, 311-14, 319, 320-22
Forest, Richard, 3, 5, 7, 9, 18, 23, 28, 32-34, 40, 49
Forest, Rosanne, 18, 48, 55, 61, 63
Fox, Dom James, 118
Frank, Anne, 86, 307
Fried, Howard, 198-99

Gandhi, Indira, 263
Gandhi, Mahatma, 28, 134, 135, 257, 264, 273
Gardner, Jerry, 189, 195
Garland, Judy, 58
Gettleman, Marvin, 198-99
Ginsberg, Allen, 59-60, 65, 91-92, 246
Ginsberg, Naomi, 91
Gogol, Nikolai, 209, 286
Goodman, Paul, 133, 136
Gorbachev, Mikhail, 284-85, 288-91
Gorky, Maxim, 209
Grady, John Peter, 148
Graf, Bob, 189, 193, 201
Gray, Francine, 195, 203-5
Greene, Graham, 288, 290
Gregorios, Paulos Mar, 289
Gregory, Dick, 193

Groppi, James, 193
Gumbleton, Bishop Thomas, 246

Harbottle, General Michael, 289
Harney, Jim, 189
Harvey, Phil, 137
Hassler-Forest, Daniel, 20, 232-33, 250-51, 267-68, 279, 319-20
Hassler-Forest, Thomas, 20, 320
Hassler-Forest, Wendy, 20, 250, 267-69, 275, 279, 320
Hassler, Alfred, 178-80, 182, 233-35, 246, 317, 320
Hassler, Laura, 221, 224-25, 229, 232, 250, 266-67
Heidbrink, John, 114-15, 140, 142, 146, 148, 168
Hendrickson, Charles, 3-4
Hendrickson, Hendrick, 13
Hennacy, Ammon, 92-93, 96
Henry, Linda, 168-71, 177, 203, 211, 221
Henson, Jim, 304
Hepburn, Audrey, 73
Hersey, John, 38
Heschel, Abraham, 165
Higgenbotham, Jon, 189
Hintlian, George, 281
Hoffman, Allen, 120
Hollander, Mel, 310
Hoover, J. Edgar, 31, 48, 217-18
Huxley, Aldous, 181

Inglis, Douglas and
  Robert, 8, 10-11, 24,
  29, 30, 32, 35, 42
Iswolsky, Helene, 106-7

Jackson, Jr., Harold, 194-
  95, 199, 202
Jägerstätter, Franz, 150-
  52
Janicke, Al, 189
Jegen, Mary Evelyn, 110
John Paul II, Pope, 259-
  61, 298
John XXIII, Pope, 107-
  8, 114
Johnson, Lyndon, 162,
  171-72
Julian, Percy, 194

Kaye, Bob, 99, 116-22
Keillor, Garrison, 310
Kelly, Walt, 30-31
Kennedy, Caitlan, 268-
  69, 279, 282, 312, 320
Kennedy, John F., 78,
  84-85, 124, 146
Kerensky, Alexander,
  107
Kerouac, Jack, 65
Kerrell,Walter, 97
Kesey, Ken, 246
King Jr., Martin Luther,
  123, 133-35, 179-80,
  201, 233
Kinnell, Galway, 209
Kirk, David, 168, 213-
  15, 230
Kok, Jan, 306
Koneazny, Jim, 211
Kuntsler, William, 194

Lacey, Arthur J., 97, 102
Lacouture, Jean, 245
LaPorte, Roger, 163-64
Larrick, Jim, 305

Larson, Charles, 194-
  202
LaVan, Theodore, 42
Lawrence, D.H., 75
Le Guin, Ursula, 44
Leskov, Nikola, 209
Levertov, Denise, 209
Lown, Bernard, 289
Lydon, Karen, 218-19
Lynd, Alice and
  Staughton, 246-47

Madden, Ralph, 93
Mahon, Kathryn, 214
Mailer, Norman, 290
Mandela, Nelson, 133
Mann, Richard, 215
Marabito, John, 88-89
Marvy, Doug, 189, 191,
  193
Mastroianni, Marcello,
  290
Maurin, Peter, 88, 91,
  93, 102
Maximos IV, Patriarch,
  214-15
McCarthy, Joseph,
  16-17, 31, 45
Melville, Herman, 68
Menuhin, Yehudi, 304
Merton, Thomas, 8,
  75-76, 94-95, 100,
  103, 111-22, 124-25,
  129, 131, 133, 142,
  144-51, 154, 163-64,
  169-72, 177-80, 194,
  260, 266, 283, 286,
  297, 306, 317-18, 331
Merwin, W.S., 246
Miller, David, 160, 188
Miller, William Robert,
  107
Mirejovsky, Lubomir,
  274
Mische, George, 188

Mitchell, Edgar, 208
Monroe, Marilyn, 100
Moore, Bishop Paul,
  230-31
Mozart, Wolfgang
  Amadeus, 267
Mullaney, Anthony, 189,
  193, 200, 202
Munnik, Len, 304, 306
Muntz, Margo, 294, 307
Murphy, Duncim, 240
Muste, A.J., 133-35,
  147-48, 151, 160-62,
  235-36, 319

Nelson, John Oliver,
  148
Nesbitt, Catherine, 52
Neuhaus, Richard John,
  165
Newman, Kathy, 60
Nixon, Richard, 217,
  236
Noble, John, 138
Nouwen, Henri, 266-
  67, 295-97, 319-20

O'Connor, Cardinal
  John, 298
O'Dwyer, Paul, 246
O'Leary, Br. Basil, 189,
  193, 199
Ojile, Fred, 189, 200
Ovsiannikov, Sergei,
  313, 320

Paret, Bennie, 126
Pasternak, Boris, 65,
  285, 291
Patchen, Kenneth, 98,
  133
Peacock, Joe, 294
Peck, Gregory, 290
Peluso, Judy, 218-19
Pimen, Patriarch, 287

Pitirim, Archbishop, 286–87
Platov, Mariquita, 305
Pohl, Frederick, 45
Pottier, Françoise, 303
Preminger, Otto, 6
Pushkin, Alexander, 209

Rand, Ayn, 64–65
Raya, Bishop Joseph, 214–15
Reagan, Nancy, 291
Reagan, Ronald, 136, 270, 290–91
Repin, Ilya, 285
Ring, Charles, 148
Roberts, Archbishop Thomas, 144
Roep, Kirsten and Thomas, 250, 252–53
Romero, Oscar, 260
Rosebaugh, Larry, 189, 193
Rosenberg, Ethel and Julius, 7
Russell, Bertrand, 80
Rustin, Bayard, 133, 135

Sagan, Carl, 208
Sakharov, Andrei, 288
Samson, Allen, 194, 199
Sandberg, Stuart, 97
Sanders, Ed, 124–26, 129
Schachter, Rabbi Zalman, 118
Schmemann, Fr. Alexander, 107

Schmorell, Alexander, 306
Schneider, Louis, 247
Schwartz, Elie, 282
Schwarzschild, Rabbi Steven, 246
Seeger, Pete, 61, 217, 304
Seraphim, Christ, 192
Shepard, Alan, 208
Skobtsova, Mother Maria, 306
Smiley, Glenn, 135
Smith, Catherine, 12–13
Snyder, Edith, 136
Snyder, Gary, 209
Solomonow, Allan, 247
Soloviev, Anatoly, 299
Solzhenitsyn, Alexander, 209, 316
Sooy, Nicholas, 305
Spellman, Cardinal Francis, 125, 165
Speth, Florence, 218
Spock, Benjamin, 175–76
Squire, Roger, 37, 40
Stadniuk, Matvei, 106, 299, 301–3
Steichen, Edward, 49
Stickgold, Mark, 194, 197

Tarengal, Catherine, 101
Tchernikova, Tatiana, 276

Thich Nhat Hanh, 177–86, 205, 220–25, 234, 245, 256, 262, 266, 317, 319, 320
Thich Tanh Van, 224–25
Thich Tri Minh, 262
Thomas, Cherian, 264
Thoreau, Henry David, 15, 65, 67, 135, 215
Tolkien, J. R. R., 312
Tolstoy, Leo, 209
Trumbo, Dalton, 59

Vericker, Carol, 219
Vidal, Gore, 290
Voogd, Alexis, 294, 298

Walsh, Tony, 148
Warren, Mobi, 247
Warren, Will, 239, 256
Welles, Orson, 309
Williams, Betty, 240, 258
Williams, John, 321
Wilson, Desmond, 237

Yoder, John Howard, 147
Young, Fr. Lyle, 173, 215–16
Yuvenali, Metropolitan, 286, 290

Zahn, Gordon, 196
Zinn, Howard, 198, 247